AF326925

An Introduction to the Australian Economy

University of
Queensland Press

An Introduction to the Australian Economy

Ron Hefford

Norman Thomson

John Foreman

Roger Vinall

© University of Queensland Press, St Lucia, Queensland, 1980

Typeset by Press Etching Pty Ltd, Brisbane
Printed and bound by Southwood Press Pty Ltd, Sydney

Distributed in the United Kingdom, Europe, the Middle East, Africa, and the Caribbean by Prentice-Hall International, International Book Distributors Ltd, 66 Wood Lane End, Hemel Hempstead, Herts., England

*National Library of Australia
Cataloguing-in-Publication data*
An Introduction to the Australian Economy
  Index
  ISBN 0 7022 1495 7
  ISBN 0 7022 1496 5 Paperback
  1 Macroeconomics. i. Hefford Ronald Keith

339

Contents

Tables

Preface

In recent years there has been a trend towards a syllabus for Matriculation Economics that consists of a compulsory course in macroeconomics and a choice of either two or three electives. The same is true of a number of introductory courses now offered in Australian CAEs. The purpose of this book is to meet the first of these requirements, namely, an introductory course in macroeconomics.

Although we have laid the foundations for some electives that have a macro bias, such as International Trade and The Role of Government, we have made no attempt to cater for the wide array of elective courses now being offered. That would require a text of encyclopaedic proportions. In any event, we believe that the interests of students would be better served by separate texts, each written specifically to meet the requirements of individual elective courses. More importantly, we have found from experience that concurrent study of both macro and microeconomic theory at an introductory level results in a great deal of confusion. For example, many students taking a first course in economics find it difficult to distinguish between aggregate supply and demand in the economy and supply and demand in markets for individual commodities. The linkages between these two bodies of theory are not readily apparent to students engaged in their first encounter with economics. For this reason we have deliberately avoided the use of microeconomic analysis — for example, in attempting to explain changes in the general level of prices.

This book has been written at a level that we believe to be appropriate to matriculation candidates of average ability. No prior knowledge of economics has been assumed. In general, a "concentric" approach has been adopted in the hope that this will allow students to advance their understanding by relatively easy stages. For example, many students find money, banking, and monetary policy particularly difficult to understand at their first encounter. We have therefore introduced these elements in separate chapters, dealing with the nature and functions of money within the context of labour specialization and investment expenditure in chapter 3, the role of financial intermediaries in chapter 7, and monetary policy, representing one set of policy weapons available to the government, in chapter 8.

Some introductory texts assume too much prior knowledge and make little attempt to relate economic theory to the real world. For example, some authors introduce the concept of taxation as though all students are already aware of the different forms of tax levied. In fact, of course, very few readers of introductory texts have ever paid taxes — except by way of excise duties, which most were never aware had been included in the prices paid. We have tried to avoid such "sins of omission" and to give substance to the theory by frequent reference to Australian data and institutions. It is to be hoped that these data and the numerous examples offered will serve to facilitate understanding of the basic concepts and theory.

Our principal purpose is to introduce students to macroeconomic theory and to familiarize them with past and present problems and policies in the Australian economy. In addition, we believe that a text such as this should have a broader educative function, so that students who read it should be better equipped to face life beyond the classroom than those who have never studied economics. Finally, we hope that this book will help to stimulate discussion of current macroeconomic issues and the policy responses of governments to the problems of our time.

Following convention, we take this opportunity to acknowledge assistance from many sources. We are grateful to Christine Bierbaum both for research and for helpful comments on the drafts of several chapters; to Kevin Davis and Merv Lewis for throwing light on the mysteries of the banking system and monetary policy; to Geoff Harcourt and Barry Hughes for clarification of some aspects of wage indexation; to John Mead and Bob Akhurst of the CES for information on labour training schemes; A. Lane of the Bureau of Customs; Ian Crawford of BHP; John Bremner of GMH; the public relations departments of both the Bank of Adelaide and the Bank of New South Wales; and for assistance provided by a number of people in the Australian Bureau of Statistics. As usual, responsibility for any errors of fact or interpretation remains with the authors.

We also thank Bert Kelly and Brolga Books for permission to reproduce an extract from *One More Nail;* Helen Wickens for the preparation of all diagrams; Kathleen Cheshire for the collection and handling of data; and last, but not least, the girls in the Department of Economics at the University of Adelaide for the typing of the manuscript.

Adelaide, May 1979   R.K.H., N.J.T., J.F., R.H.V.

Introduction

THE ORIGINS OF MACROECONOMICS

It is generally agreed that economics — or what we now regard as economics — was founded by Adam Smith (1723-90). In his most famous published work, *An Inquiry into the Nature and Causes of the Wealth of Nations* (1776), Smith dealt with many issues, many of which have occupied the minds of economists ever since. Over the past two centuries, economists have continued to seek answers to the problems raised by Smith, most of which stem directly from the knowledge that every society faces a scarcity of resources relative to wants. That is, most of the questions with which economists are concerned can be traced back to the inescapable fact that each society faces limited means but unlimited ends.

Some issues, such as the distribution of income associated with unequal ownership of resources, have been debated by each generation. The Australian Commission of Inquiry into Poverty is simply a rekindling of a long-standing area of interest. In most societies, such basic issues have led on to other questions. For example, what kinds of economic systems are possible? In what ways can production be organized? How can (or should) the product be distributed among those people who contribute to the production process? In contrast, as some economies have developed and their societies have become affluent, new issues (such as resource conservation and urban renewal) have emerged. Others such as education, health care, and environmental pollution have received more attention.

One way of describing the nature and content of economics would be to list the many questions to which economists seek answers. Alternatively, we could catalogue all of the major areas of interest within this discipline — areas like international trade, labour economics, industrial organization, economic history, and so on. However, it is probably more useful, for those engaged in their first encounter with economics, to recognize that there are two main branches within the discipline. One of these deals with the behaviour of individual units in an economic system — that is, individual consumers, firms, and industries. It is concerned primarily with the ways that prices are determined in individual markets — including markets for land, labour, and capital — and the ways that buyers and sellers respond to those prices. This branch of the discipline, sometimes referred to as Price Theory or Value Theory, is *microeconomics*. The other major branch, *macroeconomics*, is concerned with the total or aggregate features of an economy — total production, total income, total employment, and prices in general, as distinct from production, income, and employment in individual firms or industries and the prices of individual goods or services.

Within macroeconomics there are two broad areas of interest. The first of these, Growth Theory, seeks to explain changes in economic activity with changes in population, skills, quantities and types of capital equipment, and the organization of production over long periods of time. From studies of different economies in different periods, such theory also attempts to specify the conditions necessary for sustained economic growth.

The second broad area of macroeconomics — that on which we will concentrate in this book — is known as *the short-period theory of production and employment*. Why "the short-period"? The reason is that this body of theory, in contrast to Growth Theory, seeks to explain fluctuations in levels of economic activity over periods so short that it can be assumed that population, skills, technology, the stock of capital equipment, and the organization of production *remain constant*.

How did this latter body of theory develop? During the nineteenth century it was generally held that there was a natural tendency for each of the more advanced economies to operate at the full-employment level of output. Not surprisingly, debate was most vigorous when idle plant capacity and unusually high unemployment had existed for long periods. One such period was early in the nineteenth century, when high levels of unemployment followed the long period of war between Britain and France. Of particular interest are the now classic debates between two Englishmen, Thomas Malthus (1766-1834) and David Ricardo (1772-1823).

Malthus argued that it was possible to have "a general glut" of commodities, so that total demand was then insufficient to take out of the market all that was being produced. Ricardo claimed that such a situation was simply not possible. He asserted that unemployment must be due to an inappropriate balance between the production of different goods. If there was a glut in the production of some goods, there must be a deficiency in the production of others.

The views of Ricardo were reinforced by those of J.B. Say (1767-1832).

This French economist argued that, in aggregate, the production of goods generates an equal level of demand; that is (what has since been referred to as *Say's Law*) the supply of goods generates its own demand. The essence of this argument was that people supply goods or services in order to buy other goods of equal value. It was suggested, for example, that a farmer takes his products to market in order to exchange them, directly or indirectly, for other goods needed by his family or for farm requisites like seeds and implements. Such notions clearly had appeal to common sense. So, like Ricardo, Say argued that gluts would appear only temporarily and only in the markets for individual commodities. In fact, Say suggested that such a situation could be remedied simply by adjustments to prices — for example, by reductions in the prices of those goods temporarily in surplus.

Malthus and other opponents of these views were unable to produce any generally acceptable alternative theory. Yet Malthus did raise some particularly important questions. For example, what if people sell goods and save part of what they receive? Surely total demand would then be less than the value of goods supplied and this would result in a cut-back in supplies for want of demand in general? Ricardo and Say rejected this possibility. They argued that people who save will lend to others — to consumers, to businessmen, or to landlords who want to spend more than their current incomes. That is, they argued that saving by one individual would simply result in a compensating increase in the spending of another.

Although some of the questions raised by Malthus were not adequately answered, the debate lapsed and confusion between the mechanisms in *individual* markets and *national aggregate* behaviour persisted. The problem of unemployment receded. Thereafter, over the remainder of the nineteenth century, unemployment in the more advanced capitalist economies rarely exceeded 8 per cent of the workforce and generally fluctuated between 2 and 6 per cent. Interest in these issues subsided, remaining only as a strand of Marxian economics that asserted an overall lack of demand owing to poverty.

Interest in these questions was revived again in the late 1920s and in the 1930s. In Britain, for example, there was only one year over the period 1921-38 when unemployment fell to less than 10 per cent of the workforce. The year 1929 signals the beginning of what is generally known as the *Great Depression*, although there is little doubt that the foundations for that depression can be found in the years before 1929. Essentially, producers in most countries of the world found themselves with unsold goods, so that production and incomes fell.

Confidence in the market was already under severe strain by 1929. For one thing, increasing stocks of unsold goods and growing unemployment during the 1920s had induced many developed countries (notably the

United States of America) to severely restrict imports through the levy of high levels of import duties. The sudden crash, following a period of wild speculation in shares on the Wall Street stock-market in October 1929, led to a collapse in the confidence of many people — and governments — in the market as an economic regulator.

This lack of confidence, which manifested itself in a reduction of export income, consumption, and investment expenditure, is reflected in the unemployment figures shown in table 1. Both Britain and Australia show a significant increase in unemployment after 1929, reaching 22 per cent in Britain and almost 30 per cent in Australia in 1932. It is important to notice that these unemployment figures are basically derived from trade union returns only and therefore, to the extent that there were then many non-unionists, understate the full extent of the unemployment that existed.

Unemployment was not evenly distributed through either Britain or Australia. Some industries, and therefore some locations, suffered more than others. Similarly, while *money* wage rates in general fell — in contrast to the downward rigidity of wage rates today — prices also fell even further. Those fortunate to be in employment therefore experienced a gain in *real* wages. Falling prices led to a decline in profits and a consequent decline in the level of private investment expenditure.

Table 1. Unemployment in Britain and Australia 1924 to 1937 (percentages)

Year	Britain	Australia
1924	10.1	8.9
1925	11.2	8.8
1926	14.4	7.1
1927	10.1	7.0
1928	11.6	10.8
1929	10.0	11.1
1930	16.2	19.3
1931	22.0	27.4
1932	22.5	29.0
1933	19.8	25.1
1934	16.6	20.5
1935	15.3	16.5
1936	13.0	12.2
1937	11.2	10.5

Sources: Australia — *Commonwealth Year Book*, various issues, and Robert Skidelsky *Politicians and the Slump* (London: Macmillan, 1967).

Government action in Britain appeared to be dictated by the demands of international bankers, both in New York and in the City of London. Britain at first tried to maintain the value of the pound sterling. This could only be done with support from the United States and American bankers who insisted upon a balanced budget. So with incomes (and tax receipts) low and a balanced budget objective, there was little stimulus to the economy by way of government expenditure. Only when Britain went off the gold standard late in 1931 and devalued the pound did the economy show signs of recovery. Unlike the United States and Germany, where government spending stimulated the economy, Britain relied mainly upon the initiatives of the private sector.

Australia suffered more than Britain (and the United States) from the fall in incomes of primary producers, especially wool and wheat. Wool, as now, was sensitive to changes in the incomes of overseas buyers. With the onset of falls in output and incomes overseas, the demand for wool fell. World wheat supplies were high, and the price fell 60 per cent between 1929 and 1932. Even today, falls in price of this magnitude would have important implications for Australia; but in the 1930s when our reliance upon the farm sector was even greater than it is today, the effects were catastrophic.

Furthermore, with the onset of the Great Depression, Australia was caught with a heavy overseas debt commitment. By 1928/29, 28 per cent of export earnings were earmarked simply to meet interest and dividends on debt as they fell due to overseas lenders. Falls in export prices of the order of 60 per cent for wheat, 50 per cent for wool, and of similar magnitude for other primary products, such as fruit, mutton, and sugar, increased the burden of repayments dramatically. Between June and December 1929, Australia's overseas reserves in London fell by 60 per cent.

More than 70 per cent of foreign borrowing by Australia was by the public sector. With the initial refusal of the Commonwealth Bank to take up the shortfall in foreign funding of public expenditure programmes, the government could do little to stimulate economic activity. Eventually, under what became known as the Premiers' Plan, in June 1931 the Commonwealth Bank did lend money to the government, but only after the Australian pound was devalued by 20 per cent, public expenditure *reduced*, and taxation *increased.*

The Premiers' Plan and reduction in the basic wage by 10 per cent coincided with the beginning of recovery overseas. Certainly the measures in the plan itself suggest that there was little in it to stimulate the economy, except in so far as it may have improved the confidence of the more conservative section of the business community who believed in the tidiness of a balanced budget.

Meanwhile, during this period economists were being more and more influenced by the writings of John Maynard Keynes. By 1936 he had published his famous *General Theory of Employment, Interest and Money.* In the main, Keynes lent support to the views of Malthus and rejected some of the arguments of Ricardo and Say. Unlike economists in the nineteenth century, he denied that full employment was in some sense a "natural" level of activity. He also denied that there was an automatic market mechanism that would serve to restore an economy to full employment. The main thrust of his argument was that government must bear a greater measure of responsibility for the level of economic activity in any short period. They could manipulate activity by means of appropriate fiscal and monetary policies, including a willingness to spend in excess of revenue if warranted by the circumstances of the time.

Subsequently, the explanation and prescriptions offered by Keynes came to be widely accepted and practised in Western industrialized countries. In the 1950s and the first half of the 1960s, it seemed that the policy prescriptions suggested by Keynes offered a greater measure of stability in economic activity than had formerly seemed possible. However, the circumstances over the period 1945-60 were unique in many ways. There existed a great backlog in consumer demand (housing, consumer durables, clothing and so on) that had been severely restricted by wartime priorities. The capacity of industry in some countries had been sharply reduced by war damage. Demand was given further impetus by rising real incomes and expectations. The strength of aggregate demand generally served to make full employment fairly readily attainable. More often than not, governments found it necessary to take action to *dampen*, rather than to stimulate, economic activity. So, in retrospect, it would seem that the guiding principles suggested by Keynes were never seriously tested before the late 1960s. Perhaps "Blind Freddy" would have been equally capable of sustaining full employment over the two decades to 1965.

Since the latter part of the 1960s, Western industralized countries have faced higher levels of unemployment than at any time since the Great Depression. The existing body of economic theory offers no ready solutions. The very relevance of Keynes has therefore been brought into serious question in recent years. However, it is not *yet* clear that the *basic notions* of Keynes have been discredited; nor what the alternatives might be.

1 What, How, and For Whom

SCARCITY: THE BASIC ECONOMIC PROBLEM

Every society, regardless of its political, social, and economic organization, has certain physical and human **resources** which can be used to produce goods and services. For example, Australia has large reserves of iron ore, vast areas of land suitable for animal or crop production, and some of the most highly skilled people in the world. These physical and human resources make possible the supply of the wide range of goods and services used each day in this country.

Resources are often referred to in a collective sense. However, there are times when it is useful to subdivide resources into three broad categories, namely, **land, labour**, and **capital**. Each of these categories of resources has many distinct components, some of which differ widely in quality from one society to another.

Under **land**, for example, we include all natural resources available to man. So land includes not only soil and the minerals and fuels that lie beneath the earth's surface, but also rivers, forests, and energy provided by the sun and wind. **Labour** is the human resource that works on, harnesses, and in various ways modifies land. However, the effectiveness of labour depends not only upon physical effort; mental effort is also involved. So it is that a skilled farmer can produce much more than one who is unskilled, even when land is identical in quality and both are producing the same crop.

Labour rarely works without the aid of tools or other equipment. For example, the fast-flowing rivers of Tasmania and the Australian Alps would be of little use to man unless he could harness them in some way to generate electric power or, at the very least, to turn simple paddle wheels. Power stations, paddle wheels, and other tools and equipment used by labour in conjunction with land for the production of goods or services are examples of various forms of **capital**.

Resources are used to produce goods and services. The three categories of resources are land (natural resources), labour (human resources), and capital (man-made resources).

Although each economy has land, labour, and capital resources, the quantities and qualities of resources differ greatly from one economy to another. For example, while Australia has more than sufficient land to meet the food and fibre needs of her own population, Japan has not. Similarly, newly developing nations like Papua New Guinea have less labour with the technical skills necessary for industrialization than a country that has been developed industrially for many generations. Likewise, tools, machines, and other forms of capital available in developed countries like Britain or the United States are relatively more plentiful than they are in the developing economies.

In the course of time, changes in the quantity and quality of resources have been observed in many individual economies. The quantities of tools, machines, and other capital have tended to increase in relation to the numbers of workers. So we find more equipment is associated with each worker. Equally important, the quality of capital has also improved, so that labour is now equipped with better tractors, lathes, trucks, and so on than it was in the past. Many of these **improvements in technology** also reflect the fact that labour has been better educated and trained than it was formerly. Such changes have resulted in less wasteful use of natural resources, the development of alternative materials and sources of energy, and marked increases in output per worker — or **labour productivity.**

However, at any particular time the total stock of resources available to any economy is fixed. Even if all people with particular skills work long hours, there is a limit to how long they can work and how much they can produce. Similarly, at any time there is a limited quantity of land available for agricultural purposes. Certainly we can reclaim swamps or dam more rivers in the future; but until these things are done, we must make do with what is available now. In the same way, our **stock** of capital is limited. In the future, we might increase the number of desalinization plants, the number of public libraries, or the numbers and quality of beef roads in outback Queensland or the Northern Territory. But for the present we must make do with what we have.

In contrast to the fixed nature of an economy's resources, **human wants** are unlimited. Who among us doesn't want something more than we have at present? (Is it a trail bike, a yacht, a holiday in Europe, or a room of our own in which to study subjects like economics?) One problem in countries like ours is that since our incomes have passed a level at which the basic needs of food, clothing, and shelter have been met, a whole new horizon of possible wants has opened for us. Sometimes these wants emerge when we see what our friends or neighbours have. Also wants are created in us by clever advertising. The origins of these wants are not our immediate concern: it is necessary only that we recognize that they exist.

This characteristic of human behaviour is not something new. Writing late in the eighteenth century, Adam Smith noted that "the desire for food is limited in every human by the narrow capacity of the human stomach, but the desire for the conveniences and ornaments of building, dress equipage and household furniture seems to have no limit or certain boundary".

Each and every society faces a situation in which resources are limited but wants are boundless. That is, resources are **scarce** in relation to wants. This scarcity of resources is widely considered to be one of the fundamental problems of economics: in fact it is referred to by some as "**the basic economic problem**".

The basic economic problem is how to use scarce resources in an attempt to statisfy unlimited wants.

Faced with this problem, every society must find ways and means of **rationing** its available resources between the people who want them. In order to do this, there are three fundamental questions that must be answered:
1. *What* shall be produced from the available resources?
2. *How* should the economy produce the goods and services it wants?
3. *For whom* will the goods and services finally be provided?
Every society, rich or poor, is faced with each of these questions. To each question there are alternative answers, none of which is likely to suit all of the people concerned. But choices must be made.

The rest of this chapter will be concerned with these three fundamental questions, some alternative answers, and the ways in which decisions are made in different societies.

Each economy faces three fundamental economic decisions: what to produce, how to produce, and for whom the goods and services will be produced.

Questions

1. What is a resource?

2. List three resources that would be categorized (*a*) as land; (*b*) as capital.

3. How can improvements in technology lead to a greater output per worker?

4. What is "the basic economic problem"?

5. Three fundamental questions must be answered by every society. Explain briefly what is meant by each of these questions.

6. Why do choices have to be made?

WHAT TO PRODUCE

At any time the resources available to any economy can be regarded as fixed. The same can be said of technology, since changes in technique (such as improved organization or more efficient machines) take time to develop. So, even if all labour and other resources are fully employed, there is necessarily an upper limit to the volume of goods and services that can be produced in any period.

Since the scarcity of resources imposes a limit on *total* production, each society must somehow make a choice between alternative goods and services that might be produced. Some societies would probably prefer to have more food, clothing, and medical care and less military hardware. Others would prefer more schools, libraries, and theatres and fewer motor vehicles and highways.

To illustrate these choices between alternative goods and services, consider the mythical island-economy of Utopia. For the sake of simplicity, we will assume that Utopia produces only two commodities, grain and cloth. Since Utopia never has an unemployment problem, no resources are unemployed and all land, labour, and capital are used in the production of one commodity or the other using the best technology available.

Nevertheless, the people of Utopia would be faced with a choice: whether to produce more grain and less cloth or more cloth and less grain. The numerous alternative combinations of grain and cloth that *could* be produced, given existing technology, skills, and the fullest use of all available resources, can be represented on a **production possibilities curve**. The curve for Utopia is described by *A-B-C-D* in figure 1.

If all resources were concentrated on the production of grain and the production of cloth was abandoned altogether, Utopia could produce 10,000 tonnes each year (represented by point *A*). As an alternative, all resources could be used in the production of cloth, in which case grain output would fall to zero and the production of cloth would be 25,000 metres annually (represented by point *D*).

Provided Utopia had no trading links with the rest of the world, it is

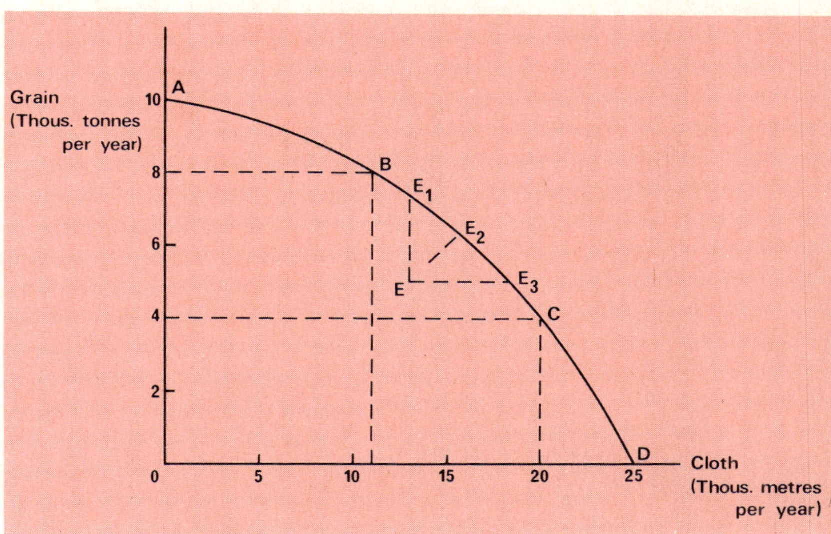

Fig. 1.   The production possibilities curve for Utopia

unlikely that the Utopians would be content to settle for production of only one commodity. Such a decision would mean that they would be either well clothed but starving or well-fed nudists. So they would probably prefer to produce some grain and some cloth. But how much of each?

If all resources were initially concentrated on the production of grain, it would be necessary to release some of these resources for the production of cloth if the Utopians wanted cloth as well as grain. As a result, they might produce the combinations of grain and cloth represented by point *B* — that is, 8,000 tonnes of grain and 11,000 metres of cloth. As an alternative, they may prefer to produce that combination represented by point *C*. But one thing is clear. If these people wish to increase their production of cloth, they can do so only by releasing resources that were formerly engaged in the production of grain.

This brings us to an important principle. **If, in any economy, all resources are already fully utilized, production of any one commodity or service can be increased only by reducing the output of some other commodity or service. In these circumstances the cost of increasing production of one commodity can be measured in terms of the loss in production of another**. This is referred to as the **opportunity cost** of that extra output. For example, the opportunity cost involved in switching from combination *B* to combination *C* — that is, in raising the output of cloth from 11,000 to 20,000 metres annually — is the 4,000-tonne loss in production of grain.

Opportunity cost is the alternative foregone when a choice is made.

The production possibilities curve in figure 1 has been drawn concave to the origin. But why should this curve take that particular shape? The reason is that some resources are more suitable, or more highly productive, if used for some purposes rather than for others. When the Utopian economy is producing the combination represented by point *B* in figure 1, it would seem reasonable to assume that the best land, the most skilful farmers, and the best available farm machinery would be engaged in the production of grain. Similarly, factory buildings, looms, and skilled textile workers would be producing cloth.

However, if a decision was made to concentrate all resources on the production of grain, the factory buildings, looms, and other textile machinery would contribute nothing to grain production and the former textile workers could do little more than fetch and carry for the skilled farm workers. Although the output of cloth would drop to zero, the resources formerly engaged in cloth production would add very little to the production of grain — in fact, only 2,000 tonnes per year. Of course, these former textile workers *could* be retrained, but that would take a great deal of time. In the event of a decision to switch all resources into the production of cloth, farm land, farmers, and farm machinery would likewise contribute very little to production.

Had the production possibilities curve been drawn as a straight line, joining points *A* and *D*, this would have suggested that the resources engaged in one industry would have been equally productive in the other. In other words, this would suggest that farm and textile machinery, as well as farm and textile workers, are perfect substitutes for each other. Clearly, this is not a realistic view.

So far, we have assumed that all resources available in Utopia have been fully employed. For that reason, an increase in the output of one commodity has necessarily involved a decrease in production of the other. If, on the other hand, the Utopian economy had been infected by the problems faced in the Australian economy in the seventies and had been operating initially at something less than full capacity — that is, with land, labour, and capital unemployed — it would have been possible to increase production of one commodity with no loss in production of the other. For example, let's assume that Utopia was initially producing that combination of grain and cloth represented by point *E* in figure 1. It would then be possible, given the resources available, to increase production of grain with no loss in the production of cloth: that is, it would be possible to switch from *E* to E_1. As an alternative, the production of cloth could be increased with no loss in the production of grain (a switch from *E* to E_3). Another alternative open would be an increase in the production of both (that is, a switch from *E* to E_2).

Whether Utopia was initally producing somewhere on its production possibilities curve or moved to such a position from somewhere inside that curve, the scarcity of resources imposes an upper limit on production in the shorter run. Until such time as there is some increase in the capacity of that economy to produce, it will be impossible to produce any combination of goods and services that would be represented by a point (such as F in fig. 2) outside the curve.

With the passing of time, it is quite likely that such an increase in total production will be possible. But this increased capacity would not necessarily require more workers or more machines. It may come about through some change in technology, such as the introduction of high-yielding varieties of grain or more efficient textile machinery. It is unlikely that technological advances would have an equal impact on all industries in any period. However, after people have been educated or trained to use the new techniques, adoption of the new technologies will serve to shift the production possibilities curve outwards to the right — as indicated in figure 2.

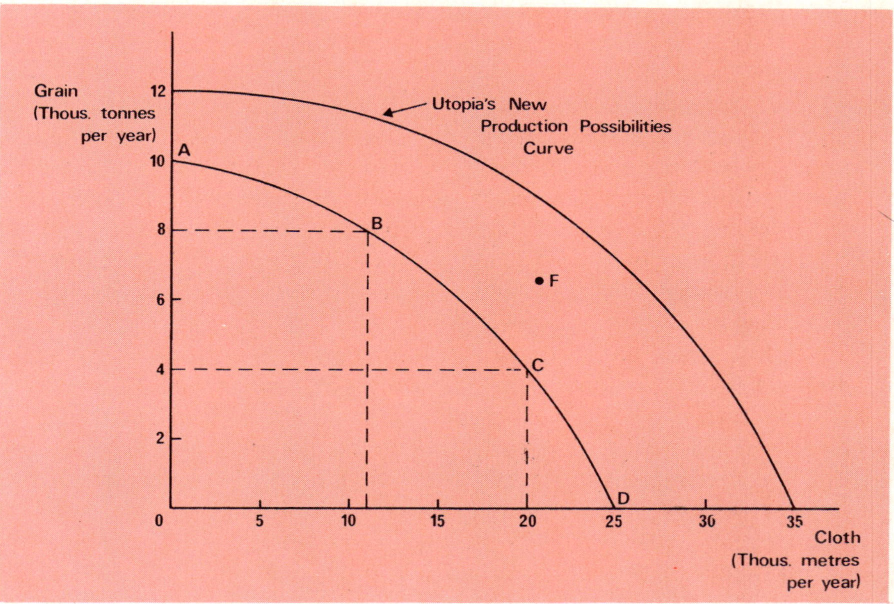

Fig. 2.   A shift in the production possibilities curve with improvements in technology

To illustrate the principles involved, we have assumed that the people of Utopia face a choice between only two commodities, grain and cloth. In the real world, of course, individual economies produce many different commodities and services. To represent the choices involved in the real world would require a multi-dimensional diagram. Nevertheless, the principles are the same.

A production possibilities curve shows the alternative combinations of two products an economy could produce with the fullest use of available resources. The resources of society serve to restrict production to combinations on or within the curve. Society's unlimited wants would require combinations somewhere outside the production possibilities curve.

From time to time, economies like Australia have operated at less than full capacity — that is, far inside their production possibilities curves. At other times, all resources have been fully employed. In fact, during World War II the loss of manpower to the armed services and the need for munitions resulted in total demand in excess of our capacity. Since the requirements of the armed services were given first priority, the production of goods and services for the civilian population was less than sufficient to meet demand. Ration books were issued to all civilians in an attempt to ensure an equitable distribution of the limited supplies of food and clothing available.

Since that time, this and other industrialized economies have periodically operated at full capacity. In those periods, as in Utopia, there has clearly been a need to choose between alternatives. These alternatives include not only things like motor cars, cigarettes, and clothing, but also school buildings, roads, and defence equipment. That is, the choice of what to produce is often a choice between the variety of goods and services available in the market-place and the collective goods and services supplied by governments.

Another choice that must be made by every society is the extent to which available resources are to be used to satisfy present wants, or to be diverted into the production of machines and other **capital goods** that will allow some increase in the production of goods and services in the future. Such choices are also faced by individual producers. For example, a farmer may decide to limit the extent of his current production activities in order to have time to clear more land or to build a modern piggery. In making such a decision, he presumably hopes to increase his output and income in the future.

Likewise, governments provide funds to encourage students to stay longer at school or university rather than leave to join the workforce. For each student who decides to remain at school, there is an immediate opportunity cost involved — hopefully, to be offset by higher earnings later. But such a government policy also implies a belief that those students who proceed with futher education will, as a result, contribute more to society in the future. In this way, a society adds to its stock of **human capital**.

Questions

1. What does a production possibilities curve demonstrate?

2.

Roads ('000 km per year)	17	16	14	10	6	0
Cars ('000 per year)	0	12	20	28	32	34

   a. Plot the production possibilities curve from this table.

   b. What is the opportunity cost of increasing production of roads (1) from 0 km per year to 6,000 km per year; (2) from 10,000 km per year to 16,000 km per year?

   c. Explain why the opportunity cost of producing 2,000 cars varies over the whole range of production.

   d. How can this society produce 8,000 extra cars per year (1) if it is producing 16,000 km of roads and 12,000 cars per year; (2) if it is producing 12,000 km of roads and 8,000 cars per year?

   e. What would be necessary for this society to produce 16,000 km of road and 28,000 cars per year?

   f. Construct a new production possibilities table to demonstrate the effect of an increase in the workforce which allows the economy's capacity to increase by 20 per cent. Show this new situation on your diagram.

   g. Construct a new production possibilities table to demonstrate the effect of the opening of a new car factory which allows car output to increase by 50 per cent relative to the original situation. Show this new situation on your diagram.

3. Why is it not possible to operate outside of the production possibilities curve?

4. Two similar economies, *A* and *B*, have identical resources which are being fully utilized. These resources may be used to produce capital goods or goods for immediate consumption called consumer goods. In *A*, more capital goods are produced than in *B*. What is likely to happen to the position of the production possibilities curve of *A* compared with that of *B*, over the next five years? Sketch production possibility curves to demonstrate this.

5. If the production possibilities curve for Utopia had been drawn convex to the origin, what would this suggest about the productivity of Utopia's resources? Explain by considering the opportunity cost of cloth at various levels of grain output.

HOW TO PRODUCE

Having decided *what* is to be produced, each society must then decide *how* its resources are to be combined to produce these goods and services. Much will depend on the labour skills and capital equipment available. If both a highly skilled workforce and the most advanced machinery are available, the productivity of labour can be very high. For example, anyone who has seen the huge machines used in the extraction of iron ore in Western Australia will know that each of those machines can do the work of a thousand hand-held shovels. Such production techniques, involving the use of a great deal of capital and very little labour, are said to be **capital intensive**.

The developing countries also face the choice of how to produce goods and services from their available resources. However, the alternatives open to these societies are generally not the same as those available in the developed countries, because they have a large pool of relatively unskilled labour and a shortage of capital and skilled operators. The result is that the techniques of production in some of these countries are not at all like those used in Australia today. For example, in the Canary Islands, some roads are constructed by men equipped only with small stone hammers: each wanders the hills until he finds a suitable stone, which he then carries back to the work site and pounds into small pieces. In the high-yielding rice growing areas on the western side of the Malay Peninsula, farm workers still cut and thresh each individual plant by hand. Techniques such as these, involving the use of large quantities of labour and very little capital, are said to be **labour intensive**.

Typically, the developing countries have large reserves of unskilled and semi-skilled labour compared with other resources. A rapid switch to labour-saving techniques would result in vast numbers of unemployed. These people would be left with no means of support, simply because people in these countries do not generally have automatic entitlement to unemployment benefits.

In contrast, the developed countries have been replacing labour with machines since spinning machines replaced hand-operated spindles during the Industrial Revolution. This is not to suggest that the substitution of machines for labour (or **automation**) does not create serious problems in our kind of society. For example, many thousands of Australian clerks, technicians, and research workers have been replaced by computers during the past decade.

Changes in techniques of production are not confined simply to changes in the relative quantities of labour and machinery used. From time to time, new raw materials have been developed — such as the wide range of synthetic fibres that now compete with Australian wool and the growing variety of building materials. The choice of technique also involves choices between alternative sources of power. In the past, every society faced a choice between human and animal power, and some developing countries are at present in the process of substituting machines for animals — just as Australian farmers did in the late 1940s. Now most economies, developed and developing, face yet another choice, namely, the future source of energy (coal, oil, uranium, or the sun) for the generation of public power supplies.

The "how" decision: goods and services can be produced in different ways. The decision how goods and services are to be produced is largely influenced by the relative scarcity of different resources. Some production techniques can be described as being land intensive, others as labour intensive, while others are capital intensive.

Questions

1. List some industries in Australia that are (*a*) land intensive; (*b*) labour intensive; (*c*) capital intensive.

2. When deciding to build a new runway at an airport, why would the Indian government be likely to decide to use different methods of construction from those used in Australia?

3. In the 1970s, considerable concern has been expressed over increased computerization in some industries, particularly telecommunications. Try to find out about and describe some instances where capital has been substituted for labour.

WHO RECEIVES THE OUTPUT?

So far, we have considered the questions of what to produce and how to produce it. Every society must find its own answers to each of these questions. Yet there still remains one particularly important question: Who is to receive the goods and services produced?

Much depends on the extent to which the community or representatives of society make these decisions and the extent to which individuals are left to choose their own "baskets" of goods. On a kibbutz (commune) in Israel, individuals are assigned to particular types of work. They may work in the fields on animal production or in some kind of manufacturing plant within the settlement. Regardless of the type of work, all take their meals in the community dining hall, all are entitled to free nursery care for their children, and so on. Over and above the goods and services available to all, each worker also receives a very small cash allowance to cover personal needs, such as bus fares or tobacco. The situation is similar in Chinese communes, except that each family also has its own small plot of land — by which it can add to its level of food consumption or add a little to family income — and each must pay a token fee for health care and other local services.

During the twentieth century a great deal of economic and political debate has centred on this question of who should receive the output of society. In very regulated societies like China and the USSR, incomes are determined by the state, and this in turn dictates to a large extent what people are able to buy. Many services are not bought and sold, as they are in Australia, but are provided by the state. The distribution of these services may depend upon how well each individual stands with the ruling party. In contrast, in economies like Australia and the United States, where most goods and services are provided privately, the decision who gets what is determined largely by who can pay. So the final distribution of goods and services depends to a large extent on the incomes received by individuals, which in turn reflect unequal ownership of resources. However, this ability to pay is modified to the extent that governments in these countries impose heavier taxes on individuals with higher incomes and provide the less privileged with cash benefits and various services under their social welfare programmes.

The "for whom" decision: not everybody benefits to the same extent from a society's production. The relative benefit that different individuals or groups get from a society's output is at the core of the "for whom" decision.

Questions

1. In the Australian economy, what determines the shares of production received by individuals?

2. In the Australian economy, some low-income earners have their income increased by government measures. List some ways in which the government may increase income.

MAKING THE "WHAT", "HOW", AND "FOR WHOM" DECISIONS

The "what", "how", and "for whom" decisions in different societies tend to be determined by the types of society in which people live. For convenience, we will distinguish only three types of society:
1. **Traditional economies**
2. **Command economies**
3. **Market economies**

Traditional Economies

In traditional economies, goods and services are produced and distributed according to the methods dictated by long-established custom. Change is uncommon and production tends to follow the pattern established by past generations.

Although less readily evident today, traditional economies were quite commonplace in the eighteenth century, when Adam Smith observed that "every man was bound by a principle of religion to follow the occupation of his father, and was supposed to commit the most horrible sacrilege if he changed it for another". Thus in traditional societies, birth normally determines one's role in life, and, with little or no change in technique, how anything is produced does not change either. In the absence of any change in production techniques, the creation of capital for future output is generally limited to maintaining the present stock of tools, implements, and other capital equipment.

The "for whom" decision is also determined by custom. In primitive hunting, fishing, and gathering societies, for example, the successful hunter traditionally takes the best cuts for himself, leaving the remainder for others in the community. In other traditional economies, the Church or the local lord may receive, as their due, a certain proportion of all output.

To some extent, *all* economies display some evidence of tradition. This can be seen in many ways, including religious and social customs and the occupations of the present generations. It is also apparent in the widely held conservative attitudes towards social, economic, and political change.

Command Economies

We have already noted that some economies, such as the USSR and China, make their "what", "how", and "for whom" decisions largely through **central planning**. That is, a large part of economic activity in these countries is regulated by an army of bureaucrats, working and planning within the policy guidelines handed down by their political masters. To this end, the planners must have access to data concerning all aspects of the economy, not only as a check on current performance, but also in order to plan for the future. Thus a characteristic feature of these (and other) command economies is the existence of forward planning, most commonly for five-year periods.

Other economies, such as Australia, Britain, and the United States, were essentially command economies during World War II. As suggested earlier, the war effort was necessarily assigned first priority. People were drafted not only into the armed services but also into those forms of production, such as munitions and foodstuffs, that were regarded as most essential to survival. Those goods in short supply (petrol, food, and clothing) were formally subjected to rationing in order to ensure equitable distribution between civilians — regardless of their incomes and capacity to pay.

But decisions reached on the basis of command are not confined to dictatorships, centrally planned economies, or wartime emergency conditions. Some far-reaching decisions have been forced upon basically traditional economies by command of ruling military juntas. Land reform, under which land has been taken from people with large holdings and re-distributed among landless peasants, is one such example.

Command is also widely evident today in countries like Australia, Britain, Japan, and the United States. Governments levy taxes, restrict pollution, and in many other ways regulate the economic behaviour of business enterprises and individuals. What this suggests is that there is an element of command decision-making in all economies.

Market Economies

The "what", "how", and "for whom" decisions in market economies are basically determined by the prices set in markets for goods and services. Production responds to the demands of buyers, who indicate their choices between alternative goods and services by the ways in which they spend their incomes. If a product or service is not wanted at a particular price very few will buy it. More people will buy it if the price is lower. Producers then respond to these indicated preferences of buyers by changing what they produce or their techniques of production. To a large extent, the relative prices of resources determines the "how" decision.

In a market economy, the final distribution of goods and services depends upon the **distribution of income** between the individual members of society. This in turn depends upon how much the market is prepared to pay these individuals for the resources they can offer — whether land, labour, or capital. In the absence of intervention by government, the clever and the industrious are likely to prosper, while those who are unable to sell their services or (like the aged and the sick) have no services to offer, will face a struggle for survival.

Elements of the market economy can be seen around us in Australia. Some **trading enterprises** (or **firms**) offer goods or services that sell very readily at current prices. The prospect of profits in these firms is good. Those firms that produce goods or services not wanted at current prices make losses, and must either change their product or their techniques of production or go out of business.

Labour also responds to market forces. Some time ago, Australia was short of doctors and the incomes of private practitioners were very high and rising. In response to these signals, many young people entered medical schools, forgoing the immediate chance of income in some alternative occupation. Now it appears that we have too many doctors. If incomes in this profession rise less rapidly in the future, it will be interesting to see how the numbers entering medical schools respond to these market signals.

The replacement of labour by computers and other mechanized equipment in recent years is another example of market forces at work in the Australian economy. Firms and governments have been substituting relatively cheap capital equipment for increasingly expensive labour. But this example serves to remind us that the "what", "how", and "for whom" decisions are subject to a mixture of forces. The production and cost of computers is largely determined by market forces. However, the price of a computer's "competitor", labour, is determined by command, in that we have laws that specify minimum wage rates in most occupations. So the price of labour is fixed and it remains for employers to decide how much labour and capital they will employ at the current prices of each.

More generally, individual economies do not fall neatly into any one of the three categories suggested. Every economy has some elements of tradition. In Australia, for example, there are large numbers of farmers who are the sons of farmers and many medical students who are the sons or daughters of doctors. Similarly, in Australia as in all other economies, there is abundant evidence of some elements of command — in that governments in all economies impose taxes, regulate trade, and intervene in economic activity in many other ways. Even planned economies must ultimately respond to market signals if a particular product is always left on the shelf long after all others have been sold.

We, in Australia, have what is referred to as a **mixed economy**. The "what", "how", and "for whom" decisions are reached as a result of market, command, and traditional forces.

The market is certainly important in many areas of our economic activity: this is readily apparent from a visit to any local shopping centre. But other forces also operate. For example, it is clear that Australian governments are not willing to leave education to be decided by market forces alone. Similarly, without the intervention of our governments, many people with low incomes would not receive adequate health care. Finally, the "for whom" question is not left entirely to the market. If that were so, only the strongest would survive. So, in addition to imposing taxes that fall most heavily upon those with the highest incomes, the government also provides the aged, the sick, the unemployed, and other underprivileged groups with pensions and other supplements to income.

Each economy makes its economic decisions by a combination of traditional, command, and market forces.

Questions

1. What evidence is there in the Australian economy of the "what", "how", and

"for whom" decisions being influenced by (*a*) traditional; (*b*) command; (*c*) market forces?

2. What type of economic system would you favour? Give reasons for your choice.

2 The Unique Nature of Individual Economies

INDIVIDUAL DIFFERENCES

We concluded the previous chapter by noting that the decisions reached on *what* will be produced, *how* it will be produced and *to whom* the benefits will accrue differ from one economy to another. Part of the reason for this is the difference in reliance on *traditional, command*, and *market* forces. The influence of past events and the consequent political philosophy of a particular country is obviously of crucial importance.

However, before a country can make the "what", "how", and "for whom" decisions, it must take account of the resources actually at its disposal. Quite obviously, it would be pointless for any economy to build a rocket to take astronauts to the moon this year if it has not the technical skills or fuel to complete the task. On the other hand, knowledge of a plentiful supply of offshore fish may quickly induce that country to become interested in maritime affairs. In other words, forces exist which make countries, like individuals, different.

In attempting to understand the economic behaviour of societies, we frequently draw upon the knowledge provided by other disciplines, such as history, politics, demography, and anthropology. For example, in seeking to understand economic behaviour in Papua New Guinea, where the traditional society was, and still is, very important, we can learn a great deal from social anthropologists.

Every society evolves in some way in the course of time. For example, Britain over the eighteenth and nineteenth centuries evolved from a predominantly rural economy to an urbanized, industrial society. Furthermore, a close examination of events in Britain will show that there were features of the transition to an industrial base which were peculiarly British and are not found in the **economic development** of, say, Japan or

Germany or the United States. To understand each case is to recognize that each country met — and has evolved from — a unique set of circumstances.

In the case of Britain, for example, most economic historians, until fairly recently, placed emphasis on the enclosure of common lands, particularly over the period 1760-1815, improvements in the techniques of cultivation and animal husbandry, and the consequent drift of landless and redundant farm workers into the towns and cities. The rising productivity of labour in agriculture was said to have had two immediate and simultaneous effects: the means of feeding the growing urban population and a growing demand for non-farm products, particularly the products of manufacturing industries.

Although an acceptable explanation of the origins of the Industrial Revolution, this fails to explain how that transformation was sustained. The reason for sustained growth is found largely in the concurrent and massive growth in Britain's **trade** with the rest of the world. For example, over the century to 1914, there was a twentyfold increase in her imports of foodstuffs and industrial raw materials. This growth in trade in turn relied in part on the existence of an extensive overseas empire and her power to impose peace on Western Europe over the century after 1815. That is, there were a number of factors contributing to the industrial development of Britain in that period.

By way of contrast, we could consider the factors involved in the economic development of Australia during the nineteenth and twentieth centuries. Australia's development was stimulated by the opportunity to sell primary products like wool and wheat to Britain and other industrialized nations in Western Europe. The growth of manufacturing industry and very sharp growth in population in these countries increased the demand for foodstuffs and industrial raw materials. This demand was met by the areas of recent settlement — not only Australia, but also other countries, including Canada, Argentina, Uruguay, South Africa, and New Zealand. In the absence of long-standing traditions or central planning, market forces acted as the strongest inducement in deciding the "what", "how", and "for whom" in these countries. As income and population grew in these areas of recent settlement, the demand for the manufactured goods of Britain and Western Europe also increased. In this way, **economic growth** in the Old World was transmitted to the New World. An important consequence of this development was the belief that, for countries able and willing to specialize in particular forms of economic activity, trade was the vehicle, or "engine", of economic growth.

Factors that contributed to the economic development and industrialization of Britain in the nineteenth century include improved agricultural productivity and a great expansion in overseas trade.

Australia derived benefit from this growth in trade as an exporter of food and raw materials and an importer of manufactured products.

Questions

1. How does an increase in trade provide an "engine of growth"?

2. Outline briefly the differences in the resources available to two countries, Australia and one other, and describe the effect of these differences on the economies of these two countries.

THE ECONOMIC DEVELOPMENT OF JAPAN: A CASE STUDY

Another country in which economic development was nourished substantially by the nineteenth century growth in world trade was Japan. Her path to development was unique in other ways. Because it serves particularly well to illustrate features of the "what", "how", and "for whom" choices peculiar to an individual economy — and also because Japan is our major trading partner — the Japanese case seems worthy of detailed consideration.

On the basis of her physical resources alone, Japan was the least likely candidate for economic development in all of Asia. About 80 per cent of Japan is extremely rugged, and frequent earthquake shocks cause the thin mantle of soil to slip off the slopes long before it attains any semblance of maturity. So something like 90 per cent of her population has long been concentrated on the narrow coastal plains. Even there, the soils are inherently low in lime and organic matter. The northern half of the country is frost free for only four or five months each year. Added to these handicaps, the streams are fast-flowing and hard to harness, transport and communication links are difficult to establish, and these islands are less well endowed with minerals and fuels than are other Asian countries.

Farming during the eighteenth and nineteenth centuries was organized on a kinship basis, with each group sharing land, tools, animals, and other resources. By the middle of this period, when population ranged between 26 million and 28 million, the pressure on land resources was already being felt. Bad harvests were followed by widespread infanticide — referred to by the Japanese as "thinning" — simply in order to allow other members of each family a better chance of survival. In order to avoid such action, some children were assigned as life servants to other families more favourably situated with respect to land and other resources. These children took the name of the family for which they worked and became part of an extended family system.

In some instances, holdings were so large that land-owners were unable to cultivate all of their own land. Rights to cultivation of small areas were assigned to members of the extended family, as well as to others outside the family. These people were given direct access to the land-owner's water supplies, tools, and beasts of burden. In return, the land-owner was entitled to call on these people for assistance during each peak in his labour requirements, particularly at times of sowing and harvesting. So it was that a high degree of economic interdependence necessarily existed between land-owners and their extended families.

This sense of obligation continued to exert a strong influence on behaviour until very recent times. In other words, *traditional* forces influenced economic decision-making and behaviour in Japan. For example, in the early 1930s, the slump in demand for their products threatened to put many Japanese manufacturers out of business. However, so strong was the sense of obligation between employers and employees that many employees volunteered to take a cut in wage rates in order to give their employers a better chance of survival. At the same time, many employers helped to ensure the survival of their employees by providing them with meals and accommodation. This traditional sense of obligation in part explains the relatively late development of labour unions in Japan and the attitude towards industrial relations of both labour and management.

Command decision-making also played its part in the development of Japan. For example, as early as 1583, official surveys were conducted to establish the ownership and size of land holdings, the quality of soil, and estimated yields. These surveys provided governments with a basis for the levy of taxes, which in turn forced people to produce more than was otherwise necessary to meet just their own family needs.

Education, among other things, serves to improve the quality of labour. Japanese governments long ago had a policy aimed at raising the level of literacy. One result was that the proportion of boys undergoing formal education in Japan during the eighteenth and nineteenth centuries was substantially higher than that in Western Europe. Despite Japan's relative isolation, remarkable advances in agricultural technology were achieved, providing yet another pre-condition for development. The increase in farm output supplied much of the food and raw materials necessary to achieve subsequent industrialization.

From late in the seventeenth century, Japanese governments deliberately restricted contact with foreigners. Some Dutch merchants were permitted access to a few ports, but people of other nationalities were denied entry. In the eighteenth and nineteenth centuries, Japanese merchants also began to make excursions to China and Korea. This trade, although limited, began to modify the totally agrarian economy that formerly existed. Foreign demand for silk and cotton fibres, as well as for lacquer-ware, mats, and other products of small-scale or "cottage" industry, led to the development of specialized markets for such commodities. In return, Japanese farmers were able to buy a growing range of products, such as hand cultivating tools, harness, paper, and tobacco.

In the process of exchanging farm output for other products available in urban centres, farmers from each district mixed with farmers from other areas and became aware of new types of agricultural production as well as new technology. So the growing volume of trade in Japan's urban centres contributed to the spread of new ideas. A still wider range of products and ideas was opened up to the Japanese in 1853, when an American naval squadron forced Japan to extend access to her ports to nations other than the Dutch. Japanese shame at bowing to the American terms, together with a fear of being colonized, led to growing unrest.

In 1868 the ruling regime was overthrown and a new government was established under the direct control of the emperor. In a deliberate break with the *traditional forces* which had so influenced the development of Japan, bright young men were sent to the corners of the world to study, at first hand, the techniques used by foreign industry and the weapons of other military forces. In the space of only ten years, the Japanese government had organized the building of shipyards, powder magazines, telegraphic communications, the beginnings of a public transport network, and other new industries.

These new activities were financed very largely by means of an increase in **land tax**. In fact, by the 1880s the farmers of Japan were paying 86 per cent of all taxes levied. In contrast, as a deliberate stimulus to the creation of new industries, manufacturers paid very little tax or none at all. In order that they might meet this tax increase, farmers responded by adopting new seeds, new fertilizers, and improved techniques of cultivation. Then, having increased their production, land tax was increased still further. Given this threat to their survival, as well as a remarkable capacity for innovation, the yields of Japanese farms raced far ahead of their Asian neighbours. In this way, the government encouraged a surplus of food and fibre sufficient to support a growing proportion of the workforce engaged in the building of new industries in the towns and cities.

One major problem faced by Japan during this period of rapid development was her shortage of labour with the training and experience to make management decisions. Some decisions, both in government and in private firms, involve the taking of risks. People trained and experienced to take these risks are often referred to as **entrepreneurs**. When Britain embarked upon industrialization she was fortunate to have an elite — particularly a long-established merchant class — experienced in making economic decisions similar to those encountered in manufacturing industry. Japan, at first, had to rely on foreigners for these skills. Later, as more of her graduates received experience in the public service and in industries established with the help of government, they were able to replace the foreigners with their own entrepreneurs.

Towards the end of the nineteenth century, the government was financing 74 per cent of all investment expenditure in Japan — still, in the main, on the basis of taxes levied on farmers. As the profitability of these new enterprises came to be recognized and both labour and managerial skills became more readily available, government was able to sell off most of these new industries to private interests. Since the profits of these industries continued to be taxed much less heavily than the incomes of the long-suffering farmers, the new owners were quick to reinvest those profits. Consequently, after the first decade of the twentieth century, investment undertaken directly by the government fell to less than half of the total.

Only forty years after the government of Japan was forced to bow to the demands of the Americans, the new-born Japanese fleet embarked on its first test of strength. The result was a decisive and humiliating defeat for the Russian navy, at that time widely regarded as one of the most powerful in the world. By 1940, in the space of barely seventy years, Japan had completed the transformation from an agrarian economy to industrial maturity.

Japan has relatively poor natural resources. Its remarkable economic development was influenced by the strong obligation between worker and employer as well as by government initiatives in education, technical development, and investment in new industries. Japanese economic development demonstrates a blend of traditional, command, and market forces at work.

Questions

1. What were the most significant factors in Japan's economic development before World War II?

2. Give examples of traditional, command, and market forces influencing the course of Japan's development.

ECONOMIC CHANGE IN THE TWENTIETH CENTURY

Not all economies have developed in the same way as Japan. Some countries owe their present economic systems to past political revolutions. This is the case in the USSR and China. In others, such as Egypt and Pakistan, the armed forces removed the former governments and ruled through military juntas who introduced numerous social and economic reforms. Developing (Third World) countries like India, Malaysia, Indonesia, and Papua New Guinea also have features in common with one another; among other things, each has a tradition-bound agricultural sector working side by side with cities that look and function like those of the industrialized countries. On the other hand, each of these economies has unique features and each relies to a different extent on tradition, command, and the market.

Regardless of the ways in which the basic economic decisions are made, very few developing countries in the world today can draw any comfort from the rapid economic growth achieved by Japan. Many of these countries have yet to establish the conditions (such as stable government and widespread literacy) necessary for sustained economic growth. Furthermore, the cultural conditions of nineteenth-century Japan were peculiar to that country, and it is doubtful whether peasant farmers anywhere in the world today would long endure treatment as harsh as that meted out by the Japanese government.

Nor is trade now the engine of growth that it was during the nineteenth century. Over that period, Britain, for example, experienced a threefold increase in population — despite substantial emigration to the New World. To sustain this growing population, as well as to take advantage of emerging opportunities for trade with areas of recent settlement, there was a twentyfold increase in Britain's imports of food, fibre, and industrial raw materials over this period. This need for rapid growth in the supply of imports also encouraged Britain, as well as other former colonial powers, to engage directly in the development of plantations, mines, railways, and port facilities in the countries of origin.

However, the rate of growth in demand for such imports is now much lower than it was during the nineteenth century. Population growth in the industrialized countries is now insignificant: in some of these countries, growth is either zero or little more than zero. Some industrial raw materials, like fibres, have been synthesized. Others, particularly metals, are now being recovered and recycled. Nor do the former colonial powers have the same interest in developing sources of supply in what are now politically independent countries.

Opportunities for trade now open to the developing countries have also been restricted in other ways. The industrialized countries have developed numerous import-replacing industries, either for defence purposes or, as in the case of the Australian cotton industry, in order to cut back on imports. Some countries, such as those within the European Economic Community (the EEC), now trade largely within such "trading blocs". The industrialized countries also rely heavily on taxes levied on imports and other measures designed to protect their own industries against foreign competition.

We see, therefore, that trade as an engine of growth has lost much of the impetus it had during the nineteenth century, and the volume of trade in relation to the incomes of the industrialized countries is lower than it was formerly. The industrialized countries, like members of a rather exclusive club, now trade more with one another than with the poorer and more numerous developing countries. Only the oil-rich economies of the Middle East can be confident that trade will continue, in the near future, to be the major force in their economic development. That is, changing world circumstances alone are sufficient to ensure that different economies develop in their own unique ways.

In the twentieth century, trade has been only one of the factors influencing the development and growth of economies throughout the world. Political and social factors have also played an important part in the economic development of many countries.

Questions

1. To what extent can Japan's economic development be used as a model for developing countries today?

2. Why has the growth of international trade slowed down over the last half-century?

APPLYING THE LESSONS OF HISTORY

This chapter has emphasized the necessity to take account of features peculiar to individual economies — as well as to particular periods in history — when seeking to explain the economic growth or development of a particular country. All countries, industrialized *and* developing, are subject to change in the course of time. John N. Keynes (father of John Maynard Keynes) recognized this in the last decade of the nineteenth century when he noted (*The Scope and Method of Political Economy*, 1891) that "economic conditions . . . vary with the legal form of society, and with national character and institutions". Despite this, his son, like most other economists before and since, assumed the customs, laws, and institutions of his own country (Britain) and, naturally enough, gave his attention primarily to the problems he regarded as the most serious of his own time.

Given that economic theory in the English-speaking world is based almost exclusively on the past experience of Britain and the United States, it is not surprising that this body of knowledge contributes little towards an understanding of problems faced currently in developing countries.

On the other hand, Australia, unlike the developing nations, has many features in common with industrialized nations like Britain and the United States. This being so, we *can* draw heavily upon the macroeconomic theory derived and developed from experience in other industrialized countries. However, we will not be concerned with changes over a long period (as we have been in explaining development of the Japanese economy) but primarily with changes in production and employment in the short period. That is, we will concern ourselves with the changes that take place from month to month and even year to year, rather than changes measured by reference to decades or centuries. These short-period macroeconomic changes will be viewed against the background of Australian institutions and policies. Australia, too, is a unique economy, and once we understand the principal reasons underlying short-run changes in Australian production, income, and employment we will then be in a better position to evaluate our economic performance and to consider possible solutions to some of our current macroeconomic problems.

Each economy is different, and much of economic theory has been developed against a background of British and American experience. The concern of this book is primarily an explanation of short-run changes in the Australian economy.

The Role of Money in Economic Activity

So far, we have seen that land, labour, and capital can be combined in different ways to produce goods or services. The choice of how to produce these goods and services and to whom they are finally distributed depends on the extent to which individual societies rely upon traditional, command, and market forces. Most economic activities in our society involve the use of money. But what is money? Most of us probably take the existence of money for granted. It will serve our purpose best if we begin this chapter by considering some of the problems faced by a society that is *without* money.

ECONOMIC ACTIVITY IN A BARTER ECONOMY

Early in the twentieth century there were still many remotely situated communities — generally in what are now referred to as "the developing countries" — in which money never entered into economic activity. Some of these people were engaged in hunting, fishing, and gathering. Others practised primitive forms of agriculture. Most families aimed for self-sufficiency, producing not only their own food supplies but also materials for the building and repair of their homes, clothing, cooking utensils, implements, and weapons.

One reason for this underlying drive for self-sufficiency was an appreciation of the problems likely to be encountered in the exchange of one commodity for another. Any individual who chose to **specialize** — producing only grain or fish or building materials — would have to rely upon the exchange of part of his own output for the products of others, in order to break the monotony of diet as well as to meet his other needs. In the absence of organized markets and some form of money, it was necessary for the specialist to engage in the very time-consuming and uncertain process of **barter** — that is, the exchange of one commodity or service for another.

For example, any family with a surplus of grain who wished to exchange grain for a piglet would first need to find another family with a surplus piglet *and* an interest in exchanging a piglet for grain. In practice, this process could prove to be more complex. It might be necessary for the family with a surplus of grain to first exchange grain for thatching, knowing that the only family with a surplus piglet had sufficient grain but a need to rethatch the roof of their home. So, in order for barter to be undertaken, it would first be necessary for the parties concerned to establish a **coincidence of wants**.

However, the problems of families seeking to barter would not end there. The parties to any barter transaction would also need to agree on **the rate of exchange**. For example, the family with a surplus of grain may have argued that one piglet was worth no more than one bag of grain. The family with the surplus piglet may have felt that a piglet was worth two bags of grain. Reference to past rates of exchange would probably not help to resolve this dispute. Much would depend upon the supplies of grain and piglets available at any one time. If it had been a particularly good season for grain, with most families holding surpluses over and above their needs, the family seeking to exchange grain for a piglet would probably have no alternative but to give up two bags of grain or to do without a piglet.

In order to exchange goods and services by barter, it is necessary to establish both a coincidence of wants and an acceptable rate of exchange for every item exchanged. This is often difficult and time consuming and therefore an obstacle to specialization.

Questions

1. What is meant by (*a*) barter; (*b*) coincidence of wants?

2. What are the major problems associated with barter?

3. In a highly specialized economy such as Australia, there are certain instances where barter is still carried on. Why do some individuals continue to engage in the barter of goods and services in Australia?

GROWTH OF OUTPUT IN A BARTER ECONOMY

In the longer run, some communities faced more serious problems. In any purely subsistence-farming community with unlimited reserves of land, output would increase with growth in population, even if the traditional techniques of production remained unchanged. All that this would require would be an extension of the area under cultivation. (Presumably hunting, fishing, and gathering societies would have responded to population growth in a similar way. They could wander further afield or set up new but distant villages.) However, if there were no reserves of land and no change in techniques, an increase in population would serve to put pressure on the means of subsistence. In these circumstances, further growth in output would require the use of better techniques — for example, more efficient use of water and better methods of cultivation, or the building of boats and use of fishing nets.

Most modern industrialized societies divert at least 20 per cent of their current production into the production of buildings, machines, and transport equipment. As a result, there is a tendency for the level of output as well as labour productivity to grow year after year. But how could the people in a barter economy, with no reserves of land, act to ensure growth in output in future periods? If such a community was already familiar with the improved techniques required and also had reserves of labour, that surplus labour could be diverted to the digging of irrigation ditches, the construction of better implements, or the production of more efficient fishing nets. The use of resources for purposes such as these would serve to increase production in future periods but would have little or no effect on the production of goods for current consumption (see fig. 3).

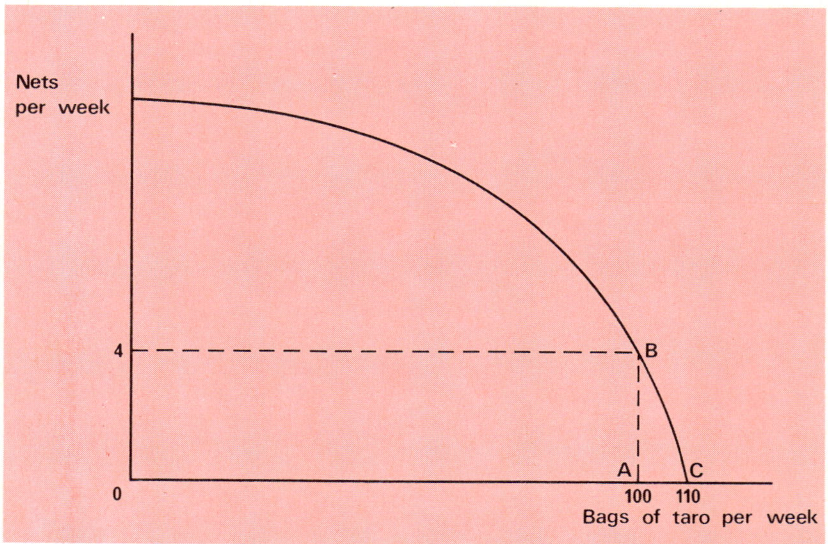

Fig. 3.   The production possibilities of taro and nets

If this community was not using all of its resources, it may be producing combination *A* (100 bags of taro and 0 nets per week). In this case, the community could produce nets, without forgoing taro, by using its resources more fully. This could be shown by a movement to combination *B* (100 bags of taro and 4 nets per week).

However, if this community was already using all available labour to produce food, the diversion of labour into other activities would result in some reduction in food supplies. That is, the **opportunity cost** associated with a switch of resources away from current production into the means of raising output in future periods (a fishing net) would be the food consumption forgone in the current period. For any society already close to bare subsistence, such a choice could not be taken lightly. If this community was using all of its resources to produce taro, it would be producing combination *C*. In this case, any production of nets would require resources to be taken away from the production of taro. The production of combination *B* results in 4 nets per week at the cost of 10 fewer bags of taro per week.

If an economy has resources which are not currently being used, it can produce more capital goods without forgoing consumption goods. It can move from a point inside the production possibility curve to a point on the curve.

Most major projects would probably require resources beyond the capacity of individual villages. For example, the setting up and operation of a shipyard to produce small boats for fishermen would require the services of many people, ranging from timber cutters to skilled craftsmen. Being a barter economy, these people could be **paid in kind**, meaning in the form of goods and services such as grain, fish, and accommodation. However, very few individuals in a primitive society would be likely to have the stores of grain and other resources necessary to initiate such an undertaking; and even fewer would be willing to accept the risks involved.

If large projects were to be undertaken in a primitive barter economy, it would probably be necessary for a government to lead the way. In order to gather together the necessary resources, the government could levy a tax. In a society without money, these taxes would be paid in kind — probably in grain, because grain can be readily transported, stored, and traded.

The government could then hire labour to build roads, dig irrigation ditches, or, for that matter, to build and operate a government shipyard. These workers — possibly farmers willing to take on work between crops, landless peasants, or unemployed from distant urban centres — would be paid in kind and it would be left to the individual either to consume or to exchange the commodities received in payment. It is likely that such a process would be necessary for projects which were beyond the immediate interests or means of individual villages but which allowed greater levels of output in future periods.

If an economy is already using fully all of its available resources, any increased production of capital is only possible by directing resources away from the production of consumer goods. The opportunity cost of more capital goods is fewer consumer goods.

Questions

1. What is meant by the term *productivity*?

2. What role would the government be likely to play in capital formation in a barter economy?

3. Why is it difficult to save in a barter economy?

4. A major problem of a barter society is capital accumulation. Suggest ways in which resources may be diverted to capital production in (*a*) a barter economy; (*b*) Australia; (*c*) a dictatorship.

THE USE OF COMMODITIES AS MONEY

If we were able to travel back through time, stopping off periodically to study economic behaviour in different communities, we would not find all societies using the same means or methods of exchange at any given time. As recently as the middle of this century, there were communities in remote and harsh environments living at the barest subsistence level by means of hunting, fishing, and gathering or the most primitive forms of agriculture. Within these communities, all families aimed for self-sufficiency. There was little produced that was surplus to family requirements. What little exchange did take place in these communities was undertaken by means of barter. In contrast, as early as 700 B.C., people in Greece and China were already using **coins** (not unlike our own) to facilitate exchange.

What, then, were the origins of money? In the barter economy referred to earlier, it was suggested that a family with a surplus of grain and seeking to exchange grain for a piglet may have found it necessary to first exchange grain for thatching. However, at a later point in time, most of the people in that economy may have come to accept payment in the form of grain. In fact, most societies in the past were at some stage prepared to accept valuable commodities — that is, *commodities valued for their own sake* — in the process of exchange or in settlement of debt.

Widespread acceptance of one commodity in payment for any other commodity or service represented a major break-through. Where grain came to be accepted for these purposes, any family with grain could exchange that commodity for any other commodity or service — simply because those who accepted the grain were aware that they could do like-wise. So, subject only to settling the matter of the exchange rate (in this case, the value of a piglet in terms of grain), the family with the surplus piglet would readily accept grain in payment, knowing that this grain would be acceptable, in turn, by any seller of thatching.

More significantly, widespread acceptance of a commodity made it possible for people with particular skills to *specialize*. Skilled craftsmen were then able to work full time at their particular trades, knowing that they could sell their own products for a widely acceptable commodity such as grain, which they could, in turn, exchange for food, clothing, or any other felt needs.

The commodities used for these purposes varied from one society to another. In some cases, it was grain; in others, it was wine or cattle or some other commodity. However, in each instance, the commodity used was initially acceptable on account of its **intrinsic value**, meaning value inherent in the nature of the commodity itself. Since **money** may be defined as **anything that is generally acceptable in payment for goods and services**, commodities assumed the functions of money when they came to be *accepted* as money.

So, with the passage of time, commodities that were initially valued for their own sake took on all **the functions of money** in a modern society. That is, these commodities served as:

1. **A medium of exchange**, the means of payment for goods and services
2. **The unit of account**, so that all other goods were valued in terms of quantities of grain or some other commodity, just as we value goods in terms of the Australian dollar
3. **A store of wealth**, that is, making it possible to set aside part of income in one period for use in a future period.

Admittedly, the use of commodities as money presented some problems. In a society prepared to accept cattle in payment for goods and services, it was impossible to engage in any transaction involving only a fraction of a live animal. A great deal of risk would have been involved in the use of either grain or cattle as a store of wealth over a long period of time. On the other hand, wine probably improved with age and therefore in value.

Problems such as these were not confined to societies emerging from the most primitive stages in the evolution of civilization. In the late eighteenth and early nineteenth centuries in Australia, officers of the New South Wales Corps established complete control over imported supplies of rum and other scarce commodities. They then traded these commodities, at prices far in excess of their original cost, for locally produced goods and services. In fact, they even insisted that their own troops accept payment in the form of these commodities. Some of these commodities were far too valuable to be consumed by any but those with the highest incomes. So rum, for example, usually changed hands many times before being consumed.

A classic and more recent example of a commodity used as money was described by R.A. Radford in his article, "The Economic Organisation of a P.O.W. Camp", published in *Economica* in 1945. The inmates of a prisoner-of-war camp in Germany during World War II were subject to near-identical camp rations plus the contents of periodic Red Cross parcels. Naturally enough, the tastes of these prisoners were not identical. Following an initial period in which trade was conducted by way of barter, these prisoners settled for the use of "tailor made" (that is, machine made) cigarettes as money. Some could not resist smoking their money! Cigarettes assumed all the functions of money and performed these functions exceptionally well — until hand-rolled (and under-filled) cigarettes were introduced, thereby debasing the currency.

Some commodities came to fulfil the functions of money, namely, as a medium of exchange, unit of account, and store of value. However, problems such as perishability and difference in quality reduce the usefulness of commodity money.

Questions

1. What are the functions of money?

2. What are the major difficulties involved in using commodities as money?

3. Why does specialization of labour need some widely acceptable form of money to enable it to work?

4. Why are people willing to accept token coins and notes as money?

THE MODERN ORIGINS OF NOTES AND COIN

Over a long period of history, various commodities served different societies as money when they came to be accepted as money.

So it was with gold, which was originally sought as an easily worked, non-rusting metal used in the making of ornaments. Like other commodities, gold was originally acceptable because it had intrinsic value. The first gold coins were hammered out between hand-cut dies and were only roughly circular. Nevertheless, in the England of Henry VIII, a one-pound gold piece *did* contain gold to the value of one pound — that is, until some people realized that a light scraping of the edges of all coins passing through their hands could result in a handsome reward. People were then reluctant to accept those coins that were clearly worth less than one pound — just as the prisoners described by Radford were unwilling to accept under-filled hand-made cigarettes. Sir Thomas Gresham, a financial adviser to Queen Elizabeth I, put an end to this practice by introducing a machine milling process that resulted in uniform coins very similar in appearance to those we use today. These coins had a milled edge and it was then clearly evident if the edges had been scraped.

The next step came with the issue of **notes**, in the first place by the storers of gold, the goldsmiths and the banks. These notes were initially acceptable because each carried the promise to pay the bearer the equivalent value in gold. There was the added advantage that notes were easier to carry than the same value in coin. Since it was believed that these notes were readily convertible into gold, they soon became widely acceptable as a medium of exchange and in settlement of debt. Notes therefore came to be accepted as money, and continued to be acceptable, even after the promise to convert into gold was withdrawn. Since coins issued in Australia and elsewhere have long since been produced from low value (base) metals, neither notes nor coin now have the intrinsic value that people required in the past. In modern societies, notes and coin are now but a small fraction of the total value of what is accepted as money.

Coinage with a metal value matched by its face value was an early medium of exchange. The notes that followed were initially a promise to pay the bearer the equivalent value in gold, but this gradually gave way to notes that also came to be acceptable as money.

Questions

1. List the properties that a commodity must possess to be acceptable as money.

2. Are Australian two-dollar notes convertible into gold?

INCOME, SAVING, INVESTMENT, AND WEALTH

In most societies, the introduction and acceptance of money has resulted in major changes in the forms of economic activity, as well as increasingly complex interrelationships between individual members of those communities. In most parts of the world, most individual families once aimed for self-sufficiency. Their economic relations with other families or with other communities were confined to occasional barter transactions. Now individuals (and groups of individuals) borrow money, erect buildings, buy machines and, in some cases, employ thousands of people in the production of goods and services sold in organized markets around the world.

In order to appreciate how money contributed to these changes in the organization of economic activity, it is first useful to consider the distinction between economic "flows" and economic "stocks". **Economic "flows" refer to quantities normally measured over a period of time** — like income per week or per annum, Australia's production of wool or motor vehicles in a particular year, or the number of books added to a school library during the twelve months to 31 December 1979. **Economic "stocks" refer to quantities measured at a given time** — like the total number of motor vehicles registered in Australia as at 1 January 1979, or the total number of books in a particular school library on the day school began this year.

Before the introduction of money, it was difficult for people in a primitive subsistence economy to hold back part of their production in one year for use in following years. One reason for this was the perishability of foodstuffs. It was also difficult to acquire, by means of barter, improved implements, fishing nets, or other means of raising the level of production in future periods. One reason was the almost total lack of communities using more advanced techniques; another was the need to establish a "coincidence of wants".

One important consequence of the introduction of money is that part of current production (a flow) can be exchanged for money and set aside (as a stock) for use in some future period. Likewise, one who works for wages and is paid in money, rather than in kind, can more readily hold back part of his current income for use at some time in the future. **Any individual who spends less than his available income over a given period is said to "save"; this process is referred to as "saving".** If an individual continues to spend less than his income, period after period, his **stock of savings** will grow — just as did the number of cigarettes accumulated by individual prisoners of war.

Once people are able to save, period after period, they have to decide what to do with these accumulated savings. Assuming that money is in the form of notes and coin, rather than some bulky commodity, an individual could hoard his savings at home. In some future period, perhaps when his current income was lower, he could draw on that hoard to increase his purchases of goods and services to a level that would otherwise have been impossible. In fact, this is precisely why people save for retirement.

However, that is not the only possibility. People who accumulate savings may draw on those savings, from time to time, to buy **durable goods**, such as motor vehicles, washing machines, and refrigerators. Any one of these could be expected to provide services to the buyer, year after year.

Another alternative open to those who save, period after period, is to use their savings to buy durable goods like farm implements, fishing nets, buildings, or machines. Like other durable goods, these will also have a market value that will tend to diminish, period after period, until worn out. However, unlike those goods that are valued for the personal comfort or convenience that they provide, the motive underlying the purchase of durable goods such as these is the contribution they can make to the production of other goods or services (and to the income of the buyer) period after period. The purchase of durable goods of this nature (that is, **capital goods**) makes up part of what is referred to as **investment expenditure**.

Yet another economic consequence of the introduction of money is that it facilitates **borrowing** and **lending**. Anyone who has savings but no immediate plans to buy durable goods may be willing to lend savings, provided there is an adequate return for the lender postponing expenditure and for the risk of loss. There are other people who wish to buy durable goods but have insufficient savings to do so. These people may aim to buy goods simply to add to their personal comfort or convenience, or for the contribution these goods are expected to make to production and their own future incomes. The borrower usually offers some form of security against loss of the lender's savings and some form of return, such as interest, for the use of those savings.

If the individual with savings is persuaded to lend, he will pass over money to the borrower. In return, the borrower will issue a piece of paper (anything from a simple IOU to a sophisticated mortgage document) in which the borrower acknowledges the extent of his debt, the date at which he agrees to repay the money borrowed, and the rate of interest payable. For the lender, this piece of paper is an asset, because it represents a claim to money at some future date. (More specifically, we refer to such claims to money as **financial assets**, to distinguish them from assets in the form of durable goods, which we refer to as **real assets**). From the viewpoint of the borrower, any financial asset that he has issued represents a **liability**: it serves to acknowledge a debt that he is required to repay at some future date.

In a primitive barter economy, the **wealth** of an individual at some point in time would have been represented by his stock of real assets — such things as a thatched home, mats, cooking utensils, implements, weapons, and if the title to land was vested in his community, the right to cultivate a certain piece of land. Following the introduction of money, along with saving, lending, borrowing, and investment, the wealth of an individual is no longer readily apparent.

In a modern economy, the wealth of any individual has several distinct components. It consists of the current value of all **real assets** (that is, durable goods — whether for personal comfort or convenience or used directly in the earning of income) **plus financial assets** (including notes and coin, as well as claims on other individuals or groups of people **less liabilities** (that is, debts outstanding) **at a particular time**. So the wealth of an individual is a stock and is not the same thing as his income.

More importantly, the introduction of money made saving easier and more attractive. The increase in saving gave an impetus to borrowing and lending, making it possible for individuals (or groups of people) to undertake investment expenditures far in excess of their own savings. So the stock of buildings, machines, transport equipment, and other real assets used directly in the production of other goods and services — often referred to as **the stock of capital** — has grown much more rapidly than could have been expected in a primitive barter economy. This, in return, helps to account for the rising productivity per worker and growing output in modern economies.

Flows are measured over a period of time while stocks are measured at a point in time. Some important economic flows are income, consumer spending, saving, and investment. Some important economic stocks are savings, wealth, and capital. Money makes it possible for some individuals to save and others to borrow.

Questions

1. What is the difference between economic flows and economic stocks?

2. What things should be included when calculating the total wealth of an individual?

3. How can an individual undertake expenditure far in excess of income in any one period?

4. What is the "stock of capital"?

5. The everyday use of the term *investment* differs from the economics definition. What is investment as economists use the term? What are some of the other uses made of this term?

6. What is the difference between *saving* and *savings*?

CONCLUSION

We have seen that "money" need not necessarily be in the form of notes and coin such as we use in Australia today. Money can be cigarettes or rum or piglets or any other item widely accepted as a medium of exchange. Some forms of money are undoubtedly superior to others. For example, a gold or silver coin is more readily stored than piglets by those who wish to accumulate savings. Similarly, a coin of a given weight and specified metal content is likely to be accepted as a more uniform measure of account — or value — than pigs or cows, which can vary in quality as well as weight.

Increasing familiarity with and confidence in money as tokens of value led people to accept printed notes which are no longer convertible into metals of equivalent value. Money in modern forms has facilitated economic activity, whereas a lack of money placed a brake on progress in barter economies. Furthermore, labour can now more readily specialize, since payment is in a readily acceptable money form. Part of the flow of income received in the course of time can be saved. In addition, individuals, or groups of individuals who own large business enterprises, can borrow money to buy durable goods in order to increase output in the future.

In the next chapter we will consider the interaction between various groups in the Australian economy. This interaction is possible because money is accepted as a medium of exchange, a unit of account, and a store of wealth.

4 Features of the Australian Economy

In the Australian economy, there are many different types of economic unit, each involved in making economic decisions and each engaged in economic relations with other units. For example, farmers hire labour and buy seed, fertilizers, livestock, and machinery in separate markets. They sell products like wool, grains, and meat at home and overseas — in some instances, through agencies of government like the Australian Wheat Board. These farmers, like others who own property and earn income, pay taxes in different forms to local, state, and Commonwealth governments. In return, they, like others in our society, derive benefit from various services provided, ranging from the maintenance of local roads to national defence. Income remaining after tax is used not only to meet the food, clothing, and other requirements of their families, but also, sometimes with the aid of loans, to undertake further investment expenditure on their farm properties.

To understand how the Australian economy works, it is first necessary to recognize the types and principal functions of the many economic units involved. To develop an appreciation of the economy as a whole, one must recognize and understand the part played by each of the principal components. The first step towards this understanding involves the classification of these units into groups — or what we will refer to as *sectors* — according to certain common and recognizable characteristics.

Some economic units are at different times members of two or even three of these groups. For example, a farmer is simultaneously engaged in economic transactions relating to both his farm and his household. Such a "split personality" need not concern us. We will be concerned mainly with sectors as a whole rather than with the behaviour of individual units within those sectors.

Once we are aware of the principal types of economic unit and relations between them, we can then proceed to examine in greater detail the functions and behaviour of each of these groups.

THE HOUSEHOLD SECTOR

What are the characteristics common to those economic units that we refer to as "households"?

The term *household* is perhaps misleading. For an economic unit to be included in this sector, it is not necessary for that unit to be a member of a family group that rents or owns a home. Some of the units included in this sector are young individuals living away from their families and old-age pensioners living alone or in institutions. However, all are *decision-making units*, in that they must decide how they will use their labour or other resources, as well as the ways in which they will use their available incomes.

Most of these units provide *resources* — most commonly in the form of labour, knowledge, and skills, but in some cases land, buildings, and machines. Most have savings lodged with banks, building societies, and other financial institutions. In return, they receive *incomes* in the form of wages or salaries, rent, interest, and in some cases, shares in the profits of firms. For the purpose of classification, it matters not whether incomes are earned in return for labour services or are derived entirely in the form of rent, interest, or shares in profits.

According to incomes earned and rates of tax specified by governments, these economic units pay what is referred to as "personal income tax" or **"direct" tax**. Taxes imposed on households are not confined to tax on income. Households also pay **"indirect" taxes** on some of the goods and services they purchase. In turn, governments use part of these tax receipts to make payments to households in the form of family allowances, age and invalid pensions, unemployment benefits, and other **social welfare payments**. We see, therefore, that the incomes of household units are not confined to payments in return for labour or other resources provided.

In addition to direct and indirect taxes, those households that own property may be subject to a **land tax** levied by state governments. Property owners also pay taxes, known as **council rates** to local government authorities, in each case according to the estimated value of their property.

Regardless of their sources of income and the forms of tax paid, the after-tax incomes of households are used, in part, to purchase goods like food and clothing and services such as public transport and personal services provided by hairdressers and dry-cleaners. Any income remaining after such **consumption expenditure** in any period is saved.

The household sector owns resources and provides these in return for

incomes. This income is taxed; the balance remaining is either spent or saved.

Questions

1. List some of the taxes levied on individuals.

2. What effect does taxation have upon a person's income?

3. Income takes several different forms. List the forms in which income can be received.

4. What uses are made of after-tax household incomes?

THE TRADING ENTERPRISES SECTOR

The term *trading enterprise* (or *firm*) refers to any unit which combines resources and management skills to produce goods and services. These goods and services are sold in the markets available. The driving force behind such economic activity is the expectation of profits. A profit is made when total sales receipts exceed the costs involved in producing and selling the product.

In some instances, what is produced and sold is a commodity like timber or steel. In other cases, firms provide services like transport or finance, or personal services like hairdressing or dry-cleaning. Some trading enterprises produce or offer for sale only one commodity or service. Others produce such a wide range of goods, or such a combination of goods and services, that they are extremely difficult to classify according to type of industry.

The classification of an economic unit as a trading enterprise is in no way influenced by the scale of its activities. Some, like the Broken Hill Proprietary Co. Ltd (BHP) and General Motors-Holden's Ltd (GMH), are very large organizations with branch operations within and between states. Each employs many thousands of people. In contrast, other trading enterprises are nothing more than backyard workshops or a few hectares of land farmed on a part-time basis by one man. So a firm may be quite small, owned and operated by an individual or a family — commonly true of farms, corner stores, and personal services — or it may be an industrial giant or a nation-wide chain of retail stores owned by thousands of shareholders and operated on their behalf by an elected board of management.

In Australia, most trading enterprises are privately owned. Apart from controls exercised by governments in areas such as public health, the environment, working conditions, and fair trading practices, the decisions about what, how, and where to produce or sell are made directly by the owners of these enterprises or, on behalf of the owners, by appointed managers.

Not all trading enterprises are privately owned. Some, like Trans-Australia Airlines, Telecom Australia, and the Australian National Railways Commission are owned and operated by the Commonwealth government. Others, like electricity and housing authorities, are operated by state governments. These organizations sell their output in the same way as other trading enterprises. However, unlike privately owned firms, these economic activities are not motivated solely by the expectation of profits. The reasons underlying government participation in such activities range from a felt need to compete with private enterprise to the supply of goods or services that private enterprise would be unlikely to provide. In most instances, it is intended that such enterprises should cover their costs. Any profits made accrue to the government concerned.

To the extent that the sales receipts of trading enterprises exceed their costs, they make profits. These profits, like wages or salaries earned by individuals in the household sector, are subject to direct taxes levied by the Commonwealth government. In the cases of trading enterprises owned by individuals or families, the owners are taxed on their profits in much the same way as wage and salary earners. In contrast, public companies like BHP are subject to what is referred to as **company tax**. Out of the after-tax profits of such companies, dividends are paid to shareholders and become part of the before-tax incomes of these individuals.

Like households, trading enterprises are also subject to taxes on property levied by state governments and local government authorities. In addition, trading enterprises face **payroll tax** levied by state governments. This tax is calculated as a percentage of wages and salaries paid, but in such a way as to give exemption to small firms.

All decision-makers in trading enterprises, whether the owners or managers acting on behalf of the owners, face the same basic questions. The most basic of these questions are *what* to produce, *how* to produce (that is, with what combinations of machines, labour, and other inputs), and, in anticipation of market demand, *how much* to produce in the current period. Beyond these most immediate questions, decisions must also be made with regard to *future* levels of production — which requires, in turn, that decisions be made with regard to replacement of worn-out machines, building repairs or extensions, and other changes in capital considered necessary to the realization of such plans. In many cases, trading enterprises also have to consider the training of the specialized skilled labour which makes the future output possible.

Trading enterprises are economic units that combine capital resources with labour services, raw materials, and other inputs used up in production processes to produce goods or services. These goods or services

are sold in markets, and success or failure of such economic activities tends to be measured in terms of profits. Some trading enterprises are wholly or partly owned by governments.

Questions

1. List by name some local firms and describe their operations in terms of what they produce, their size, and their ownership.

2. What is the major motivation for a trading enterprise to produce? Can you state any other factors that motivate production?

3. Why do you think governments in Australia have chosen to own certain types of trading enterprises?

THE GOVERNMENT SECTOR

In order to appreciate the role of government, it may be useful first to consider briefly an economy consisting of households and trading enterprises only. Within such an economy, the ownership of land and capital resources may be concentrated in the hands of relatively few people. In contrast, some people would have nothing more than their own labour services to offer for hire. Among these people, there would be some who had relatively scarce skills and who could command high prices for their services. Alternatively, there would be those with very commonplace skills, or no skills at all, who would have to accept much lower wage rates. This unequal ownership of resources would no doubt be reflected in the distribution of income between individuals.

With no taxes to pay, people could use their incomes in any way they pleased. Such an arrangement would be very satisfactory for those with high incomes. On the other hand, the people who were too old or too sick to work, as well as those unable to find employment, would have no income whatever. If not cared for by their families, these people would suffer great hardship — just as millions do in the developing countries today.

Health care and education would depend upon arrangements made by individual families or groups of households. Those that could afford to do so would hire the services of doctors and teachers; those that could not afford such services would have to do without. Law and order would probably be restricted to arrangements made by those families that could afford to hire people to protect their own members and property.

So elected governments, in economies like ours, have some important and necessary functions. The principal functions of government are concerned with the **distribution of income, allocation of resources,**

regulation of certain economic activities, and stabilization of the economy.

The *distribution* function involves issues such as the redistribution of income between those who are well off and the disadvantaged, such as the physically and mentally handicapped and the aged. The government attempts to achieve redistribution through taxation and **transfer payments**, such as unemployment benefits and various pensions. Other redistribution objectives of government may concern themselves with the income and welfare of people in specific *areas* like people in remote outback areas or inner city slums.

The main *allocation* function of government is to provide goods and services that it judges to be inadequately provided by the market. This is obviously an area of considerable subjective judgement, but in our economy today it is commonly accepted that the government must become involved in the provision of services such as comprehensive health care, education, and defence. The government also has ways and means available to influence the allocation of resources in the market. For example, if it wanted to encourage the use of public transport it could lower all fares while raising the taxes on private motor vehicles and fuel sold to the general public.

The *regulative* function influences the nature of economic activity by way of certain laws and regulations. For example, we have minimum safety standards to protect workers and some commodities cannot be imported into Australia without a licence from the government.

The *stabilizing* function of government is designed to influence the level of economic activity by varying the amount of government spending, altering the levels of taxes, and exercising control over the money supply. For example, if the government decided to spend an extra $100 million on schools and roadworks, this would increase the receipts of firms supplying the government and the incomes and employment opportunities of the workforce.

The system of government differs from one country to another. In Britain, for example, all power rests with the **central** (or **unitary**) government at Westminster. Quite limited powers, relating to local matters such as housing and education, are delegated to local government authorities like city or county councils. Britain therefore has two levels (or tiers) of government: central and local.

Up to the end of the nineteenth century, each of the Australian states had a system of government very much like that of Britain. For example, each state levied taxes on the incomes of its residents and imposed taxes on imported goods. Each had its own defence forces and met the cost of health care, education, and other services provided.

After years of heated debate and a great deal of compromise, the states agreed, at the beginning of this century, to join together within a federation of states. In doing so, they agreed to the creation of a central **federal** or **Commonwealth** government, and under the Constitution that set out the powers and responsibilities of the several governments involved, they transferred certain powers (such as responsibility for defence and the sole right to tax imported goods) to the new government.

So Australia, like Canada and the United States of America, has three tiers of government. In Canberra, we have a central government with far-reaching responsibilities towards all people in Australia. We also have separate legislative bodies, the various state governments, in each of the several states. Finally, we have local government authorities within each state, each of these *councils* having limited powers and responsibilities delegated to them by their state governments and relating to their own particular areas — such as part of a metropolitan area, a country town, or a rural district or shire. In other words, we have not one but many governments that together make up what we will refer to as "the government sector" in Australia.

The governments at all three levels function in basically the same ways and have certain features in common. For example, at each level of government:
1. Members of government are elected periodically and have powers defined in the Constitution to enact legislation (make laws) binding on the people they represent.
2. Taxes are levied, primarily in an attempt to meet the cost of services provided.
3. Tax revenue is often supplemented by borrowing, usually for investment projects like dams or public buildings.
4. The day-to-day administration of the various activities of government is left in the hands of *public servants.*
5. Apart from the costs associated with investment projects, continuing (or recurring) expenditures, such as the salaries of public servants, maintenance of buildings, and the running expenses of motor vehicles have to be met.

On the other hand, **these three levels of government differ in the types and geographical extent of their responsibilities, as well as in the forms of taxation which they impose.** For example, our Constitution gave to the Commonwealth government sole powers concerning foreign policy and defence, while the states were left with the right to administer their own industries, education, and other services within their borders. The powers of local government are derived from the individual state governments, but generally include regulation and supervision of building construction, road maintenance, and matters relating to public health (including garbage disposal). Under the Constitution, the right to tax imported goods was transferred to the Commonwealth, while the states retained the power to impose taxes on income. The states, in turn, delegated to local governments the right to levy taxes on real estate within their boundaries.

Whatever the division of responsibility between these three tiers of government and the various means of financing their expenditures, how do governments exert an influence upon the types and levels of economic activity in Australia? As indicated earlier in this chapter, our governments are to some extent directly involved in the production and sale of goods and services. For example, the Commonwealth government operates TAA and the Australian National Railways Commission, while state governments are involved in electricity undertakings and the construction of houses either for rental or for sale. However, these enterprises represent only a small part of the economic activities of governments in Australia, and all such undertakings will be treated, for our purposes, as part of the trading enterprises sector.

By far the greater part of expenditures by Australian governments is concentrated on the provision of services such as defence, social welfare, education, health care, and law and order. Since no formal markets exist for the sale of many of these services, there is generally no direct charge levied on the people who use them. **This failure to make any direct charge, or to charge only a very small fraction of the costs involved in the provision of services, is the distinguishing feature of those economic activities characteristic of the government sector. At the same time, this is essentially the reason why all governments find it necessary to impose taxes.**

These taxes imposed by governments and the various services they provide have substantial effects upon the allocation of resources between alternative uses. If there were less government intervention we would presumably have more *private* goods such as motor cars, colour television sets, yachts, and private art collections, but less *publicly* provided hospitals, schools, art galleries, and libraries. Futhermore, the distribution of the ownership of these goods would be less even than is the case at present and we would have more people living in poverty, without adequate food, education, or health care.

Questions

1. What are the principal functions of government?

2. What do we mean when we refer to the three tiers of Australian government?

3. What document spells out the limits of power of government in Australia?

4. Can you argue a case for the complete *private* provision of education or health care?

5. Is it necessary for the government to license people to practise medicine in Australia?

6. In what ways can the Commonwealth government influence the level of economic activity?

THE OVERSEAS SECTOR

In the Australian economy, as in many other economies, most of our economic transactions are conducted between the domestic sectors — that is, between Australian households, trading enterprises, and governments. However, as was suggested in chapter 1, resources are not evenly distributed over the earth's surface. For example, Australia has abundant reserves of minerals, such as iron ore and coal. In contrast, Japan relies very heavily on manufacturing industry but has negligible mineral resources. For the Japanese, again in contrast to Australia, land suitable for agricultural purposes is also a particularly scarce resource. As a result, Australia sells iron ore and coal to Japan, as well as farm products such as wool and beef, and in return buys manufactured goods such as machinery and electrical equipment.

So part of the sales of our trading enterprises, particularly enterprises engaged in mining or farming, are sales to buyers overseas. These sales are referred to as **exports** and represent part of the production of Australia's trading enterprises. Likewise, Australian firms and governments make some of their purchases overseas. For example, we buy crude oil from the Middle East because our own production is insufficient to meet our needs. We buy military and commercial aircraft, particularly from the United States, because the Australian market is too small to justify production. Such purchases are referred to as **imports** and represent part of the output of trading enterprises overseas.

However, overseas transactions are not confined to commodity trade. Foreign ships and airlines transport goods and people to and from Australia, while Australian ships and Qantas provide similar services. Associated with this movement of goods and people are insurance services provided against damage or injury. As in commodity trade, payments are made for freight and insurance services — either to overseas or to Australia, depending on the country of origin of the company providing a service.

When people overseas buy Australian-produced goods or services, this serves to generate employment and income in Australia. In contrast, when Australians buy goods or services produced overseas, this generates employment and income in other countries.

In addition to sales of goods and services, there are other economic transactions between Australia and other countries. For example, multi national companies that operate in Australia periodically remit part of their profits to their parent companies. Overseas residents who hold shares in Australian companies periodically receive dividends from those companies, just as Australian citizens receive dividends paid on shares they hold in trading enterprises overseas. Other payments flow into or out of Australia where people resident in Australia receive pensions paid by overseas governments, or Australian citizens temporarily resident overseas receive pensions or other forms of income paid by the Commonwealth government, such as the salaries of servicemen or diplomatic staff posted overseas.

The overall picture becomes even more complex when we take into consideration other kinds of transactions. For example, individuals and companies overseas not only buy shares in *existing* Australian trading enterprises, but often initiate the development or expansion of these enterprises by directly engaging in investment projects, such as the development of mining leases in Western Australia or the Northern Territory. Likewise, Australians buy shares in overseas companies and have increasingly engaged in direct investment in new ventures abroad, particularly in South-East Asia. In addition, Australian governments raise loans overseas — on government-to-government basis, through foreign banks or in major capital markets — and are then faced with periodic payments of interest and repayment of the principal sums. On the other hand, the Commonwealth government lends support to various United Nations agencies and provides quite substantial grants and loans by way of aid to developing countries.

So commodity imports and exports represent only one aspect of our economic transactions with other countries. In order to assess our total trading position in relation to other countries, it is necessary to take into consideration other types of transaction of the kind referred to above.

Australia's links with the rest of the world involve not only the import and export of goods, but also transactions related to services, the financing of investment, and government.

Questions

1. List five Australian commodity (*a*) exports; (*b*) imports.

2. Suggest some ways in which overseas trade can influence economic activity in Australia.

3. Find out the names of at least five firms in Australia that owe their origins to investment by companies overseas.

AN OVERVIEW

We have seen that the Australian economy consists of four sectors — households, trading enterprises, government, and overseas — each with certain characteristics and functions, each interrelated in many ways. In order that we may see how our economy operates, it will be necessary to have a thorough understanding of these functions and interrelationships.

Looked at in another way, the interaction and functioning of the various sectors result in features of the economy which are peculiar to Australia. For example, some key characteristics of these sectors in Australia are:

1. Over 80 per cent of our workforce are wage or salary earners, the vast majority of whom live in urban communities. The remainder are self-employed in the professions, small business, and farming.

2. By far the major part of our productive resource base is privately owned and more than three-quarters of our wage and salary earners are employed in the private sector. That is, the bulk of our production is organized by privately owned firms that buy and sell in organized markets at home and abroad.

3. Overseas transactions play a significant part in Australian production, employment, consumption, and investment. For example, about one-sixth of our total output finds its way into exports, and borrowing from overseas (net of our lending) accounts for about 10 per cent of all funds invested in Australia.

4. Although production and investment decisions are predominantly in the hands of private firms, our governments also own resources and directly operate some of our trading enterprises. However, the influence of these governments on the Australian economy is far greater than their direct participation in economic activity would suggest — for example, through the levels and types of taxes imposed and various controls exercised in industry and commerce.

These characteristics serve only to illustrate the character of the Australian economy. It will be our task in the chapters that follow to consider each of these sectors in some detail as a prelude to our analysis of the behaviour of the economy as a whole.

5 The Household Sector

As suggested in chapter 4, the household sector consists of all people who receive income and are therefore involved in making decisions on how these incomes are used. The source of household income varies between individuals. Some households work their own farms; some own blocks of flats; others are part-owners of large trading enterprises and receive incomes in the form of rent or profits. Many Australians also receive income by way of interest on their savings. However, the main source of household income in this country is from wages and salaries received in return for the labour and other skills supplied to employers.

In practice, most households receive income from a mixture of sources, like wages and salaries, interest, dividends, and even payments from the government, such as family allowances. After payment of any tax due on their income, households then spend or save the balance remaining according to their assessment of current and future needs.

This chapter looks at the receipts of households in Australia and the principal ways in which they spend that income.

THE AUSTRALIAN WORKFORCE

Within the Australian workforce (sometimes referred to as the labour force), there are vast numbers of different occupations. Each of these occupations requires different skills, many of which are in some way peculiar to the individual industries in which people work. The distribution of this workforce between major occupational groups as at May 1978 is indicated in table 2.

These broad groups tend to disguise a much wider variety of occupations. The first group, for example, includes architects, engineers,

Table 2. Employed Persons by Major Occupational Groups, May 1978

Occupational Group	Males (%)	Females (%)	Persons ('000)	Percentage of all Employed Persons
Professional, technical, and related workers	55	45	799.9	13.3
Administrative, executive, and managerial	88	12	377.0	6.3
Clerical	30	70	1,037.0	17.3
Sales	47	53	535.0	8.9
Farmers, fishermen, and timber-getters	80	20	414.4	6.9
Miners, quarrymen, and related workers	98	2	40.3	0.7
Transport and communications	86	14	323.4	5.4
Tradesmen, production-process workers, and labourers	87	13	1,900.7	31.7
Service, sport, and recreation	38	62	571.1	9.5
Total			5,998.7	100.0

Source: Australian Bureau of Statistics, *The Labour Force, May 1978.*

surveyors, chemists, geologists, veterinarians, medical practitioners, dentists, nurses, teachers, lawyers, writers, and draftsmen. The "tradesmen, production-process workers, and labourers" group includes weavers, tailors, instrument makers, jewellers, mechanics, plumbers, electricians, bricklayers, bookbinders, millers, brewers, and so on.

In addition to those in employment, there are others who have a capacity and willingness to work but are unable to find jobs. These people are unemployed but are also part of the workforce. Subject to certain rules, they may receive unemployment benefits.

The household sector also includes people who are *not* in the workforce. For example, some people have retired from the workforce and are now drawing on past savings or superannuation benefits provided by their former employers. Some receive income as owners of capital. Some are too old or too sick to work and receive pensions or other forms of social welfare (that is, social security) benefit paid by the Commonwealth government. These pensions, like the unemployment benefit, are small compared with the incomes of wage and salary earners. Nevertheless, these people, as part of the household sector, must also make decisions on how their incomes are to be used.

The Australian workforce is engaged in a wide variety of income-earning activities. The household sector also includes persons who receive payment from other sources, such as government pension funds and property ownership.

Questions

1. What is the largest occupational group in Australia? What is the smallest occupational group?

2. Who is included in the household sector?

3. What are the sources of income for people included in the household sector but not in the labour force?

SOURCES AND USES OF HOUSEHOLD INCOME

In the **financial year** 1977/78 — that is, from 1 July 1977 to 30 June 1978 — the total *gross income* (total income before tax) received by Australian households was estimated in the 1978 *Budget Papers* at $77,086 million. Part of this income was estimated on the basis of knowledge concerning the economic activities of individual households. For example, allowance was made for the value of farm produce consumed by farm families, as well as for the private use of motor vehicles used also in family trading enterprises. If no allowance had been made for the consumption of such goods and services, income would be understated to that extent.

The principal sources and uses of household income in 1977/78 are indicated in table 3.

"Other" sources of income include rent on dwellings, benefits received on retirement, payment of insurance claims, and income received from overseas. "Other" uses include taxes and fines paid to state and local governments and payments made overseas.

Total direct tax paid by households amounted to 16.8 per cent of total income. However, this understates the total tax burden of households, because consumption expenditure includes indirect taxes — such as sales tax on motor vehicles and excise duties on alcoholic beverages, tobacco, and petroleum products. In 1977/78, indirect taxes paid to the Commonwealth government amounted to $4,492 million. A very large part of this sum would have been paid by households. But part, in the form of sales

Table 3. Sources and Uses of Household Income in Australia, 1977/78

Sources	Percentage of all Sources	Uses	Percentage of all Uses
Wages and salaries	65.0	Consumption expenditure	69.6
Social welfare benefits	11.2	Income tax	15.7
Family trading enterprises	10.7	Saving	11.8
Interest received	6.9	Interest paid	1.3
Dividends received	0.9	Other	1.6
Other	5.3		
Total	100.0	Total	100.0

Note: The total value of sources and uses in 1977/78 was $77,086 million.
Source: Australian Bureau of Statistics, *National Income and Expenditure, 1977—78*.

tax on motor vehicles and excise on petrol, would have been paid by trading enterprises. We have no means of knowing how much indirect tax was paid by these different economic units. All we can say with certainty is that the tax burden met by households was considerably greater than is suggested in table 3.

Income remaining after taxation is referred to as **household disposable income**. Of household disposable income in 1977/78, 83.6 per cent was spent on the consumption of goods and services, such as food, clothing, rent, and entertainment. In fact, if we assume that payments overseas were made in return for goods and services provided and that all interest payments were related to past purchases — for example, purchases of houses and consumer durables — then household disposable income was either consumed or saved.

A large part of Australian household income is in the form of wages and salaries. Of all income remaining after direct taxation, that is, "household disposable income", a very large part is spent on consumption.

Questions

1. What is household disposable income?

2. What is the principal source of household income in Australia?

3. What is the principal use of household disposable income in Australia?

THE DISTRIBUTION OF INCOME

In the Australian economy, the ownership of resources is unequally distributed. This applies as much to labour as it does to land and capital, in that the individual members of each society do not have equal opportunities either to learn or to enter various trades or professions. Unequal ownership of resources *does* result in unequal distribution of income.

At first sight it might appear that some indication of the distribution of income can be obtained from an inspection of income tax statistics. However, these data suffer from a number of disadvantages. For one thing, income tax data are published on an *individual* basis, rather than by *households*. Furthermore, households with an income too low to be taxable — as is the case with many aged or invalid pensioners — will not appear in data of this type. Other difficulties are experienced when trying to relate individual tax data to households, including the ability of some families, such as those carrying on a family business like farming or retailing, to *split* income receipts between several members of the household. Individual incomes in these families might be quite moderate, or even low, yet the combined household income is high compared with others. This makes comparisons with households in which there might be only one or two wage or salary earners very difficult.

In an attempt to learn more about the distribution of *household* income, the Bureau of Statistics has, in recent years, begun to collect income data from families living as households: that is, people making joint decisions and sharing expenses. Although the data collected are limited to a sample of Australian households, we can be confident that they reflect the general pattern of household income distribution at that time.

The most recently published data are for 1973/74, and this is summarized in table 4. It can be seen that while almost one-third of

Table 4. Family Household Income Before Tax, Australia, 1973/74

Income Classes	Percentage of Households
Less than $3,000	10.5
$3,000–$5,999	20.5
$6,000–$8,999	28.6
$9,000 $11,999	20.0
$12,000–$14,999	10.4
$15,000–$20,999	7.1
$21,000 and over	2.9
	100.0

Source: Australian Bureau of Statistics, *Income Distribution 1973–74*, part 3, Supplementary Tables, Canberra, 18 May 1978.

households had incomes less than \$6,000, 10 per cent of households had incomes over \$15,000. It is clear that there is an unequal distribution of household incomes in Australia.

Income is unequally distributed between households in Australia.

Questions

1. Why is income unequally distributed in Australia?
2. Why do tax data tend to understate the income available to Australian households?

FACTORS INFLUENCING CONSUMPTION EXPENDITURE OF HOUSEHOLDS

We saw in table 3 that consumption expenditure of households represents a very important element in Australian economic activity. It is important, therefore, to consider some of the factors likely to have a bearing upon consumption expenditure decisions.

Consumption expenditure depends in the first instance upon the level of household disposable income — that is, income remaining after the payment of direct taxes. Individual households with very low disposable incomes tend to spend a large part of their incomes and to save little. What they can spend on goods and services in any period depends largely upon the incomes available to them. In the shorter run, such households can spend more than their incomes, either by borrowing or by drawing upon past savings. However, if they borrow, it is likely that they will be forced to consume less in future periods when repaying such loans; and if disposable incomes in past periods have been low, savings are likely to be very limited.

In contrast, people with high incomes are able to spend more on goods and services. Also, those with higher incomes tend to accumulate savings, period after period, whereas those with low incomes draw upon past savings or borrow in order to allow higher current levels of consumption expenditure.

Generally the higher the disposable income of a household, the higher is the level of consumption expenditure. But the higher the income, the higher too is the proportion of income generally saved.

The contrasts between low-income and high-income households are not confined only to total expenditure per period. They also differ markedly in the types of goods and services consumed. Households with low incomes tend to rent poor quality accommodation, eat high-calorie-low-protein foods, and rely on public transport. Those with high incomes are more likely to have their own homes, to eat out more frequently, and to have their own motor vehicles. Some of these characteristics are evident in table 5.

Table 5. Household Expenditure by Income, Australia, 1975/76

	Weekly Household Income					
	Less than $80	$80—140	$140—200	$200—260	$260—340	$340 or more
Average weekly expenditure ($)						
Food	18.0	25.5	31.7	35.7	39.7	48.8
Clothing and footwear	5.4	8.7	11.6	15.3	18.4	25.2
Housing	9.6	19.4	22.1	25.2	29.4	34.4
Transport and accommodation	9.5	20.8	29.1	34.5	45.0	59.0
Alcohol and tobacco	3.2	7.0	9.3	10.6	13.4	16.9
Recreation and education	4.9	8.1	11.0	18.4	18.9	31.6
All other	18.9	24.8	32.4	43.7	53.1	69.6
Total expenditure ($)	69.5	114.3	147.2	183.4	217.9	285.5
Average weekly income ($)	50.8	111.3	169.5	229.3	295.1	465.2
Average weekly saving ($)	−18.7	−3.0	22.3	45.9	77.2	179.7
Percentage of income consumed	136.8	102.7	86.8	80.0	73.8	61.4
Other household characteristics						
Average age of head (yrs)	61.7	49.7	41.5	40.9	40.3	42.9
Average persons/household	1.8	2.7	3.2	3.4	3.5	3.8
Nature of housing: percentage of all households						
rented	31.0	37.7	34.2	27.7	31.4	19.3
buying	8.1	23.5	37.8	45.5	47.5	54.0
owned	60.9	38.8	28.0	26.8	21.1	26.7

Source: Australian Bureau of Statistics, *Household Expenditure Survey, 1975—76*, bulletin 1.

Table 5 reveals a number of important features of household consumption and saving behaviour. As suggested earlier, households generally spend more on goods and services per period as their income rises. For example, households with weekly incomes of $340 or more in 1975/76 spent an average of $285.5 per week on goods and services. In contrast, those households with incomes of less than $80 spent only $69.5 per week. Admittedly, there were generally more persons per household the higher the level of income. So weekly *income and size of family* appear to have strong influences upon the consumption expenditures of individual households.

At the same time, it is apparent that the higher the level of household income, the smaller the proportion of income consumed and the greater the proportion saved. On average, the households with the highest incomes consumed 61.4 per cent of their incomes and saved 38.6 per cent. Those in the two lowest income classes spent in excess of their incomes, presumably by either borrowing or drawing upon past savings.

In the lowest income class, the average age of the household head was 61.7 years, suggesting that many of these people had already retired from the workforce. Most of these people owned their homes and were therefore neither paying rent nor making housing loan repayments: hence their low housing expenditures compared with those of other income groups. It also seems likely that these generally older people would have accumulated savings in past periods, making it possible to draw upon those savings and thus spend in excess of their incomes. So *wealth*, as distinct from *income*, also helps to explain the consumption behaviour of individual households.

Consumption expenditures undertaken by individual households are also influenced by other factors, particularly the *age of the householder* and the *number and ages of children* in the family. Young married couples tend to spend in excess of their incomes. Typically, at the outset, they borrow money in order to buy and furnish their homes. The pressure on current income continues as their children reach the stage of secondary (and possibly tertiary) education. With home mortgage repayments still required, saving out of current income is generally low and confined mainly to arrangements such as life assurance or superannuation designed to give security to their families. But after the children leave home to pursue their own careers or to marry, households tend to spend less on food, clothing, transport, education, and other goods and services. Furthermore, as people grow older, their own felt needs diminish. At the same time, these older people become increasingly conscious of a need to provide for their own retirement. So there is a tendency for the proportion of income consumed to fall and the proportion saved to rise. Usually on the eve of retirement, mortgages are paid off and housing costs are then reduced to maintenance expenditures and taxes of the kind payable by all property owners. Then, during retirement, past savings make it possible to spend in excess of income received.

Another factor that has a bearing on total consumption expenditure in any period — particularly among households with low incomes — is the *availability of credit.* In periods when lenders are willing and able to lend, many people borrow money to assist them in buying motor vehicles, refrigerators, washing machines, and other consumer durables. In this way, people are able in some periods to spend in excess of their incomes. At other times, households find it more difficult to borrow. Without the aid of borrowed funds, those with low incomes are less able to buy consumer durables. So the sales of such goods tend to fall. In fact, if all supplies of credit were closed off suddenly and completely, many households would be left paying off debts contracted in past periods and would have no alternative but to consume less than their current incomes or to draw upon past savings.

Since consumption expenditure depends heavily upon household disposable income, changes in the rates of income tax have the effect of changing household disposable income and consumption. For example, if all other things remain equal (including the gross incomes of households), we would expect that an increase in taxation would result in some reduction in consumption. The reverse could be expected if tax rates were reduced. In this way, rates of taxation influence consumption expenditure.

Unlike day-to-day requirements such as food and accommodation, most households can either put off or bring forward the purchase of consumer durables like motor vehicles or television sets. For example, if the prices of motor vehicles are generally expected to fall in the near future, most of the households that would otherwise buy within a month or two would be likely to delay their purchases until the expected fall in price is realized. If, on the other hand, prices are expected to rise, most buyers are likely to bring forward their purchases in order to beat the price rise. So, in the purchase of consumer durables in particular, consumption expenditures in any period are also likely to reflect widely held *expectations with regard to future prices.*

Household expectations about future income will also influence consumption expenditure. For example, if there is uncertainty about job security and the threat of unemployment, expenditure patterns will differ from households with secure employment. The more widespread is uncertainty regarding future employment and income, the less are households in general likely to spend on the consumption of goods and services.

The main factors influencing consumption expenditure are:
1. **Income**
2. **Wealth**
3. **Age of consumer and family size**
4. **Availability of credit**
5. **Taxation**
6. **Expectations about the future**

Questions

1. List the factors that influence consumption expenditure.

2. Explain how the age of the householder and family characteristics determine the level of expenditure. Use several representative groups such as a school leaver, newly marrieds, a household with children at secondary school, a couple with married children, and age pensioners to help explain your answer.

3. How is it possible for the less than $80 income group in table 5 to have negative savings?

4. From the data in table 5 calculate the proportion of income spent on food for each of the income groups. In your calculation, use the *average* income for each group.

THE AVERAGE AND MARGINAL PROPENSITY TO CONSUME

The consumption and saving behaviour of different groups of households in Australia is often summarized by reference to their "*propensity to consume*". This refers to their tendency to spend part of their disposable income on goods and services. For this purpose, it is useful to distinguish between the *average propensity to consume*, which refers to the ratio of total consumption expenditure to total disposable income, and the *marginal propensity to consume*, which refers to the increase in consumption expenditure associated with some specified small increase in disposable income.

The meaning of these terms may be clearer if we substitute some standard symbols for words. If C represents consumption expenditure and Y_d represents household disposable income, then the average propensity to consume of an individual household or a group of households is given by C/Y_d. If we now use the symbol $\triangle$ to signify "a small increase in", then $\triangle C$ indicates a small increase in consumption expenditure and $\triangle Y_d$ represents the small increase in household disposable income — say an increase of one dollar per week — that brought about this increase in consumption. Then the marginal propensity to consume can be represented by $\triangle C/\triangle Y_d$. The marginal propensity to consume is often referred to as the m.p.c., or simply by the small letter c.

$$C \qquad = \text{Consumption expenditure}$$
$$Y \qquad = \text{Income}$$
$$Y_d \qquad = \text{Disposable income}$$
$$\triangle \qquad = \text{A small change}$$
$$\frac{C}{Y_d} \qquad = \text{Average propensity to consume}$$
$$\frac{\triangle C}{\triangle Y_d} = \text{Marginal propensity to consume} = \text{m.p.c.} = c$$

From table 5, it was apparent that the households in the two lowest income groups were generally spending in excess of their incomes. In each of these groups, the average propensity to consume (or a.p.c.) was greater than 1. In contrast, the a.p.c. of the highest income group was only 0.61.

How might these groups have responded to an increase of one dollar in their weekly incomes? The information contained in table 5 does not allow us to calculate directly the marginal propensity to consume for any of these groups. Since households in the two lowest income groups were spending more than their current incomes, presumably they would have continued to spend in excess of their incomes had all incomes been raised by one dollar a week. If this were so, then the m.p.c. for each of these lowest income groups could have been at, or very near to, unity (1).

On the other hand, it is clear that the proportion of income consumed declines at higher levels of income. In other words, as the level of household income rises, there is a tendency to consume a smaller proportion (and to save a larger proportion) of income received. Households in the group with average weekly income in the range $140-$200 had an a.p.c. of 0.87. They were already saving an average of $22.30 per week. If all households in that group had received a one dollar increase in weekly income, it seems likely that they would have consumed a smaller proportion of that dollar than they were formerly consuming on average. That is, we would expect the m.p.c. to be less than the a.p.c. and perhaps as low as 0.8.

Alternatively, since we can in general assume that what is not consumed is saved, we could describe this latter group's response to a one-dollar increase in weekly income as having a *"marginal propensity to save"* of 0.2. Either of these measures (the marginal propensity to consume or the marginal propensity to save) would suggest that, out of an increase in income of one dollar, households in this group would increase their consumption expenditures by eighty cents and their saving by twenty cents.

Low income households have high m.p.c.'s — meaning that they tend to consume a high proportion of any increase in their incomes. In contrast, households with high incomes have relatively low m.p.c.'s.

Questions

1. What is meant by the term *propensity to consume*?

2. What is the average propensity to consume?

3. What is the marginal propensity to consume?

4. A person's disposable income increased from $10,000 to $12,000 and consumption expenditure increased from $8,000 to $9,000. Calculate the a.p.c. at both levels of income and the m.p.c.

CONSUMPTION EXPENDITURE IN AGGREGATE

We have been considering the consumption behaviour of individual household units, or groups of households, depending on their disposable incomes and other characteristics. From this point onwards, we will be concerned more often with total (or aggregate) consumption expenditure in the Australian economy, reasons for changes in consumption expenditure from period to period, and some of the consequences of these changes for the economy as a whole. Nevertheless, it will be necessary to bear in mind the contrasts between individual households and the factors influencing their consumption behaviour. If the government wishes to stimulate or dampen aggregate consumption expenditure, the effectiveness of the measures the government chooses to adopt will depend upon the composition and characteristics of all households in the economy.

Over the past two decades, there have been some marked changes in aggregate or total consumption expenditures of Australian households. It is clear from table 6 that Australians in general are now spending greater proportions of their incomes on housing, transport, and communication and smaller proportions on food and clothing than they did in the past. These changes do not mean that we are less well fed and clothed than we were in the 1950s. In fact, the lesser emphasis now given to food and clothing and greater emphasis on housing, motor vehicles, and so on is consistent with growth in the purchasing power of our incomes.

Table 6. Percentage Distribution of Aggregate Consumption Expenditure in Australia (selected years)

	1956/57	1966/67	1976/77
Food	25.8	22.6	17.1
Clothing and footwear	12.2	9.9	8.2
Housing	8.2	11.8	15.5
Transport and communication	12.6	14.5	15.4
Alcohol and tobacco	10.9	9.7	8.7
Household durables	7.7	7.3	7.8
Health	4.8	5.7	6.3
All other	17.8	18.5	21.0

Source: Australian Bureau of Statistics, *Australian National Accounts* (various issues).

Over this same period, household disposable income has remained a fairly constant proportion of total Australian income, ranging from a low of 66 per cent of all income in 1969/70 to a high of a little over 70 per cent in 1974/75. Aggregate household disposable income and aggregate consumption expenditure have each been plotted as a percentage of total Australian income in each year from 1963/64 to 1977/78 in figure 4. Although household disposable income has remained a fairly constant proportion of total income and consumption expenditure has remained at around 90 per cent of disposable income, some variations are apparent from the graph. For example, after the slump in economic activity occurring from 1973/74 onwards, consumption expenditure as a percentage of household income fell slightly. This is reflected in the increase in the percentage of household saving from 1973/74 onwards, apparent in the graph both by the size of the gap between household disposable income and consumption expenditure and in the separate series of points showing the percentage of income saved by households.

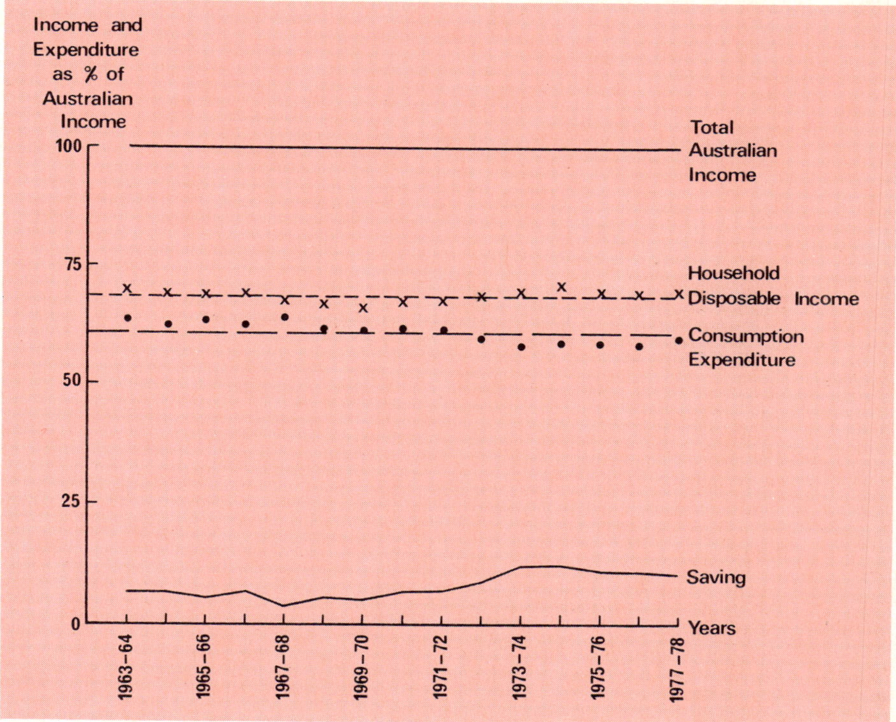

Fig. 4.   Relationships between income, saving, and consumption expenditure: Australia 1963/64 to 1977/78. (Source: Australian Bureau of Statistics, *Quarterly Estimates of National Income and Expenditure*)

There are many possible reasons for changes in the relationships between income, saving, and consumption expenditure. For example, if the Commonwealth government increases tax on incomes, household disposable income will fall, and, if nothing else changes, households will probably consume less. If there is a reduction in taxation or an increase in social security benefits, like pensions or the unemployment benefit, household disposable income will rise; presumably consumption expenditure will also rise. If there is a marked decrease in rates of interest paid on savings, this may encourage people to save less and to consume more. On the other hand, if many people begin to worry about the possibility of losing their jobs, they may tend to save more out of their current incomes as a form of insurance against the loss of employment in the future.

Some of these possibilities will be considered at length in later chapters. Meanwhile, because other sectors also contribute to production, income, and expenditure, we now need to consider the economic behaviour of trading enterprises in the Australian economy.

From this point we focus on aggregate consumption expenditure. Over the past twenty years household disposable income has been around 70 per cent of total income and households have consumed around 90 per cent of disposable income.

Questions

1. How has the proportion of consumption expenditure spent on food changed over the last twenty years? Why has this occurred? Does this mean that less food is being consumed now than twenty years ago?

2. Since the mid seventies, the proportion of household disposable income saved has changed. How has this proportion changed and what are some possible reasons for this change?

6 The Trading Enterprises Sector

Australian trading enterprises are engaged in many different kinds of economic activity, ranging from farming, mining, steel production, and motor vehicle assembly to the provision of services such as those supplied by retail stores, hairdressers, and building societies. Some of these enterprises are very small, employing only one person or one family. In these cases, all decisions concerning purchases and sales are made by an individual or a family, who also represent the firm's workforce. Others are quite large, providing jobs for many thousands of people. Most are owned privately: but some, like telecommunication and electricity undertakings, are owned and operated by governments.

Although our trading enterprises vary greatly in size, forms of ownership, and types of goods and services produced, they also have many features in common. They all combine resources to produce goods or services. All firms are faced with decisions about what and how to produce, as well as the quantities to be produced in each period. Likewise, all trading enterprises must make decisions concerning investment expenditures, such as the replacement of worn-out equipment, the purchase of additional buildings and plant, and desired levels of stocks. Investment decisions determine their capacity to produce in *future* periods.

In our kind of society, the driving force behind decisions of these kinds is **the expectation of profits**. However, profits are by no means certain. All trading enterprises face a great deal of uncertainty — not only with regard to future demand for their own goods or services in preference to those of their competitors, but also concerning future economic conditions at home and abroad and the likely impact of any change in these conditions on total demand for goods and services. While the prospect of profits is a strong motivating force underlying the economic activities of trading enterprises, there is always the risk of periodic losses or even complete failure.

Production and investment decisions are influenced largely by the expectation of profit.

FEATURES OF AUSTRALIAN INDUSTRIES

The importance of a particular industry may be judged in terms of the numbers of people employed, the value of output and its contribution to export earnings, or the extent to which the production of the industry reduces our import requirements.

Table 7 lists industry groups according to the numbers of people employed. Manufacturing, wholesale and retail trade, and "community services" (such as health, education, and other services provided by government) together accounted for more than half of the Australian workforce in 1977. In contrast, agriculture and mining directly accounted for only 6.0 per cent and 1.2 per cent respectively of the workforce. If we were to judge the importance of these industries only according to employment provided, we would be likely to conclude that agriculture and mining contribute relatively little to the Australian economy. Yet these two industries together account directly for more than one-tenth of the

Table 7. Australian Workforce by Industry, November 1977

Industry Division	Percentage of persons Employed		Persons Employed ('000)	Employment as Percentage of Total Workforce
	Males	Females		
Agriculture	78	22	388.6	6.0
Forestry, fishing, and hunting	92	8	17.3	0.3
Mining	93	7	79.2	1.2
Manufacturing	75	25	1,300.0	20.0
Construction	93	7	508.3	7.8
Wholesale and retail trade	58	42	1,220.9	18.8
Transport and storage	84	16	311.2	4.8
Finance, insurance, real estate, and business services	54	46	488.1	7.5
Community services	37	63	907.5	14.0
Entertainment, recreation, restaurants, personal services	42	58	392.1	6.0
Other industries	74	26	521.9	8.0
Registered unemployed	67	33	357.0	5.5
Total workforce			6,492.1	100.0

Source: Australian Bureau of Statistics, *The Labour Force, 1977*; and Reserve Bank of Australia, *Statistical Bulletin*, June 1978.

total value of our production. They also provide raw materials for processing by manufacturers and together account for more than three-quarters of our exports. These exports, in turn, allow us to import raw materials, components, and machinery essential to other industries. Also, productivity varies between industries, so employment alone is an insufficient basis for judging the importance to the economy of individual industries.

Within these broad industry classifications, there are marked contrasts in the sizes of individual firms. The measure of size can be indicated by numbers employed, value of annual sales, or value of real assets employed in production. However, many trading enterprises have two or more plants, such as a factory in each of several states. Also, many firms produce a range of goods and services, implying that their output is classified under more than one industry grouping. Hence published data tend to understate the sizes of trading enterprises in Australia.

Bureau of Statistics figures show that in June 1976, 91.4 per cent of all manufacturing plants employed less than one hundred people, while only ninety-five plants (or 0.3 per cent) employed one thousand or more. Not surprisingly, the smallest plants are found in the wood, wood products, and fabricated metal products industries, where individual plants in most instances serve only relatively small local markets. The largest plants were mainly those associated with transport equipment (largely the production and assembly of motor vehicles) and basic metal products (such as steel).

Two widely known examples of firms in these latter two industries are GMH and BHP. A thumbnail sketch of these two trading enterprises is provided on pages 72 and 73. Examination of the characteristics of these two firms indicates that the economic activities of BHP are much more diversified than those of GMH. That is, many of the activities of BHP would be classified under separate industries, such as ship-building, mineral and fuel extraction, and steel milling. One consequence of this diversification by BHP is that although that firm suffered losses in ship-building and steel production in 1977/78, it made an overall profit before tax of $271 million — largely owing to the profits earned in the production of minerals and fuels.

The two examples of GMH and BHP serve to remind us of the *financial* side of trading enterprise activities. These results are expressed in money terms in statements of account from which the tax liability is determined as well as the profitability (or otherwise) of the firm. In addition, public companies (those in which shares in the company can be freely traded on the stock exchange) periodically appraise their net wealth in the form of a *balance sheet*, which sets out the assets and liabilities of the company at a given time. This information is contained in *annual reports*, and in the case of public companies these are published and freely available to all who want to see them.

GENERAL MOTORS–HOLDEN'S LIMITED

GMH is primarily engaged in the assembly of passenger and commercial motor vehicles and currently sells about 150,000 vehicles each year. It also produces crawler tractors, front-end loaders, diesel engines, gas turbines, and various motor vehicle parts and components. During 1977 this trading enterprise operated manufacturing and assembly plants throughout Australia and employed, on average, 21,555 people.

Some of the operating results for GMH over the twelve months to 31 December 1977 were as follows:

	$m.
Receipts from sale of motor vehicles	726.9
Wages and salaries paid	213.4
Parts and components purchased from other Australian enterprises	460.7
Depreciation of fixed assets	200.3
Loss on overall operations	8.4
Taxes paid to governments	26.8

After allowance for depreciation of buildings, plant, and equipment over this period, these fixed assets were together valued at $189.3 million. Inventories of finished and partly finished motor vehicles and other products were reduced by $24.8 million to $197.9 million. So total real assets as at 31 December 1977 were valued at $387.2 million.

Despite the loss on operations over this period, GMH paid $8.1 million in dividends to shareholders and undertook investment expenditures amounting to $53 million—in part financed by the borrowing of $30 million, in part by drawing upon undistributed profits accumulated in past periods.

Source: *Annual Report, 1977* and other information provided by General Motors —Holden's Limited.

Apart from day-to-day running expenses, such as wages and the raw materials and services purchased from other firms, trading enterprises must make allowance for the fact that their **buildings, machines, and other equipment wear out with use** in producing their output or become outdated and too costly to operate. **This wearing-out process is referred to as "depreciation" and the funds that firms set aside to replace these assets at some future date are referred to as "depreciation allowances".**

After deducting from sales receipts all expenses other than depreciation and tax payable on its income, the firm is left with what is known as its **gross profit** (or loss). In the case of BHP in 1977/78, for example, its gross profit was $405.6 million. However, BHP had more than $2,000 million worth of plant, buildings, and equipment that was

THE BROKEN HILL PROPRIETARY COMPANY LIMITED

BHP is engaged in a wide range of economic activities. Over the twelve months to 31 May 1978, production included iron ore, coal, coke, manganese, steel, ships, tinplate, a wide range of steel products, and, jointly with Esso, 62 per cent of Australia's crude oil requirements as well as natural gas, liquefied petroleum gas, and ethane. These and other economic activities were located throughout Australia, as well as in New Zealand, Papua New Guinea, Indonesia, and the Philippines, and employed 59,414 people.

Some results of operations over the twelve months to 31 May 1978 were as follows:

	$m.
Total sales receipts	2,373.9
Wages and salaries paid	713.1
Depreciation of fixed assets	134.2
Royalties to governments	51.7
Profits on operations	271.4
Taxes paid to governments	179.3
Profits available to BHP shareholders	81.5

After allowance for depreciation on buildings, plant, and equipment, fixed assets were valued at $2,110.9 million. Inventories, after an increase in value of $28.5 million during 1977/78, were valued at $648.3 million. So total real assets as at 31 May 1978 were valued at $2,759.2 million.

Profits net of tax amounted to $81.5 million. Of this sum, $69.5 million was paid out in dividends to BHP's 176,555 shareholders. The balance ($12 million) was added to undistributed profits, lifting accumulated undistributed profits to $255.3 million. Investment expenditures over this period included $28.8 million spent in the continuing search for minerals and fuels.

Source: *Annual Report, 1978* and other information supplied by The Broken Hill Proprietary Company Limited.

being used in producing its output. In order to be able to go on producing in the future, these assets must be periodically replaced. So $134.2 million was put aside as a depreciation allowance. Its gross profit ($405.6 million) less $134.2 million depreciation allowance resulted in a **net profit** (before tax) of $271.4 million.

Although GMH and BHP are both giants when compared with most other firms, their activities serve to illustrate some of the features common to all trading enterprises. In any given period, all firms are concerned with decisions not only about current operating activities, like the hiring of labour and the purchase of raw materials from other trading enterprises, but also about the replacement of or additions to their real assets. These latter decisions will determine their future capacity to produce. Decisions of both kinds — that is, those regarding current levels of production and those regarding the purchase of capital equipment — have a strong and very direct bearing upon the level of economic activity in Australia. Each of these areas of decision-making will therefore occupy our attention for the remainder of this chapter.

All firms make production decisions and investment decisions.

Questions

1. Why is it difficult to assess the importance of an industry to the Australian economy by using only (*a*) number of persons employed; (*b*) the market value of production?

2. What industries would you expect to have mainly small firms? Why?

3. Why would a firm perhaps prefer to produce several different products, rather than concentrate on producing only one product?

4. What is a depreciation allowance?

PRODUCTION DECISIONS

Once an individual firm has decided what it is going to produce and how it intends to produce these goods or services, it has committed itself to use particular types of capital equipment, together with the labour skills and other inputs required by those machines, until such time as it buys re-placements. **In the short run, each trading enterprise can be assumed to have a given stock of fixed capital equipment. Likewise, the technology employed and the skills of labour and management can be taken as given.** The result is that, in the short run, there is an upper limit to the output capacity of each individual firm, just as there is for the economy as a whole.

But how long is "the short run"? This varies from industry to industry. A firm producing simple tools and machine parts can probably buy an extra lathe and employ an additional fitter and turner to increase its production capacity in the space of a week or two. In contrast, others, such as electricity supply authorities or those who produce petrochemicals, may need several years to plan and complete any programme of expansion. In the meantime, and until expansion has been undertaken, there is a short-run ceiling on the level of output that is possible.

However, **trading enterprises do not automatically produce to their full capacity at all times**. Quite often, individual firms and industries operate at less than their capacity. This was particularly evident during the latter half of the 1970s, when plant was idle and fewer people were employed than would have been the case had all trading enterprises operated at full capacity. For example, in 1978, the metal industries in Australia were estimated to have been working at a little less than 70 per cent of their designed capacity. In other words, **subject only to some upper limit to the level of production that is possible, trading enterprises can (and often do) produce at less than capacity and can also change their levels of production in the short run.** They may do this by varying the labour they hire and raw materials they purchase as well as using more (or less) fully their designed capacity to produce.

These short-run changes in production are not brought about by chance. Individual firms, from time to time, make decisions concerning their own levels of production. But how do they make these production decisions?

The future demand for output is *unknown*. On the other hand, individual firms must necessarily produce today in anticipation of sales next week, next month, or even further into the future. So, in making their production decisions, **trading enterprises face uncertainty** — simply because they cannot predict all important future events. For example, changes in day-to-day weather conditions will affect the production decisions of farmers as well as ice-cream and soft-drink manufacturers. In addition, other events of various kinds have an impact upon the demand for goods and services. Some of these economic "shocks" are imported from overseas — for example, the sharp increase in crude oil prices during the 1970s or the cut-back in economic activity in Japan, which resulted in reductions in their demand for our coal, iron ore, and farm products. Other economic shocks originate within Australia — for example, through changes in the rates of direct or indirect taxation imposed by the Commonwealth government.

Some changes, such as a reduction in income tax, leave households with higher disposable incomes. Others, such as an increase in world demand for wheat, perhaps resulting from the failure of crops in the Northern Hemisphere, can have a favourable impact on the sales of our trading enterprises. However, other changes in economic conditions may have the effect of reducing sales below the levels expected.

Most trading enterprises hold **inventories** — that is, **stocks of finished or semi-finished goods** — for a number of reasons. These include increase in demand for their products, the seasonal pattern of sales in some industries, and a need for protection against the effects of strikes, breakdowns, and uncertainties in the supply of inputs necessary to the production process. The sales of some firms are so erratic that firms have no choice but to hold large inventories as a reserve to meet changes in demand.

If, at the beginning of a production period, demand is expected to grow in future periods, producers may set production at a rate in excess of expected current sales in order to build up their inventories. In the reverse situation, or where firms feel that their inventories are larger than necessary, they may set production at a rate less than expected sales in a deliberate attempt to reduce their inventories. However, it is important to note that there is a **planned** (or **intended**) level of inventories at any time.

The production decisions of firms are heavily influenced by immediate past sales, generally in the belief that sales in the next period will be similar to those in the last. However, in deciding upon their levels of production, the decision-makers also take into account the reports of salesmen, market research, the expected effects of sales promotion, expected changes in government policies, and other information, as well as an element of intuition. Finally, the levels of production set by individual firms also allow for an increase or decrease in inventories wherever this is intended.

However, the expectations of producers are seldom realized. Economic conditions change and sales are invariably greater or less than expected. As a consequence, inventories held at the end of each production period are usually greater or less than planned. Earlier, we noted that BHP increased its inventories over the twelve months to May 1978. In contrast, GMH reduced its inventories. Whether these changes were precisely as planned is another matter. A change that is not intended is known as an **unplanned change.**

Production costs are involved whether a firm produces for immediate sale or for additions to its inventories. If inventories are permitted to grow unchecked, period after period, a firm may find itself with a mountain of unsold goods but no funds to pay wages or buy raw materials. For example, one clay brick manufacturer in England whose doors were closed in 1974 was reported to have a stockpile of bricks sufficient to build 220,000 houses. That firm was unable to use those bricks to pay wages or to meet other expenses. So most firms see unexpected changes in their inventories as a signal and respond by adjusting their levels of production.

As an illustration of the kind of changes in the level of production experienced in some industries, figure 5 shows changes in the quarterly production of motor vehicles, steel, and cement over the period 1971 to 1978. These data, as well as data for other basic industries, show that levels of production change quite substantially from one period to the next. In the industries considered here, there is evidence of a *seasonal pattern in production*, with output tending to peak in the September quarter of each year. This is particularly evident in the cement industry but is less evident in the steel industry. It is clear from the peaks and troughs seen in

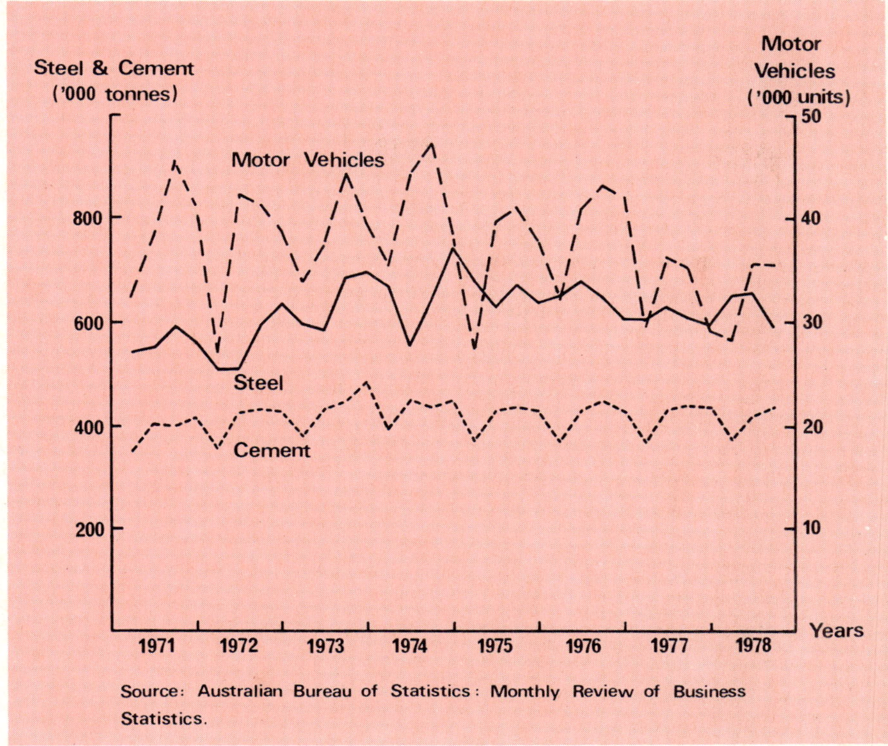

Fig. 5.   Production of steel, cement, and motor vehicles by quarters, Australia, 1971-78 (Source: Australian Bureau of Statistics, *Monthly Review of Business Statistics*)

figure 5 that seasonal factors alone are not sufficient to explain *all* of the changes observed. So other changes in economic conditions also exerted some influence.

Production decisions are affected by such factors as:
1. Expected future sales
2. Immediate past sales
3. The business climate
4. The time of the year

Questions

1. What are the uncertainties faced by trading enterprises?

2. Explain why firms hold inventories.

3. Explain why there is a seasonal trough in production early in each calendar year.

4. Would you expect demand for vehicles, steel, or cement to be greater in some quarters of the year than others? Why?

INVESTMENT DECISIONS

We have seen that the output of individual firms is limited, in the short run, by their plant capacity, technology, and the skills of their workers. Admittedly, sales can exceed output if firms have inventories upon which they can draw to meet unexpected increases in demand for their products. However, it is only in the longer run, through investment expenditures, that a firm can maintain and if necessary increase its capacity to produce.

For our purposes, it is useful to distinguish between **two types of investment expenditure**. Firstly, purchases of **fixed capital equipment**, such as buildings, machines, tools, and transport equipment. Secondly, investment in **inventories** of finished and semi-finished goods — that is, goods completed and ready for sale or which have been partly processed by the firm concerned.

Firms are said to "invest" in inventories because there are costs involved in producing and holding inventories and the purpose is to allow greater sales in future periods than would otherwise be possible. Demand for a firm's output in future periods may be greater than was expected. Alternatively, there may be an unexpected fall in production resulting from disputes between labour and management, interruptions to supplies of raw materials, or a need to shut down to allow plant maintenance. In any of these circumstances, the holding of inventories makes it possible for a firm to draw upon its finished goods to meet current orders, or to use semi-finished goods to increase its rate of production quickly.

If a trading enterprise produces at a rate in excess of its sales over any period, this will result in an increase in that firm's inventories. Whether or not this inventory build-up was intended, this is referred to as **inventory investment**. The reverse situation — that is, where current sales exceed current production, resulting in a reduction in inventories — is referred to as **inventory disinvestment.**

The other type of investment expenditure, that involving the purchase of fixed capital equipment, is of two broad kinds. One is the **replacement** of existing buildings or equipment that have worn out with use or which no longer fit in with current production techniques. The other kind is in the form of **additions** to the stock of such assets. These additions are also of two kinds — those that simply duplicate existing buildings and plant, so that a firm increases its capacity to produce, but uses the same techniques as formerly — referred to as **capital widening** — and investment in new, more sophisticated equipment which requires less labour per unit of output — referred to as **capital deepening**.

This suggests that technical changes occur only when capital deepening is undertaken. However, this is not so. Technological change is a continuous process in a modern society; replacements, except for the most elementary tools and machines, are seldom likely to be precisely the same as the plant or equipment being replaced.

The sum of increases in the value of inventories and purchases of fixed capital equipment over some given period — for example, a financial year — is referred to as the **gross investment expenditure** over that period, whether we refer to an individual firm or to all trading enterprises in aggregate. This measure of investment expenditure includes the purchase of replacements and is "gross" in the sense that no allowance is made for depreciation over that period: that is, it refers to investment of all kinds, regardless of whether buildings or machines are purchased as replacements or as additions. **Net investment expenditure** is gross investment less depreciation over the period considered and, although also including changes in inventories, is sometimes used as a rough measure of growth in the stock of fixed capital equipment.

Although considerably less than the consumption expenditures of households, the gross investment expenditures of trading enterprises represent an important element in the total demand for goods and services in the Australian economy.

Production decisions relate only to the immediate future production period. Even so, such decisions are made in the face of a great deal of uncertainty. Hence the need to hold inventories. But sales seldom measure up to expectations, and this is reflected in changes in output as well as changes in inventories from one period to the next. For example, the

Table 8. Gross Investment Expenditures of Trading Enterprises as a Percentage of Total Expenditure, Australia, 1968/69 to 1977/78

Year	Investment in Fixed Capital Equipment	Inventory Investment	Total
1968/69	22.1	2.4	24.5
1969/70	22.5	1.7	24.2
1970/71	22.4	1.4	23.8
1971/72	22.3	−0.3	22.0
1972/73	20.8	−0.8	20.0
1973/74	19.5	2.6	22.1
1974/75	18.8	1.5	20.3
1975/76	19.1	0.0	19.1
1976/77	19.0	1.3	20.3
1977/78	19.0	−0.3	18.7

Source: Australian Bureau of Statistics: *National Income and Expenditure* (various issues).

inventories held by our trading enterprises increased by $1,073 million in 1976/77. In the following year, the total value of inventories fell by $225 million.

Investment expenditure is made up of investment in fixed capital equipment and in inventories. Gross investment expenditure includes all purchases of fixed capital equipment, whether used as replacements or added to the total stock of capital.

Decisions concerning the purchase of fixed capital equipment, like production decisions, are also motivated by the prospects of profit. However, fixed capital is expected to contribute to output over a *number* of production periods, extending into the more distant future. Some machines may last only five years, others ten years. Buildings can usually be expected to last for forty years or more. But the longer the expected economic life of an investment project, the less certain can decision-makers be concerning the economic conditions under which that project will be operating. Hence, when economic conditions are changing and businessmen are even less certain than usual about the future, they tend to concentrate their investment expenditures on inventories or short-term projects — simply because their expectations about the next year or two seem more likely to be realized than expectations concerning the more distant future.

In order to make a decision concerning a new investment project, what factors need to be taken into account? All investment projects involve additional expenses. The initial cost of new buildings or equipment is usually known with a fair degree of certainty. Following erection or installation of the new buildings or equipment, there will be additional operating expenses, such as labour and raw material costs associated with the project. However, in circumstances such as we have faced in recent years, the prediction of wage rates and raw material or crude oil prices two, five, or ten years hence would be a particularly hazardous exercise.

Since any investment must be financed either from borrowed funds or by drawing on the firm's own reserves, another factor of importance to decision-makers is the possibility that rates of interest may change. The interest charge on borrowed funds, or the interest that could have been earned if the firm's own funds had been lent out, is part of the cost of investment. A sudden increase in interest rates on borrowed funds, for example, *after* the firm has purchased new capital equipment, could seriously jeopardize the profitability of the venture.

A third area of uncertainty faced by those responsible for investment decisions is the likely future demand for their product and the prices they are likely to receive. Apart from the success or otherwise of sales promotion, the responses of rival firms, and a number of other possible changes in the future, the government may legislate to alter taxes. These and other changes could influence demand for the firm's products.

A change in any one of these variables could threaten the survival of a trading enterprise. Operating costs could increase unexpectedly, interest rates could rise, and the price received per unit of the firm's output could fall. Decision-makers can and do make allowance for these uncertainties — for example, by making conservative estimates of sales and prices, or pessimistic guesses about what is going to happen to wages, fuel, and other costs in the future. None the less, during periods of great uncertainty about the future, trading enterprises will be reluctant to undertake new projects because estimates of sales receipts, costs, and interest rates appear subject to errors of very considerable magnitude.

So the situation faced by each individual firm is rather "circular" in nature. The ability to meet all financial commitments depends very heavily upon the firm's gross profits. The level of profits in any period depends, in turn, on investment expenditures undertaken in past periods. Decisions concerning investment projects are heavily dependent upon expectations about the future, particularly the expectation that the flow of cash, after allowance for additional operating expenses, will prove sufficient to restore reserves or to meet debt commitments associated with these projects.

Although profits are the incentive, the risks associated with many investment projects are very substantial. In the event that a trading enterprise is unable to meet its commitments, its creditors can bring an end to the life of that firm. In the longer run, new firms and industries emerge. Other firms wither away with a steady decline in demand for their products or come to an abrupt end as a result of what some may prefer to describe as misadventure.

Investment decisions are influenced by the expectations of profit. These decisions are affected by uncertainties concerning possible changes in operating costs, interest rates, prices, demand, and government policies.

Questions

1. In any one period, how can sales exceed output?

2. What are the two broad types of investment expenditure?

3. What is the difference between capital widening and capital deepening?

4. Investment this year may increase the capital stock next year and hence increase production potential.
   (*a*) In what circumstances will investment increase the capital stock?
   (*b*) What is the opportunity cost to society of investment expenditures?

5. Give possible reasons for the inventory disinvestment that occurred during the 1970s.

6. Describe the factors that influence investment decisions.

CONCLUSION

In this chapter we have seen that the managers of trading enterprises are faced with two sets of decisions. One concerns the quantities of goods and services to be produced during the current production period — given the ceiling imposed by its existing stock of capital equipment and the skills of labour and management. The other set of decisions concerns investment. These decisions are more difficult, since they involve the management in making judgements about the more distant future. The greater the uncertainty in the minds of the decision-makers, the more difficult the task. In periods when the future looks grim and unpromising, new investment expenditures are invariably lower and concentrated on short-term projects. Similarly, when there is optimism about the future, investment expenditures are higher.

7 Financial Intermediaries: Trading Enterprises of a Special Kind

The principal distinguishing feature of **financial intermediaries** is that they earn their incomes mainly by borrowing and lending. They gather together funds by offering attractive returns to lenders, and they provide loans as well as specialized financial services. They earn income by charging higher rates of interest on funds they lend than on money they borrow.

BORROWING AND LENDING WITHOUT INTERMEDIARIES

In chapter 3 we saw that one of the functions of money is to make it easier for people to save part of their current incomes for use in future periods. Those economic units that save in a given period can be referred to as **surplus** units, because their incomes exceed their expenditures over that period. These surplus units are mainly households. In contrast, there are other economic units that spend in excess of their incomes in a given period. These can be referred to as **deficit** units, because their incomes are less than their expenditures in the period considered.

Some households spend in excess of their current incomes in order to purchase consumer durables — like buying a motor vehicle with the aid of a loan. Sometimes the borrowing makes possible the consumption of a commodity over many years, as is the case when households borrow to purchase a home. Other economic units spend in excess of their incomes in order to acquire assets, like buildings or machines, in anticipation of income that those assets may earn in future periods.

In order to spend in excess of their incomes in any period, deficit economic units have only two alternatives: either they must draw on savings accumulated in past periods or they must somehow find some-body willing to lend to them.

From the viewpoint of a person with accumulated savings, there are a number of possible ways in which these accumulated savings may be held. Firstly, they may be held in the form of money, sometimes as cash in the pocket or in a tin under the bed, or more likely in a bank. People desire to hold their savings in this form to finance transactions in the future, both expected and unexpected. For example, a person may be saving to purchase a consumer durable, such as a new motor cycle. This is an expected transaction. However, there is also the prospect of unexpected expenditure, and for this reason there is a need to have money in case of an emergency such as an urgent house repair. For this reason, people may prefer to keep their savings in a **liquid** form — that is, in a form that is readily convertible into cash at short notice with little or no loss in value.

Secondly, a person may wish to hold accumulated savings in the form of assets other than money. Assets are of two broad kinds, *real* and *financial.* **Real assets** consist of physical goods or property, such as a block of flats, land, paintings, jewellery, or a motor vehicle. **Financial assets** include such things as debentures, government bonds, house mortgages, and IOUs. People hold financial assets mainly because of the income they provide, usually in the form of interest. A common way of acquiring financial assets is to lend money. In return, the lender receives an under-taking from the borrower to repay the loan at some time — and to pay a certain rate of interest.

One major factor that determines whether or not a person decides to lend money is the rate of interest. Interest payments can be regarded as compensation to lenders for not spending and gaining satisfaction from current consumption. It is also compensation for the risk that the money may not be repaid. In this sense, the higher the risk, the higher generally is the rate of interest. So borrowers must persuade others to lend by offer-ing a suitable rate of interest, depending upon the risks involved for lenders.

Given the uncertain conditions under which they operate, trading enterprises generally prefer to borrow for long periods of time at low rates of interest. Better still, they would rather have no fixed-interest commit-ments and would prefer to pay those who provide the funds for invest-ment according to the success (or otherwise) of these projects. Public companies can do this by issuing what are known as **ordinary shares**, which entitle the buyers (shareholders) to periodic **dividends**, the right to sell these shares at any time (possibly for more than the initial purchase price, providing shareholders with **capital gains**), and, in some circum-stances, a share in the assets of the company in the event of its failing and being declared bankrupt. However, shareholders run the risk that after outstanding debts have been settled, there may be nothing left for them to share. In the event of operating losses, period after period, they are unlikely to receive dividends. Worse still, if the firm fails completely, their shares may be worthless.

If borrowers and lenders had no alternative but to deal directly with each other, there would be relatively little borrowing and lending. Many individuals and households have such small savings that they would not be prepared to accept the risk involved. They would probably prefer to hold their savings in other forms, rather than buy financial assets issued by trading enterprises. Also borrowers often require amounts greater than the small savings possessed by any one individual. Few would be willing to lend for ten or twenty years, and most would probably require higher rates of interest, as an offset to risk, than borrowers would be willing to offer. So large, long-life projects, even if potentially very profitable and socially desirable, would depend very heavily upon the savings that trading enterprises themselves were able to accumulate. Otherwise they might be abandoned for want of finance.

Savers split their accumulated savings between cash, other financial assets, and real assets. Without financial intermediaries, the required conditions of reasonable return and minimal risk on financial assets would be difficult to find. Few savers would hold financial assets and few potential leaders would have access to suitable finance.

Questions

1. Why do some people wish to spend in excess of their income?

2. Wealth may be held in a number of different forms. Describe the forms in which wealth may be held, and give reasons for holding wealth in these forms.

3. Interest rates may change a lender's willingness to lend and a borrower's willingness to borrow. What factors would be taken into account when fixing a rate of interest by (*a*) the lender, (*b*) the borrower?

THE GENERAL ROLE OF INTERMEDIARIES

The *conflict of interests* between the *wants* of potential lenders and the *preferences* of potential borrowers has given rise to financial intermediaries, which intermediate, or act as *middlemen*, between surplus and deficit units.

Financial intermediaries have skills in borrowing and lending that are not usually acquired by members of the public, particularly in some specified areas. For example, a short-term money market dealer has to be particularly adept at finding lenders of large sums of money, often millions of dollars, for periods of a few days. Building societies have to match lenders with small savings who wish to lend only for short periods with borrowers who require large amounts for long periods. What this means is that some financial intermediaries borrow relatively small amounts from many people with small savings, in order to lend out larger amounts to borrowers.

Savings banks and building societies offer interest on deposits, security against loss, and, if required, repayment without prior notice. Such arrangements are particularly attractive to surplus units with small savings. So people lodge deposits with these intermediaries and receive, in turn, **passbooks** which record deposits and withdrawals, interest paid by the intermediary, and the balance of their accounts at any time. To each individual depositor, the balance of his account represents a financial asset. From the viewpoint of the intermediary, however, the balance in each passbook represents its liability towards an individual depositor.

Having borrowed from their depositors, these intermediaries then lend out funds to households, trading enterprises, and governments. On these loans they charge higher rates of interest than they pay on their own deposit liabilities. It is the difference between interest received on loans and interest paid to depositors that allows these intermediaries to cover their operating expenses and to make profits.

Some loans provided by intermediaries are for short periods, measured in weeks or months, helping an individual or a trading enterprise to bridge a temporary shortage of funds. Others, like housing loans, are provided over a long term, extending up to twenty years or more. In the great majority of cases, the borrower is required to provide some form of security against the possibility that he may not repay the loan when it falls due. In this event, the intermediary may be legally entitled to sell the borrower's assets in order to recover the debt outstanding. **Unsecured loans** are provided by some intermediaries. In this case there is no security offered by the borrowers, but they are subjected to close scrutiny and the interest charged is substantially more than that on secured debt because of the extra risks involved.

Financial intermediaries also spread risk. A lender who has lent to an enterprise that cannot repay the loan will probably lose part, if not all, of his money. However, financial intermediaries have a large number of borrowers, few of whom are going to fail to repay their loans.

From time to time there are borrowers who fail to meet their debt commitments. Despite security held against this possibility, inter-mediaries do incur losses on these individual loan transactions. However, a safeguard against losses is provided by expertise in the screening of those who apply for loans, as well as deliberate spreading of risks over many individual borrowers, different types of industry, and different geo-graphical areas. So the occasional failure of a borrower to repay a loan is usually offset quite readily by the large numbers of loan transactions and the interest rates charged.

How is it that some intermediaries are able to tie up a large proportion of the funds deposited with them in illiquid assets, like house mortgages, while at the same time allowing their depositors to withdraw their deposits without notice? Again, large numbers make this possible. From experience, such intermediaries know that relatively few of their depositors are likely to reduce their deposits over any period; furthermore, such reductions are likely to be offset by increases in the deposits held in other accounts.

Financial intermediaries receive deposits in the form of notes and coin. These assets do not earn income for the financial intermediaries. In order to make profits, financial intermediaries keep some of these liquid assets as reserves and convert the balance into income-earning assets by making loans or buying government securities or other financial assets. The financial intermediaries arrange their asset holdings to maximize the income from the assets they hold while meeting certain liquidity and security requirements. For example, they need to keep more than enough notes and coins to meet the expected demands for withdrawals and try to minimize the risk of losses on the loans they make in order to retain the confidence of depositors.

In these ways, financial intermediaries are able to offer both surplus and deficit units essentially what each requires. Given that intermediaries are willing to finance long-term investment projects, of which housing is but one example, the level of investment expenditure is also higher than could be expected if borrowing and lending were restricted to direct negotiation between borrowers and lenders. So, through the services they provide, financial intermediaries help to increase the productive capacity of the economy.

Financial intermediaries are middlemen between lenders and borrowers, providing each with the financial services they require. Their existence encourages the flow of finance between lenders and borrowers and thus a larger amount of investment.

Questions

1. Why do you think financial intermediaries are better at borrowing and lending than individual members of the public?

2. How does a financial institution spread the risk of lending?

3. Why do savings banks and building societies hold a certain amount of cash instead of using this to purchase income-earning but less liquid assets?

4. In recent years there have been a number of "runs" on building societies. Find out what a "run" is, and give some reasons why they occur.

5. Find out what are the current rates of interest being offered on (*a*) savings accounts; (*b*) investment accounts with savings banks; (*c*) building society deposits.

BANKING AND NON-BANKING TECHNIQUES

In Australia there is a wide range of financial institutions. To simplify the task of learning about the operations of each of these institutions, those with similar functions are grouped together. One such group consists of what are referred to as **trading banks**. Trading banks offer **non-interest-bearing cheque accounts**. Those who have cheque accounts (also called current accounts) with a trading bank are issued with cheque books containing a number of forms like the one illustrated in figure 6. Each cheque, when completed and signed by a customer, represents an instruction to the bank to transfer part of that customer's balance of account to the credit of some other economic unit. There is no need to visit or notify the bank before making out each cheque. To make a purchase or settle a debt, all the customer has to do is "draw" the cheque in favour of the other economic unit. This implies that the recipient of the cheque knows or can trust the person giving the cheque and that there are sufficient funds in the account to make the payment specified.

For example, John Smith has a cheque account with the Bank of Adelaide. He receives an account for $200 from the XYZ Trading Company for timber purchases during January and settles this account in February by drawing a cheque in favour of that company.

If the XYZ Trading Company also has an account with the Bank of

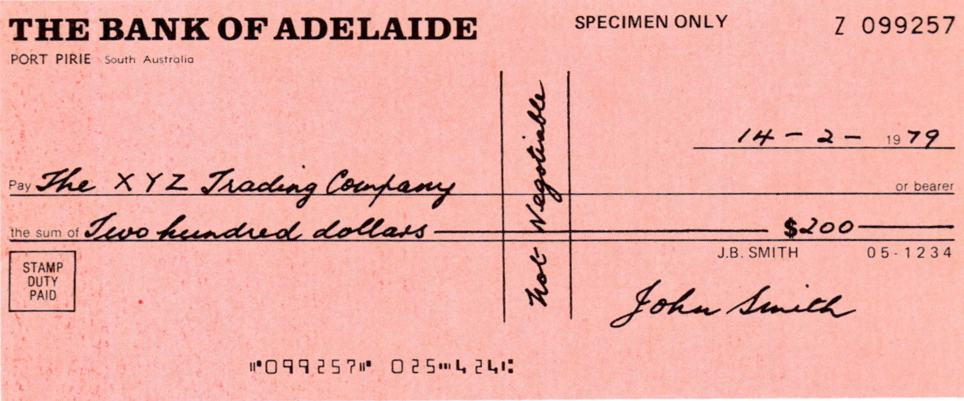

Fig. 6.   Specimen bank cheque

Adelaide, it is a fairly simply matter for the bank to deduct $200 from the balance of Smith's account and to add this amount to the credit of the XYZ Trading Company. However, it is more than likely that the XYZ Trading Company has its account with one of the other major banks, such as the Bank of New South Wales, and will deposit Smith's cheque with its own bank.

As a result of many such transactions, each bank gathers together cheques drawn by the customers of other banks and, on a daily basis, settles any of the balances outstanding. For example, the Bank of Adelaide, on a particular day, may be holding $9 million in cheques drawn on accounts held with the Bank of New South Wales, while the latter may be holding cheques amounting to $10 million drawn by customers of the Bank of Adelaide. To correct this imbalance, the Bank of Adelaide would be required to pay $1 million to the Bank of New South Wales. This is done by using the exchange settlement account each bank has with the Reserve Bank of Australia.

In this and other ways, the costs associated with cheque accounts are greater than for other deposits. So the banks pay no interest on balances in these accounts; in fact they levy a small charge on each customer, according to the numbers of cheques drawn in each period. However, some banks are now offering interest on the minimum monthly balances in such accounts — apparently in an endeavour to win custom from their competitors.

In addition to cheque accounts, trading banks accept interest-bearing **fixed deposits**. These deposits are of some specified minimum size and cannot be withdrawn before a certain minimum period of time without loss of interest. Customers are required to give notice of withdrawal of fixed deposits.

In addition to other activities which will not concern us in a book such as this, trading banks make loans of a unique kind to their customers — namely, loans by way of **overdraft**. What this means is that customers who are granted loans in this form are given the right to draw cheques to some specified limit in excess of the balances in their accounts. For example, before drawing a cheque in favour of the XYZ Trading Company, the balance of John Smith's account may have been $200. After drawing that cheque, his balance would have been reduced to zero and he would no longer be entitled to draw cheques against that account. However, if the bank had granted him an overdraft limit of $4,000, he could then draw further cheques, up to that limit, without making further deposits. The bank would simply make payment on each of Smith's cheques as though the balance in his account was sufficient to cover those withdrawals. In due course, Smith would be required, over some agreed period, to reduce his overdraft and to finally restore (to zero or better) the balance of his account. Meanwhile, Smith would also be required to meet interest and other charges associated with that loan.

In Australia, the major banking groups usually operate both their trading bank and savings bank business from the same premises. They are, however, separate financial intermediaries and undertake different types of business. Savings banks restrict their lending largely to government and semi-government authorities, and to housing loans. For a housing loan, the security held is a mortgage on the property concerned.

Building societies operate in much the same way as savings banks. They both accept deposits repayable on demand and issue passbooks which allow their customers to make day-to-day withdrawals in precisely

THE BANK OF NEW SOUTH WALES

The Bank of New South Wales is one of the major banking intermediaries in Australia. At the end of September 1977 it had 983 banking branches operating throughout Australia and 143 branches overseas. In addition, this bank was the sole owner of numerous subsidiary companies, each supplying specialized financial services. These activities were together employing 21,137 people—almost as many as were employed by GMH at that time.

Like other banks, the principal expenses are wages and salaries paid to employees and interest paid on savings accounts. The main source of income is interest received on loans, advances, and government securities; but income also includes charges levied on cheque account customers for services provided.

The economic activities of the Bank of New South Wales, like those of some other major banks in Australia, now extend far beyond what were not long ago regarded as traditional banking services. The activities of this bank are now much more diversified than they were formerly. Apart from branch banking overseas and travel services employing about four hundred people, the bank also has a number of wholly owned subsidiaries, each of which is a specialized intermediary. One, for example, concentrates upon the purchase and development of building sites. Another offers a choice of superannuation arrangements to contributing members of the public. Yet another concentrates on the operation of "unit trusts", which offer, to the buyers of these units, a small share in the ownership of large numbers of Australian companies and dividends based on the operating results of those companies.

During the twelve months to 30 September 1977, profits earned by this group of companies amounted to $71.0 million. Of this sum, $53.1 million accrued to the shareholders of the bank, $20.4 million was set aside for payment of dividends, and the remainder (undistributed profits) was added to reserves ("shareholders' funds").

the same way. If customers agree to lodge deposits for a minimum period of, say, six months, higher rates of interest are paid on those deposits. Where customers agree to leave their savings untouched for longer periods, still higher rates of interest are offered.

Subject to the need to hold a proportion of their deposit liabilities in cash or in other very liquid forms to meet the day-to-day requirements of their savings account customers, the building societies, as their names suggest, lend almost exclusively for the purchase of homes by their customers. So, apart from their land, buildings, furniture, and office equipment, the assets of building societies are largely in the form of mortgages held as security on housing loans.

Finance companies attract funds in other ways, in part by issuing ordinary shares, but mainly through the sale of debentures. The **shareholders**, as in other public companies, receive **dividends** that tend to reflect profits over each period of operation. If profits fall sharply or losses are incurred, they may receive nothing at all. In contrast, **debentures** are issued for specified periods — for example, for three to five years — and debenture-holders must then be *repaid in full* or encouraged to subscribe to a new issue. **Thus debenture issues are simply a means of raising loans and represent part of a finance company's debt.** In contrast to shareholders, those who buy debentures are guaranteed a fixed rate of interest, generally equal to or more than the rates paid on fixed deposits by banks and building societies. These interest commitments must be met, whether or not a company makes a profit: otherwise, debenture-holders may force a company into bankruptcy in order to recover payments due to them.

In their lending of funds, the finance companies take greater risks than the banks and building societies and, as is generally the case, expect to earn higher rates of return. Most of these companies are heavily involved in financing time-payment arrangements on the purchase of motor vehicles and other consumer durables. Some offer personal loans for any purpose, in some instances without requiring borrowers to provide any form of security. They also purchase ordinary shares in other companies and, like other shareholders, face the same risk of losing their funds. However, unlike most individual shareholders, the finance companies attempt to minimize such losses by spreading their shareholdings over many different types of industry.

Life assurance organizations are another kind of non-bank intermediary. They gather together funds by offering lump-sum compensation or regular payments of income in the event of death, accident, or sickness suffered by those insured. These benefits are offered in return for regular premiums paid by, or on behalf of, the people concerned. The risks (or probabilities) of death, accident, or sickness are well known within the industry, being based on periodic assessments of the frequency of such

AUSTRALIAN GUARANTEE CORPORATION LTD

The Bank of New South Wales has a controlling interest (53.25 per cent of the shares) in Australian Guarantee Corporation Limited, a major finance company. Like other finance companies, AGC does not conduct banking business, but raises its funds by the issue of shares and debentures—the latter being offered at fixed rates of interest (usually higher than available on fixed deposits with the banks) and issued for specified periods. For example, during the twelve months to 30 September 1978, AGC issued 17.5 million new debentures and redeemed (that is, repaid in full) 8.7 million, leaving a debenture debt of $1,709.6 million outstanding.

For a long time after it opened for business in 1928, AGC was engaged almost exclusively in the financing of time-payment arrangements on the purchase of motor vehicles, tractors, and other farm machinery. Although instalment credit still accounts for about 70 per cent of its business, AGC (like the Bank of New South Wales) has become increasingly diversified. It now has a number of subsidiary companies in Australia, New Zealand, Papua New Guinea, and South-East Asia. Some of these subsidiaries are also involved in short-term financing arrangements. Others are engaged in such diverse activities as property development, fire and general insurance, short-term rental of motor vehicles, and the manufacture of bricks.

After meeting expenses, including payments of interest to debenture holders, during the twelve months to 30 September 1978, the AGC group of companies earned profits amounting to $79.8 million. Of the after-tax profit of $44.5 million, AGC distributed $16.0 million to shareholders and added the balance (undistributed profits) to its reserves, which then stood at $177.7 million. At that time, the real and financial assets of the AGC group of companies were together valued at $2,243.7 million.

events within the Australian population as a whole. On the basis of this knowledge, the premiums are set at levels higher than necessary to meet the risks involved.

Each of the major insurance organizations has vast numbers of policies current at any one time. So each is able to lend out funds in the knowledge that it will have a large and regular inflow of premiums as an offset against fairly predictable payments to policy-holders. The lending of these intermediaries tends to be widely spread between households, trading enterprises, and governments. This is reflected in the many types of financial assets held as security against loans — mainly government securities, ordinary shares and debentures in numerous Australian companies, mortgages on house properties, and insurance policies temporarily surrendered by their own customers as security for personal loans.

Other non-bank intermediaries gather together funds by the sale of other kinds of financial assets. Some offer very specialized services. Others are engaged in a wide range of economic activities. However, all are involved in financial intermediation, in that they borrow from surplus units (offering as security their own liabilities) and lend to deficit units (accepting mortgages, debentures, and other financial assets as security for these loans).

THE AUSTRALIAN MUTUAL PROVIDENT SOCIETY

The Australian Mutual Provident Society (AMP) is an important example of a *non-banking* financial intermediary operating in the Australian economy. The AMP is a life assurance organization and has no shareholders. Nor does it issue debentures or accept current savings or fixed deposits like the banks. The funds at its disposal are received, in the first instance, as premiums on life assurance policies of various kinds. In addition to offering insurance against disability or death and policies that provide for payments after the insured survive to some specified age, the AMP also offers employer-subsidized superannuation arrangements which, in recent years, have accounted for two-thirds of all premiums received.

**Balance Sheet for the Australian Mutual Provident Society
as at 31 December 1977**

Liabilities	$m	Assets	$m
Provision for taxation	65.8	Government securities—	
		Australian	1,305.7
Bank overdrafts	61.6	Other	183.6
Amounts owing on		Ordinary shares	754.5
purchase of assets	44.7		
		Debentures of companies	280.1
Policies in process of			
settlement	33.6	Other securities	199.7
Other liabilities	41.9	Loans—	
		on mortgage	715.5
Policy-holders' funds	4,663.8	on AMP policies	162.1
		other	36.0
		Outstanding premiums,	
		dividends, rent	161.1
		Cash in hand	10.6
		Fixed assets (land,	
		buildings, etc.)	1,102.6
	4,911.5		4,911.5

Source: Australian Mutual Provident Society, *129th Annual Report, 1977.*

At the end of 1977, the AMP held 15.4 per cent of its total assets in the form of ordinary shares. Clearly, the AMP is providing a great deal of risk capital for other Australian trading enterprises. In fact, a list of the society's share holdings has the appearance of a "who's who" of major Australian companies—extending through mining, banking, transport, retailing, the media, food, drink and tobacco manufacturing, textiles and clothing, steel and engineering, building supplies, consumer durables, paper, oil, and gas. In forty of these companies, the value of AMP's share holding was in excess of $5 million.

During the twelve months ended 31 December 1977, income amounted to $1,009.9 million—of which $666.4 million was received in premiums paid by policy-holders and the balance was interest, dividends, or rent received on the AMP's financial and real assets. Payments to policy-holders (or their beneficiaries) amounted to $433.8 million. After operating expenses (largely wages, salaries, and commissions paid to its own employees), provision for taxation, and allowances to cover depreciation, the remainder represented after-tax profits. Since the AMP has no shareholders, their profits are in part credited to policy-holders, in the form of bonuses on policies, and in part held as a reserve against future policy commitments.

Questions

1. List the major trading banks in Australia. What forms of deposit are accepted by trading banks?

2. How are savings banks and building societies (*a*) similar; (*b*) different?

3. What is the main way that finance companies borrow money?
   What is the rate of interest currently being offered on three-year debentures issued by finance companies?

4. Why do finance companies offer higher rates of interest on money borrowed from the public than savings banks?

5. Investigate the activities of a financial institution of your choosing.
   Describe the sources and uses of funds.
   Describe the operations of the institution.

FINANCIAL INTERMEDIARIES AND THE MONEY SUPPLY

In chapter 3 we defined money as "anything that is generally acceptable in payment for goods and services" — including payments in settlement of debt. There is no doubt that notes and coin serve this purpose particularly well. However, as we suggested earlier, when considering the use of cheque account facilities offered by some of our major banks, bank deposits transferred by cheques also are generally acceptable in payment for goods and services purchased as well as in settlement of debt. So, if we accept that money is "anything that is generally acceptable . . .", then the total supply of money at any time consists of *notes and coin in the hands of the public plus the sum of all bank deposits subject to withdrawal by cheque.*

In Australia, our best approximation to this measure is that referred to officially as **the M1 supply of money**, which includes **all notes and coin in the hands of the public — plus those cheque account deposits held by the trading banks.** This definition of money is clearly a better approximation to the money supply than notes and coin only.

Although the supply of money is conventionally defined in this way, some economists feel that this definition is too narrow. Some assert that the money supply also includes all other deposits held by the banks. This broader definition includes fixed deposits that normally cannot be withdrawn without prior notice. Furthermore, it should be remembered that people who hold either current savings or fixed deposits cannot make payments simply by offering evidence, to storekeepers and others, that they have made such deposits. They must first make withdrawals either in notes and coin, or by transferring funds to their cheque account, or, for the payment of a small fee, purchase a bank cheque which is drawn in favour of the person to whom they wish to make payment.

If we accept that current savings and fixed deposits represent part of the supply of money, perhaps we should also include deposits with some non-bank intermediaries — particularly those held with building societies.

Definition of the money supply is not as precise as we would like. However, for the want of better measures, we will refer only to those used officially in Australia: namely, **M1**, which represents all notes and coin in circulation, plus cheque account deposits with the trading banks; **M2**, being all notes and coin plus *all* deposits held by the trading banks — that is, whether or not subject to withdrawal by cheque; and **M3**, which refers to notes and coin in circulation, plus the sum of all deposits with *all banks* (savings plus trading banks) — regardless of the forms in which those deposits are held.

In recent years, notes and coin have represented only 8½ to 9 per cent and cheque account deposits with the trading banks approximately 20 per cent of the M3 supply of money. Yet the alternative definitions of the money supply suggest that deposits subject to withdrawal by cheque are in some way of special significance. This is certainly so. In fact, trading banks are able to *create* additional deposits. They can do this by buying financial assets, such as debentures and government bonds, from the public. In this way they increase their asset holdings, while increasing the value of customers' deposits. Since deposits subject to withdrawal by cheque represent part of the money supply, this means that **banks are able to create money.** Furthermore, they are also able to do this through their *lending* policy. To illustrate the process involved, it may be useful to return

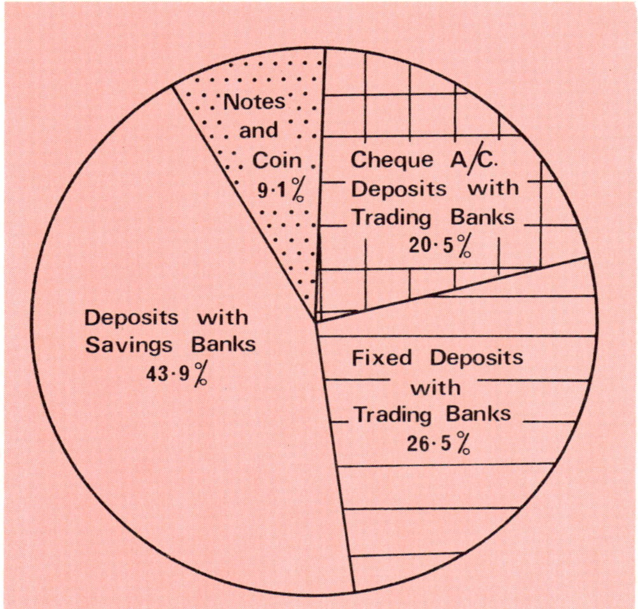

Fig. 7.   Components in the supply of money (M3) Australia, December 1978 (Source: Reserve Bank of Australia, *Statistical Bulletin*)

again to John Smith's request for a loan of $4,000 from the Bank of Adelaide.

For the sake of simplicity, let us first assume that the Bank of Adelaide is the only banking intermediary in Australia. Having established that Smith is creditworthy, the bank agrees to make the loan. In doing so, it makes a note in Smith's account to the effect that even when that account falls to zero, Smith can go on writing cheques to the value of $4,000 and the bank will honour the cheques for the people receiving them. It is unlikely that the bank would hand over notes and coin to Smith to the value of $4,000.

The people who receive Smith's cheques in return for their goods and services will, for the most part, especially if they are trading enterprises, deposit them in their own cheque accounts. If the recipients live overseas, then deposits in Australia will not increase as a result of these payments by Smith. Similarly, if some or all of the new deposit is used to pay taxes to the government, the deposits of customers will not increase. Furthermore, some of the people or firms who receive Smith's cheques will simply use them to reduce their own overdrafts and so payments to these people will not increase the deposits held by the Bank of Adelaide. Finally, some of the cheques drawn by Smith may be converted into notes and coin. If this happens, notes and coin will be transferred from the bank to the pockets and purses of customers and deposits will not increase.

Both by purchasing assets from the public and making loans, trading banks create deposits. The ownership of these deposits may change as cheques are written on them. However, a large proportion remain as customers' deposits in the banking system except where there are—
1. **payments made overseas;**
2. **payments to government;**
3. **repayments of bank loans;**
4. **withdrawals of deposits in the form of extra notes and coin.**

Notwithstanding "*leakages*" such as these, some — or possibly most — of Smith's $4,000 overdraft will serve to increase the deposits of others. That is, this **advance (loan) creates deposits**. This not only increases M1 — the supply of money — but also alters the balance between the banks' holding of liquid assets and the amounts in depositors' accounts. As we noticed earlier, banks hold a reserve of liquid assets, such as notes and coin, to meet the demands of depositors. In this example, even if the advance to Smith and his subsequent payments to customers does not reduce the bank's holdings of notes and coin, it *will* increase the bank's liability, "deposits".

These principles can be applied to an economy with many banks, as is the case in Australia. Some of the people and trading enterprises paid by John Smith would have paid these cheques into their accounts with the Bank of Adelaide. However, others would have made their deposits with the Bank of New South Wales or one of the many other banks, raising deposits held in *those* banks. Meanwhile, Smith is not the only person to seek and receive approval for a loan. Some of the customers of the Bank of New South Wales, operating either on an overdraft or on their deposits with the bank, draw cheques which are deposited in accounts with the Bank of Adelaide.

As in our simple illustration of John Smith borrowing from one bank, if all banks with cheque accounts were in the process of granting *additional* loans to customers, then the general level of deposits in banks in total would be rising.

Banks like to lend as much as they can. After all, this is how they make their income. However, apart from the possibility of government regulation, there must be *self-regulation* by the banks if they are to retain the confidence of the public. Banks must always retain a proportion of their assets in a form that can be readily converted into notes and coin should some depositors wish to make cash withdrawals. These are known as *reserves*. Unless a bank starts off with an excess of these liquid assets, any growth in deposits as a result of a sustained lending programme will so alter the proportions of liquid assets to deposit balances that the ability of a bank to meet the day-to-day requirements of customers could be threatened. This relationship between the value of liquid assets and depositors' balances is known as the **reserve ratio**.

If, for example, the sum of the deposit liabilities of Australian banks was \$10,000 million and the reserve ratio necessary to meet the requirements of customers is 20 per cent, then the banks would together need to hold \$2,000 million in liquid reserves. If they were holding \$2,100 million in these reserves, they could increase their deposit liabilities through lending by $\$100\text{m} \times \frac{1}{\text{the reserve ratio}}$. They know that if they increased loans by the \$100 million excess reserves, this would increase deposits by \$100 million and they would still hold more than the required reserves of 20 per cent of deposits. These excess reserves of \$100 million will support an expansion of loans so that deposits increase by \$500 million — so that the \$100 million initial excess reserve is 20 per cent of the final increase in deposits.

There is a simple relationship between the initial increase in deposits and the total increase in deposits it will support. This relationship is termed the **credit multiplier**. In fact, the initial change in deposits multiplied by the credit multiplier equals the total increase in deposits. In the example above,

$$\$100 \text{ m} \times \frac{1}{} {}^{1}/_{5} = \$500\text{m}.$$

The term $\frac{1}{\text{the reserve ratio}}$ is the credit multiplier. So long as the extra advances do not result in an increase in the volume of notes and coin in circulation in the community, liquid reserves would stay at \$2,100 milllion and deposit liabilities in Australia would rise to \$10,500 million. The reserve ratio would then be precisely 20 per cent.

Bank loans create bank deposits. Because of this, an initial increase in deposits is subject to a credit multiplier. The value of the credit multiplier is the number of times the total increase in deposits is greater than the initial increase in deposits.

We have seen that by lending, banks can increase deposits and thereby the supply of money. So far we have talked only in terms of self-regulation by the banks to ensure that they retain the confidence of the public. However, this ability to generate money has some obvious implications for the amount of economic activity taking place in a community and is therefore of crucial interest to governments attempting to regulate the economy. For example, an economy could be operating at much less than its capacity, that is, well inside its production possibility curve. The banks, if only looking to their own interests, might view this depressed state of the economy with some pessimism and be reluctant to lend to trading enterprises because of the bleak outlook in the market-place. The government, on the other hand, might be keen to see an increase in lending and spending to generate the production of more goods and services and therefore employment and income in the community. In the following chapter we examine the ways in which the government, in a modern economy, makes use of policy instruments to regulate lending and the supply of money.

Questions

1. (*a*) Distinguish between the M1 and M3 definitions of money.
   (*b*) What are the approximate proportions of the components of M3?

2. How can a trading bank create money?

3. Describe "leakages" from the banking system.

4. What is the reserve ratio?

5. Why do banks retain a proportion of their assets as reserves?

6. Credit cards are becoming widely used in Australia. Describe the effect of the use of credit cards on (*a*) the desire to hold cash; (*b*) M3.

8 The Government Sector

In chapter 4 we discussed the functions and structure of government in Australia. In this chapter our major concern is the stabilizing measures available to government, particularly with respect to the level of economic activity.

There are a number of ways in which governments exert an influence on economic activities in Australia. For example, local and state governments have "zoning" laws that restrict economic activities of some kinds to certain areas. Concern for the environment has resulted in various restrictive measures, ranging from limits on motor vehicle exhaust emissions to prohibition of mining in some parts of Australia. Governments also prohibit some forms of economic activity, such as the production and sale of certain drugs; closely scrutinize methods of sales promotion, particularly advertising; and have laws designed to prevent the use of unfair methods of competition between individual firms.

Nor are all of our markets entirely free to determine how much of each commodity or service will be supplied. For example, minimum wage rates are fixed by law. So, even if there are large numbers of people without jobs, employers cannot offer work at lower wage rates. Prices of some goods and services are subject to administrative approval, by either the states or the Commonwealth or both. For example, the prices of some farm products are fixed by state or Commonwealth marketing boards, and the Commonwealth government determines the prices at which our crude oil producers sell their product to the refineries. Some industries are deliberately subjected to competition from government-operated trading enterprises. Others are protected against competition by means of taxes imposed on imported substitutes, making those imported goods more expensive than home-produced goods. Some receive direct financial assistance from government; other industries are left to fend for themselves.

Governments also affect economic activity in more general ways. For example, if all of our governments were to increase their taxes, we would expect our households and trading enterprises to spend less. If, following an increase in taxation, there were no increase in government spending, there would be an overall reduction in demand for goods and services and some reduction in production and employment. Alternatively, our governments may decide either to reduce taxation or to increase their own expenditures — employing more public servants and increasing their purchases from trading enterprises. In either case, we would expect an increase in total demand for goods and services and an increase in the numbers of jobs available.

In ways such as these, governments can either reduce or stimulate the overall level of economic activity in Australia. The influence of individual governments on economic activity is very closely related to their taxing powers and the relative sizes of their expenditures. On both these counts, the Commonwealth government overshadows all others.

TAXATION AND EXPENDITURE BY AUSTRALIAN GOVERNMENTS

Under the Constitution, the Commonwealth government has the sole power to impose taxes on imports — that is, **customs duties**. On the interpretation of the courts, it appears that the Commonwealth also has the sole power to levy taxes on goods and services sold. These are **excise duties**, such as we pay on beer, tobacco, and petroleum products, and **sales tax** (see table 10). After transferring their income-taxing powers to the Commonwealth in 1941, the states were left with very limited taxing capacity, confined mainly to death duties, land taxes, and stamp duties on various transactions.

Since 1941, the Commonwealth has entered into tax-sharing arrangements with the states and has provided additional assistance by way of special grants. For example, the Commonwealth makes funds available to state housing authorities. More recently, the Commonwealth government has transferred to the states the right to gather **payroll taxes** from trading enterprises within their own borders. In 1977 the Commonwealth allowed the states to levy additional taxes on the personal incomes of their own residents. The *political* as well as economic implications of tax-sharing between the states and Commonwealth are very complex. The example quoted by Bert Kelly in the accompanying "Tax-Sharing Arrangements: Another Viewpoint" serves to illustrate just one of the issues involved.

In addition to tax-sharing arrangements and grants, the states (like the

TAX-SHARING ARRANGEMENTS: ANOTHER VIEWPOINT

From time to time, members of state governments have stated publicly that the quality of services provided by their governments would be improved, or certain new projects would be undertaken, if only the Commonwealth government would return a "fair" share of the taxes gathered in their states. The Commonwealth has responded by offering to return to the states the power to impose tax on incomes. However, the states have not yet accepted the Commonwealth government's offer. So the heavy reliance of the states on tax-sharing arrangements and grants of various kinds continues.

After each round of negotiations on tax-sharing arrangements, the Commonwealth government appears to be "the villain of the piece" and the state governments the oppressed but true representatives of the people. However, as C.R. (Bert) Kelly has suggested, these tax-sharing arrangements suit the states quite well:

> Soon after I became a member of Parliament, Mr. (later Sir Thomas) Playford was our State's distinguished Premier. Every now and then he used to give tongue about the shoddy deal South Australia was getting from the Commonwealth and he would proclaim that what he wanted above everything was for South Australia to get our income taxing powers back so that we could have a fair go again, as we used to before the evil Commonwealth took away our right to levy our own income tax. Being rather dewy-eyed, I sidled up to the great man and volunteered the information that, from now on, he could count on me as an active ally in his struggle to get back his taxing powers so that the State could progress once again. Mr. Playford was rather startled to hear these glad tidings and asked me to repeat my statement to make sure that he had heard right. Then he took me into the privacy of his office and, carefully closing the door, admitted that, though this was the song he sang in public, he didn't really want his taxing powers back. "The present system rather suits me, Bert", he explained, "the Commonwealth gets the odium for raising the money and I get the credit for spending it." [The Hon. C.R. Kelly, *One More Nail* (Adelaide: 1978), Brolga Books, p.163]

Commonwealth) borrow funds from time to time, mainly through the **Australian Loan Council**. This council consists of representatives of both the Commonwealth and the states. It meets periodically and attempts to co-ordinate the borrowing plans of all Australian governments. But even in the Loan Council, the Commonwealth has such voting strength that it virtually has the power to determine the extent of borrowing by the states.

Despite the various sources of funds available to the states, the Commonwealth has a very significant hold on the purse strings of governments in Australia. In 1977/78, for example, the states together spent $13,991 million. Our *National Accounts* show that taxes gathered by the states themselves accounted for only $5,467 million or 39.1 per cent of all funds used. Of the remainder, $6,690 million (or 47.8 per cent) was received from the Commonwealth under tax-sharing arrangements or in the form of grants, and $1,434 million (or 10.2 per cent) was borrowed through the Loan Council.

In contrast, as shown in the 1978/79 *Budget Papers*, the Commonwealth government gathered $21,346 million in tax revenue during 1977/78, representing 79.6 per cent of all taxes gathered by the Commonwealth and state governments over that period. Its total expenditure, including payments to the states, amounted to $26,802 million — representing 29.7 per cent of the sum of expenditures by all sectors of the economy in that year.

One of the consequences of these taxing, tax-sharing, and borrowing arrangements has been that the division of responsibility for the provision of some services has become less distinct than it was formerly. For example, if the Commonwealth gives to a state a grant to assist in the financing of a specific project such as urban renewal or decentralization of population, this is, in effect, a sharing of responsibility.

Likewise, local government authorities are to some extent limited in their freedom to allocate available funds between alternative uses, owing to their heavy dependence upon state government assistance. Local government tax revenue is restricted mainly to rates levied on real estate within their own boundaries. The sum of all tax revenues raised by local government authorities accounts for only about 5 per cent of all taxes collected in Australia. Local governments rely heavily upon both the Commonwealth and states for funds.

The importance of state and local government activities in Australia should not be underestimated. They provide many employment opportunities, both directly and indirectly, as well as many services essential to our way of life.

However, the Commonwealth government overshadows all other governments in the scale of its economic activities; furthermore, the Commonwealth is in a position to influence strongly the expenditures of the states and, through the states, the expenditures of local government authorities.

For these reasons, but also because the Commonwealth government alone bears responsibility for management of the Australian economy as a whole, we will now concentrate our attention on the ways and means by which the Commonwealth is able to influence the level of economic activity.

Each of our major political parties — in fact, each successive government — has different policies and different sets of priorities. For example, some favour greater emphasis on defence or encouragement of private enterprise. Others prefer to expand the government sector and to improve education, health care, and other services. But in their management of the economy, all Commonwealth governments since World War II have stressed **three major economic policy objectives — full employment, price stability, and a reasonably balanced trading relationship with the rest of the world**. In pursuit of those policy objectives, the Commonwealth government relies heavily upon two principal sets of weapons: fiscal policy and monetary policy.

Questions

1. What taxing powers are held by (a) the Commonwealth; (b) the states?

2. What proportion of state government spending is financed by state revenue raising?

3. Why is it desirable for the Commonwealth government to be solely responsible for the economic management of the Australian economy?

4. List and explain the three major objectives of Commonwealth government economic policy.

FISCAL POLICY

Fiscal measures are those in which the government raises revenue and spends in the community. The extent and direction of spending and sources of revenue can be varied according to the policy objectives of a particular government. The fiscal policy of a government is therefore expressed in the way that it behaves — that is, how it raises its revenue and how it spends its funds.

A fundamental and preliminary decision of government fiscal policy concerns the division between private and public goods that the government considers desirable. Within that broad framework, fiscal policy decisions must be made concerning variations in the levels of taxation and government sector expenditure to counter booms or slumps in economic activity. Decisions must also be made about the distribution of the burden of taxation and the distribution of the benefits of government sector expenditure. For example, taxes that fall heaviest on those with high incomes and means-tested social welfare payments serve to redistribute income from those on high incomes to those on low incomes. Means-tested social welfare payments ration benefits to those most in need by only providing funds to individuals who can demonstrate that their personal income receipts are either low or zero.

In the past, there have been occasions when governments have introduced changes in fiscal policy within the space of a few months. Economic conditions sometimes change quite rapidly. At other times, governments have made further changes because they have incorrectly assessed the economic "climate". However, very short-run changes in fiscal policy tend to have undesirable effects on the economy. Rapid changes in policy add to uncertainty, leading households and trading enterprises to expect further changes in the future. Generally, however, the fiscal policies of governments are set in their annual **budgets**, which are usually introduced in August. Budget decisions are reached after searching attempts to assess the state of the economy, including discussions with representatives of employer and farm organizations, the trade unions, and other wide-ranging interests.

Fiscal policy is a weapon of economic policy which involves the use of taxing and spending. The annual government budget is the way in which fiscal policy is expressed.

However, it is important to recognize these detailed statements of revenue and expenditure for what they are, namely, *estimates*. For example, the government sets the rates of tax that are to be applied during the following year. It makes certain assumptions concerning employment and income over that period. But it cannot be certain, in advance, how many people will be employed or the incomes those people will earn. So income tax receipts may prove to be greater or less than expected. Likewise, even though the rates of sales tax on motor vehicles may he held constant throughout the coming year, the government cannot be certain how many motor vehicles will be sold. Nor can governments be certain about their expenditures. For example, even if there is no change in the level of the unemployment benefit, government payments to the unemployed will be greater or less than estimated if unemployment rises above or falls below the level expected.

As a result, **we can be certain that total revenue actually received in any fiscal year will be either greater or less than estimated. Likewise, we can be certain that actual expenditures will be greater or less than expected.**

Before the Great Depression in the 1930s, governments regularly planned to raise just sufficient revenue to cover their intended expenditures — that is, they planned to have **balanced budgets**. Not that this meant that actual revenue proved to be precisely equal to their actual expenditures. Governments in those days encountered unexpected changes in economic conditions and ended each period with more or fewer funds than expected. Nevertheless, they *intended* that they should have balanced budgets and considered it improper to plan for any other outcome.

After World War II, mainly as a consequence of the economic management policies proposed by John Maynard Keynes, governments came to accept that fiscal policy can be used as a means of regulating the economy. This requires the government, during a boom, to plan for a **budget**

surplus, the intention being to raise more revenue than they intend to spend. During a recession, or slump, they plan for a **budget deficit**, intending to spend more than they raise. If the Commonwealth government has a surplus, this means that it is in a position to repay public loans, to repay money borrowed from its own bank, the **Reserve Bank of Australia**, or to use its revenue surplus to make loans to the states. In contrast, a budget deficit means that the government's expenditures over a certain period have exceeded its revenue. Like households and trading enterprises, this can only be financed by borrowing. The Commonwealth government does this by raising new public loans, selling bonds and Treasury notes to households and particularly to financial intermediaries. Also it can go to its own banker, the Reserve Bank, and issue securities in return for the right to draw on credit provided by that bank. In due course, some of these debts must be repaid. Meanwhile, interest must be paid on debts outstanding. Hence the "all other" item in table 9, which includes "interest on public debt".

How does a budget surplus or a budget deficit affect the level of economic activity in the economy? If the total Australian demand for goods and services grows until it exceeds our capacity to produce, this excess demand can be satisfied only by increasing our imports. This presents no great problem in the shorter run, provided we have the means of paying for more imports. If, on the other hand, we must somehow limit our purchases overseas, the pressure of demand cannot be met by increased production in the short run. This will probably push up the prices of Australian produced goods and services. Alternatively, the government can reduce the total demand for goods and services in the

Table 9. Commonwealth Government Revenue and Expenditure, 1977/78

Sources of Revenue	Percentage of all Revenue	Types of Expenditure	Percentage of all Expenditures
Taxation revenue:		Social security and welfare	27.9
Income tax:		Health	10.1
individuals	51.7	Defence	8.9
companies	13.2	Education	8.8
other	0.5	Transport and communication	3.2
Customs duties	5.2	Foreign affairs and overseas aid	2.1
Excise duties	11.6	Housing	1.9
Sales tax	7.5	Industry assistance and development	1.2
Other taxes*	1.2	Payments to the States	25.0
Other revenue	9.0	All other (including interest on public debt)	10.9
Total revenue	100.0	Total expenditure	100.0

Source: *Budget Speech 1978—79 and Statements* (Canberra: AGPS, 1978).
Note: Total receipts and revenue in 1977/78 amounted to $26,802 million.
*   Includes payroll tax collected in the ACT.

Australian economy by the use of fiscal measures. The measures available include:

1. Increased taxation, which reduces disposable incomes and hence household expenditure
2. Reduced government expenditure, which has the effect of reducing the demand for goods and services

As a result of such measures, demand may be reduced to match the capacity of the economy. This reduces our demand for imports as well as reducing the upward pressure on prices in Australia.

In contrast, the government may have good reason to expect that the total demand for goods and services will prove to be less than the capacity of the Australian economy. The fiscal measures available to government to increase total demand include:

1. Reduced taxation, which increases household income
2. Increased government spending, which increases the demand for goods and services
3. Encouragement of investment expenditure by providing tax concessions or subsidies

As a consequence, we would expect an increase in aggregate demand, a higher level of economic activity, and fewer people unemployed than if the government had aimed for a balanced budget. If these measures prove successful, there may be a hidden bonus involved. The actual deficit may then prove to be less than was planned, simply because there would then be more people employed and paying taxes and fewer people receiving the unemployment benefit.

For the fiscal year 1977/78, the Commonwealth government, facing a high level of unemployment, budgeted for a deficit of $2,217 million, expecting revenue from all sources of $24,439 million and expenditures amounting to $26,656 million. However, the *actual* deficit in that year was $3,333 million. Total expenditure was $146 million more than expected, mainly owing to social security payments being $242 million above the estimates. Tax receipts in that year fell short of the estimate by $977 million. So the *actual* budget deficit proved to be $1,116 million more than was expected at the time when the government introduced its budget for the period.

Governments, like households and trading enterprises, are unable to forecast future economic events accurately.

Tax Receipts

For revenue, it is clear that the Commonwealth government relies heavily upon taxes on income, particularly taxes on the incomes of individuals.

Taxes levied on income are intended to reflect **capacity to pay**. So the rates of tax, as indicated in table 10, are structured in such a way that the higher is **taxable income** the greater is the proportion of income lost in this way. Such a system is referred to as **progressive taxation**. The rates of

Table 10. The Principal Commonwealth Government Taxes, 1978/79

A. INCOME TAX

(a) Personal: This tax is levied on the incomes of individuals after allowing for deduction of expenses incurred in earning those incomes, as well as concessional allowances available to all taxpayers.

Rates of tax

Taxable Income	Tax Levied
less than $3,893	nil
$3,894 to $16,608	0 + 33.5c for each dollar over $ 3,893
$16,609 to $33,216	$ 4,259 + 47.5c for each dollar over $16,608
$33,217 or more	$12,148 + 61.5c for each dollar over $33,216

(b) Company: On profits distributed—46 cents in the dollar. On profits that remain undistributed—50 cents in the dollar.

B. EXCISE DUTY (examples only)

Products	Rates of tax
Beer	$ 0.52 per litre
Spirits	$18.75 per litre
Motor spirit and diesel fuel	$ 0.0515 per litre
Aviation gasoline	$ 0.0455 per litre
Cigarettes	$24.75 per kilogram
Manufactured tobacco	$12.58 per kilogram

C. SALES TAX: This tax is levied on certain goods, whether manufactured in Australia or imported. The tax is applied at the wholesale level according to the following schedules:

Classes of goods	Rate (%)
First schedule (exempted goods, including most food and clothing)	0
Second schedule (jewellery, plateware, ornaments, etc.)	27½
Third schedule (household furniture and furnishings)	2½
Fourth schedule (commercial vehicles and other goods)	15
Fifth schedule (private motor vehicles)	15

D. CUSTOMS DUTY: These duties are levied on goods imported into Australia. Each item attracts a different rate, according to the amount of protection judged to be necessary to Australian industries and the country of origin of each imported item.

Sources: *The Budget Speech, 1978—79* and Commissioner of Taxation: *57th Report, 1977—78.*

tax, as well as the various concessional allowances, are subject to change from time to time. Nevertheless, the rates of tax payable in 1978/79 will serve to illustrate the progressive nature of these taxes.

An individual with a taxable income up to $3,893 would have paid no income tax at all. People with taxable incomes in the range of $3,894 to $16,608 were subject to a **marginal rate of tax** of 33.5 cents in the dollar. This means that, for each dollar of taxable income in excess of $3,893, they were required to pay 33.5 cents in tax. So an individual with a taxable income of $16,000 would have paid $4,044.85 in tax, representing 25.3 per cent of taxable income. Any person with a taxable income of $30,000 would have faced a marginal rate of tax of 47.5 cents in the dollar and would have paid $10,620.73 in tax, equal to 35.4 per cent of income. Anyone with a taxable income of $50,000 would have paid a marginal rate of 61.5 cents in the dollar and total tax amounting to $22,470.49 or 44.9 per cent of taxable income. Hence **a progressive tax system is one in which the marginal rate of tax is higher at high levels of taxable income, so that tax on higher taxable incomes represents a greater proportion of those incomes.**

Probably a majority of our people agree with this principle. However, the Commonwealth government has generally been reluctant to increase the progressiveness of tax on income in the belief that extremely high rates of tax are likely to blunt incentives to earn higher incomes.

In contrast to income tax, which is levied **directly** on individuals or companies, **indirect taxes** are levied on the production or import of certain goods at a point of sale. For example, a wholesaler buying jewellery from a manufacturer had to pay 27½ per cent **sales tax** in 1978/79. This means that the buyer of a piece of jewellery has to pay the jeweller a price that includes the tax, regardless of his or her income. Likewise, all buyers of beer, spirits, tobacco, and petroleum products paid **excise duties** included in the prices of those products.

Since indirect taxes are paid by the buyers of goods, irrespective of their incomes, they are a relatively greater burden on people with lower incomes. Consider two individuals, one with an annual income of $10,000, the other with an income of $20,000. Each buys thirty litres of petrol a week. During 1978/79, each would have paid 5.155 cents per litre in excise duty or $80.42 in duties over a period of twelve months. However, the proportion of total income paid out in this form of tax would have been much higher for the individual with the lower income. In the example above, the individual with an income of $10,000 would pay 0.8 per cent of his income in excise duty, whereas the individual with an income of $20,000 would pay 0.4 per cent. In fact, where it can be safely assumed that the rates of consumption of certain products are independent of levels of income — quite likely the case where beer and tobacco are concerned — **the proportions of income lost by way of**

indirect taxes are higher at lower levels of income. This means that indirect taxes are usually regressive in relation to the incomes of individuals.

The amount any individual pays out in the form of income tax is usually known, either from weekly pay advice notes or the annual process of preparing a tax return. In contrast, it is highly unlikely that anyone knows exactly how much he or she has paid out in the form of indirect taxes over a period of one year — simply because few people are aware of the rates of tax applied and even fewer keep a record of the quantities of beer, tobacco, petrol, and other goods purchased over a long period. For these reasons, increases in indirect taxes are politically much more attractive than increases in tax on income.

Changes in rates of income tax will change the level of household disposable incomes. This leads to a change in the demand for goods and services *in general.* In contrast, indirect taxes are levied on some goods, but not on others, so that changes in the rates of indirect tax can be expected to show up mainly in the demand for the *particular* products concerned. Successive governments have claimed that indirect taxes represent a necessary weapon of fiscal policy. However, many of the changes in the rates of indirect tax have been introduced simply as a means of increasing revenue. Admittedly, the rate of sales tax on motor vehicles was reduced from 27½ to 15 per cent on two occasions during the latter half of the 1970s in an attempt to stimulate sales and production in that industry. This suggests that indirect taxes *have* been used as part of the Commonwealth's fiscal policy. However, since most other industries were *also* in trouble at that time, reduced income tax would have seemed more appropriate. This would have stimulated *all* Australian industries rather than the motor vehicle industry in particular.

The Commonwealth government raises revenue with a variety of taxes. Income taxes tend to be progressive, while indirect taxes tend to be regressive. Fiscal policy may include changes in any of these forms of tax.

Payments by the Government

Payments are made by one tier of the government sector to another, such as the payment of $6,690 million from the Commonwealth to the state governments in 1977/78. Our concern in this section is with payments by the *government* sector — in particular the Commonwealth government — to the *household* and *trading enterprises* sector.

The government sector is a major purchaser of goods and services.

Much of its expenditure generates employment and incomes in the trading enterprise sector as well as paying the wages and salaries of public servants. For example, a school building programme stimulates activity in the trading enterprise sector and causes incomes to flow into households. Similarly, an expanded defence force or Customs Bureau will result in people (and therefore households) being paid for services rendered.

We also saw in chapter 4 that the government provides **transfer payments**, by means of pensions and benefits which are not in exchange for goods and services, to redistribute income. These payments are not translated into a demand for goods and services until they are spent. The aged pensioner or unemployed parent may spend all the benefits straight away. However, transfer payments to others not immediately in need of consumer goods and services may be saved.

Benefits of various kinds are paid out both to individuals and to trading enterprises. Payments to firms are mainly in the form of **subsidies** (fixed sums, usually divided between individual firms according to their output) or **bounties** (where the government agrees to pay a certain amount per unit of input used, or per unit of output). In 1977/78, for example, the government paid out $326 million by way of industry assistance and development.

A large commitment of the government is in the form of payments to individuals. We have already seen from table 9 that, in 1977/78, 27.9 per cent of Commonwealth government payments were in the form of social security and welfare benefits. Individuals are supported by way of various pensions and allowances, the most important of which are listed in table 11.

The major intention of social security (or welfare) payments is to ensure that those in need receive help from the government. Age pensions are therefore provided for people who are excluded from employment because they are too old to work. The sick, supporting parents, and widows who are unable to earn sufficient income to keep themselves and their dependants at some judged minimum level of subsistence are also eligible to receive benefits from the government. The unemployed receive support because they are unable to find a job so that they can earn an income.

It also happens that, since these payments are largely funded from tax receipts, they are *redistributed* from those who "have" to those who "have not". However, the degree of redistribution from those judged to have the capacity to pay taxes to those most in need is modified in to ways:
1. Some of the tax revenue comes from indirect taxes on commodities bought by those in receipt of social security payments (such as the excise on beer and cigarettes and sales tax on goods).
2. Some of the payments made to individuals under the general heading of "social security payments" are made to people on quite high

Table 11. The Principal Commonwealth Government Social Security Benefits, 1978/79

Pension or Benefit	Recipients	Means Test	Amount of Benefits
A. Age pension	Resident males 65 years and over, females 60 years and over, who have lived in Australia for 10 years or more.	Full pension for individuals with incomes of less than $20 per week or $34.50 for married couples. Part pension to a maximum income of $126.40 per week (single) or $211.90 (married couples).	Single, $53.20 per week, married couples, $44.35 per week each. Add $7.50 per week for each dependant.
B. Invalid pension	People who are permanently blind or 85 per cent (permanently) disabled and 16 years of age or over.	As for age pension.	As for age pension.
C. Widows' pension	A widow is defined to include a divorcee, a deserted wife or one whose husband has been committed to an institution for at least six months.	As for age pension.	As for age pension.
D. Supporting parents' pension	A sole parent supporting at least one child and who has lived in Australia for 10 years or more.	As for age pension.	As for age pension.
E. Unemployment benefit	People who are 16 years of age or more who are able and willing to work and actively seeking employment (registered with Commonwealth Employment Service).	Full benefit where income is less than $6 per week (or $3 per week if under 21). Part benefit where earnings up to $94.70 per week for married couples or $57.45 if single and over 21. (Lower limits on income if less than 21 years.)	$88.70 per week if married and $51.45 if single and 18 years or more. $36 per week if single and under 18 years. $7.50 per week for each additional dependant.
F. Sickness benefit	People who are temporarily unable to work owing to sickness.	As for unemployment benefits.	As for unemployment benefits.
G. Family allowance	Parents of dependent children, including students to the age of 25 years.	On child's own incomes only.	One child $3.50 per week. Two children $8.50 per week. Three children $14.50 per week. Four children $20.50 per week. Add $7 for each additional child.

Source: Department of Social Security, *Pensions Benefits and Allowances,* November 1978, and Reserve Bank of Australia: *Statistical Bulletin.*

Note: Some benefits also carry with them certain "fringe benefits", such as free or subsidized travel and medical care. The means test and benefits also vary according to the number of children dependent upon a pensioner. Over this period, the minimum adult male wage in Australia was about $155 per week and the average of adult male earnings was about $225 per week.

incomes. The best example of this is the family allowance, which is paid to the parents of children regardless of parents' income.

These payments in the reverse direction, that is, *from* the government to households, are often referred to as **negative taxes.** As with taxes, the types and rate of social security benefits, as well as the rules concerning eligibility, have also been changed from time to time. These changes have only rarely reflected an attempt by government to increase or decrease spending — even though it is clear, from the relations between income and consumption expenditures considered in chapter 5, that any small increase in payments to people with low levels of income would probably add to consumption by the same amount. In the main, changes in the types and levels of benefit have reflected the views of successive governments concerning the welfare of people widely regarded as in need of assistance.

One important component of government expenditure is transfer payments such as social welfare benefits. Changes in government expenditure in these areas may be for reasons other than management of the level of economic activity.

Questions

1. What fiscal measures are available to government when faced with (*a*) a booming economy; (*b*) a depressed economy?

2. What is the largest source of taxation revenue to government in Australia?

3. What is meant by the term *progressive taxation?*

4. Why is it often claimed that indirect taxes are regressive?

5. Explain what is meant by *negative taxation.*

6. If the government were to restructure income tax so that people with higher taxable incomes were taxed more heavily and those with lower taxable incomes were taxed less heavily, how would you expect this to affect consumption expenditure? Why?

MONETARY POLICY

Monetary policy is concerned primarily with changes in the supply of money, interest rates, and the availability of finance. Monetary policy has an influence on the level of economic activity and hence is an important weapon of Commonwealth government economic policy. For example, when aggregate demand for goods and services exceeds our capacity to produce, restrictions on the amount of lending and an increase in interest rates make it more difficult and more costly to borrow. So households find it more expensive to buy consumer durables with the aid of borrowed funds. On the other hand, at higher rates of interest, saving is a more attractive alternative. At the same time, some trading enterprises — particularly small or new firms that would need to borrow in order to undertake investment — would be likely to abandon some of their planned investment projects. This is because higher rates of interest on borrowed funds reduce the profitability of an investment project. In the reverse situation, where demand is less than the capacity of the economy, an increase in the availability of funds to borrowers and a reduction in interest rates *should* result in less saving and more spending by households, together with an increase in the investment expenditures of trading enterprises.

Monetary measures such as these provide other means by which government seeks to achieve its economic policy objectives. That is, monetary policy is supplementary to fiscal policy. Not that one is either more or less important than the other. For some purposes, such as the redistribution of income, fiscal measures are clearly more useful; for other purposes, monetary measures are more appropriate. Both sets of weapons are necessary.

Apart from the contrasting nature of the different weapons involved, one major difference is in timing. Fiscal policy tends to be determined annually, so that the budget represents a statement of what the government regards as an appropriate course for the economy over the following twelve months. On the other hand, monetary policy is exercised on a day-to-day basis and is left in the hands of our central bank, **the Reserve Bank of Australia**.

Monetary policy is directed towards attaining the government's macroeconomic objectives through changes in the money supply, interest rates, and the availability of loans. Monetary policy is managed by the Reserve Bank and generally involves frequent but small adjustments.

The Reserve Bank has numerous functions. For example, it is responsible for the issue of notes and coin, as well as for the total supply of money. It acts as the government's banker and raises public loans on the government's behalf. It is also the banker for all other Australian banks, accepting deposits, paying interest on those deposits, and allowing withdrawals either by cheque or in notes and coin. The Reserve Bank, in conjunction with the government, announces changes in interest rates and engages in the sale or purchase of government securities in order to reduce or increase money in the hands of the public, as well as to influence the general level of interest rates. The bank is also responsible for our reserves of gold and foreign currencies and, together with the government and the Treasury Department, for the rate of exchange of the Australian dollar against the currencies of other countries.

Control over the quantities of notes and coin in circulation presents no problems. When the public needs more notes and coin for their transactions — for example, over the last few weeks before Christmas — the reserves of cash in the vaults of the banks are reduced, and the banks in turn simply draw on deposits they hold with the Reserve Bank and ask for payment in cash. When the public needs less cash and the banks find their vault reserves more than sufficient to meet their day-to-day requirements, they convert this excess cash into deposits with the Reserve Bank.

However, control over the *total* supply of money, as well as lending and interest rates, is a more complex business. As we saw in chapter 7, there is more to the supply of money than notes and coin. Whether we accept the MI or M3 definitions of the money supply is not immediately important. What *is* important is that trading banks are in a position, by lending, to increase their deposits and therefore to increase the supply of money. In the absence of any regulation by an outside authority, this process is only limited by the need to hold sufficient cash and other liquid assets to meet the day-to-day requirements of their customers.

Control over Trading Bank Asset Holdings

In its endeavour to control the money supply, the availability of credit, and interest rates, the Reserve Bank has four major types of weapon. The first is control over the way trading banks hold their assets. In chapter 7 it was seen that the expansion of the money supply through lending was influenced by the size of the credit multiplier. The size of the credit multiplier is determined by the reserve ratio. The larger the reserve ratio, the less is the ability of banks to expand deposits. Clearly, controls on the reserve ratio will influence bank lending and the money supply.

The value of this reserve ratio is determined in part by the Reserve Bank and in part by the banks themselves. It consists, in essence, of three different components.

1. The SRD (Statutory Reserve Deposit) requirement. Each trading bank is required by law to maintain an SRD account with the Reserve Bank. The Reserve Bank determines the minimum amount that each bank must have on deposit in its SRD account. For example, if the SRD ratio was 10 per cent, then each bank must deposit in its SRD account with the Reserve Bank a total of 10 per cent of all deposits it holds. Banks do not hold any more SRD than required, as it only earns a very meagre

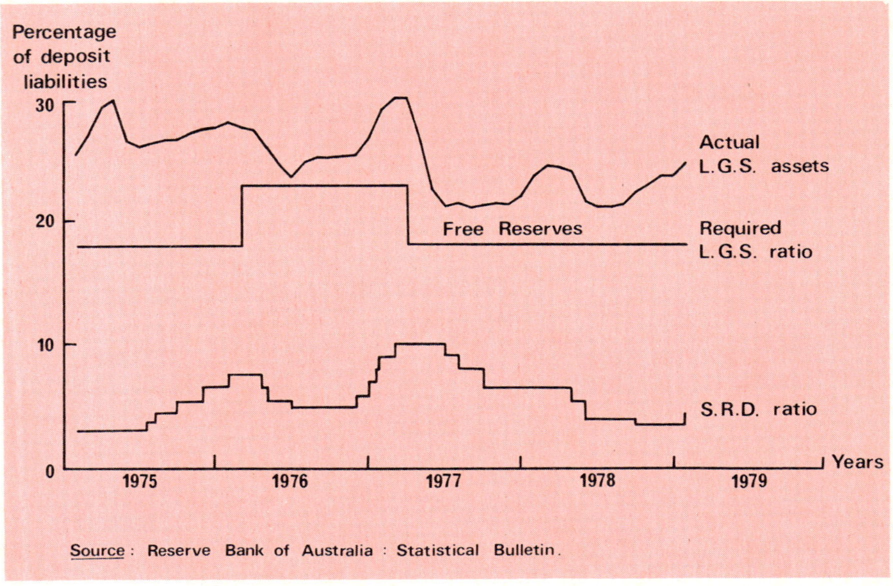

Fig. 8. Major trading banks: LGS assets and SRD ratios 1975-79 (Source: Reserve Bank of Australia, *Statistical Bulletin*)

rate of interest when compared with other financial assets. These reserves cannot be used to extend lending. Figure 8 indicates that the SRD ratio has changed frequently over the period 1975-79. Since January 1961, the SRD ratio has varied between 17.5 and 3.0 per cent.

2. The LGS (liquid assets and government securities) convention. LGS assets are defined as notes, coin, Treasury notes, Commonwealth bonds, and other Commonwealth securities and deposits with the Reserve Bank, but excluding those deposits "locked away" in the SRD. Trading banks, by this convention, undertake to hold LGS assets at some minimum specified proportion of their deposit liability. As is indicated in figure 8, the requirement for most of the period since 1975 has been to hold LGS assets at a minimum of 18 per cent of deposits. An LGS convention of 18 per cent has in fact been in operation for most of the time since 1962. If a bank is at any time unable to meet this requirement, then it must borrow on short term from the Reserve Bank. This can be at a very high rate of interest.

3. The Free Reserve Ratio. Banks usually hold LGS assets in excess of the minimum requirement. These assets are called **free reserves** and allow the bank to take advantage of attractive lending opportunities when they arise. Free reserves may also act as a safeguard against an unusually high withdrawal rate by customers as well as a source of assets in the event that the Reserve Bank increases the SRD ratio. The level of free reserves in the period 1975-79 is indicated in figure 8 and depends very much upon the policies of the various trading banks. If the free reserve ratio is higher than the desired level, trading banks will be keen to increase their lending to earn more income from the assets they hold.

Taken together, the SRD controls and the LGS convention give the Reserve Bank considerable power over trading bank free reserves. By setting the SRD at high levels, it can reduce the banks' free reserves to negligible proportions and thus reduce their lending power. Conversely, when the Reserve Bank wishes to encourage spending, the SRD ratio can be reduced to increase free reserves. This gives trading banks scope to increase their lending.

Advances	S. R. D.	Free Reserves	L.G.S. Convention
63%	10%	9%	18%

Fig. 9.   Typical asset holding of a major trading bank. (Source: Reserve Bank, *Statistical Bulletin*, 1978)

Open Market Operations

A second weapon of monetary policy is **open market operations**. These open market operations refer to the buying and selling by the Reserve Bank of government securities. Open market operations are transactions involving the public and the Reserve Bank's holdings of government securities, usually through the stock exchange and money market dealers. They do not include transactions with the banks or with the Australian government, although the banks may operate on behalf of their customers in the normal course of business.

If the Reserve Bank acts as a buyer of government securities, its operations have two effects. Firstly, it will increase the money supply, because payments made to the sellers of securities will be lodged as bank deposits. This is illustrated in diagrammatic form in figure 10.

A second effect when the Reserve Bank buys government securities is

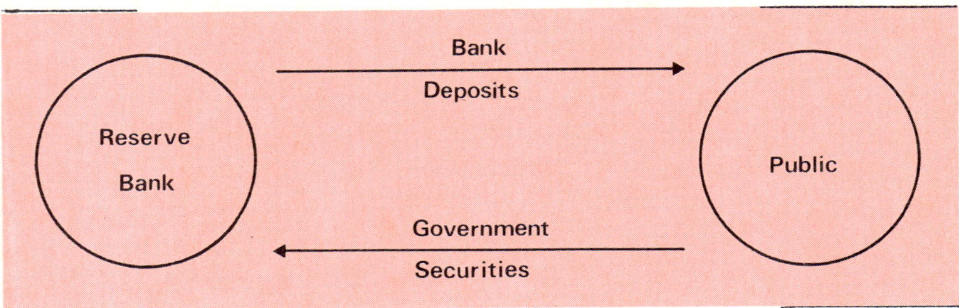

Fig. 10.   Purchase of government securities by the Reserve Bank

that the increased demand for these securities will increase their price. Given that there is a nominal yield on the face (original) value of these securities, the effective interest return will fall. For example, a $100 bond with a nominal yield of 10 per cent per year may be sold for $120. This means that the buyer still only gets $10 in interest, which implies an effective annual yield (on his $120 purchase price) of $8^{1}/_{3}$ per cent. The lower yields on government securities will exert downward pressure upon other interest rates in the finance market. In this way, the Reserve Bank can use open market operations to boost economic activity.

Conversely, the sale of securities by the Reserve Bank reduces the money supply and exerts an upward pressure on interest rates. The continuing development of Australian money markets is allowing the Reserve Bank to make greater use of open market operations.

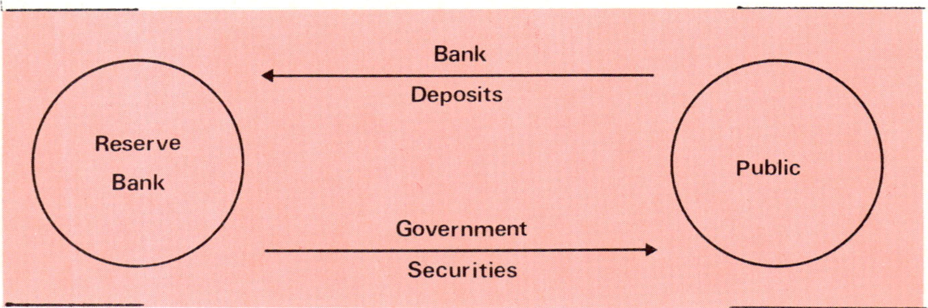

Fig. 11.   Sale of government securities by the Reserve Bank

Other Influences of the Reserve Bank

A third weapon of monetary policy is control over interest rates payable to, or by, the major Australian banks. The use of this direct control is decreasing and the Reserve Bank tends to confine its actions in this area to specifying maximum key interest rates and allowing individual banks to set their own rates within these ceilings.

Finally, the Reserve Bank influences monetary policy through regular consultation with the trading banks. In this way the Reserve Bank can influence the level of interest rates and the rate of lending, as well as the direction of lending. The Reserve Bank may modify the effects of a contraction in lending or an increase in the rate of interest by expressing the wish that some industries be exempted. On the other hand, new lending may be discouraged for other specific purposes.

Reserve Bank Monetary Controls:
- Statutory Reserve Deposits and the LGS convention
- Open market operations
- Interest rates
- Consultation

In these ways, it would seem that the Reserve Bank can exert considerable influence over borrowing and lending in Australia. Furthermore, the required strategies seem quite straightforward. When demand exceeds the capacity of Australia to produce, an increase in the SRD requirement, the sale of government securities and an increase in interest rates each serve to reduce the ability of the banks to lend and generally make borrowing more costly. In the reverse situation, a release of funds from SRD accounts, the buying of government securities from the public, and a reduction of interest rates increase the capacity of banks to lend. Interest rates are then lower and households and trading enterprises are encouraged to borrow more and increase their spending.

LIMITS TO MONETARY POLICY

There are several reasons why the weapons of monetary policy mentioned above are less effective than might be expected. The effects of increases in SRDs have been cushioned to the extent that the banks have held free reserves. The Reserve Bank may call upon the trading banks to increase their SRDs by, say $100 million, with a view to reducing the banking system's capacity to lend. There would be no immediate need to reduce lending unless this reduction in the LGS assets of the banks had also come close to wiping out the free reserves. Likewise, relatively small releases from SRDs would not automatically result in an increase in bank lending; for example, the banks may believe these reductions in SRDs to be temporary.

Equally important is the fact that many of our larger trading enterprises are not heavily dependent upon the financial intermediaries for the funds they use in financing investment projects. These firms usually accumulate undistributed profits and, in most cases, hold large reserves in fairly liquid forms. Under boom conditions, when further increases in sales are widely expected, restrictions on lending by the banks and an increase in interest rates of, say, 1 per cent are unlikely to deter such firms from proceeding with what they consider to be profitable investment projects.

In contrast, small and newly established firms are generally more dependent upon borrowed funds than the larger, long-established companies. An increase of 1 per cent in the rate of interest or a restriction on lending is more likely to have an impact upon the investment expenditures of these firms than on trading enterprises that have adequate reserves of their own. Similarly, young couples buying their first home are likely to be dependent upon the banks for a loan, and a reduction in lending by the banks would probably have a marked impact upon the building industry. So restrictions on the ability of the banks to lend or increases in interest rates may not serve to reduce aggregate demand either to the extent or in the directions that the government and the Reserve Bank would prefer.

In the reverse situation, that is, where we have surplus capacity and a need for an increase in aggregate demand, we would expect releases from SRD accounts and some reduction in interest rates. However, firms are only likely to increase their expenditures if they can see profitable avenues for investment. Even so, if they have reserves of their own they would be more inclined to draw upon these rather than borrow from the banks. On the other hand, it is by no means certain that, if the economy has excess capacity, the banks would be willing to lend to small or newly established firms or to young couples with low incomes seeking to buy or build homes.

In the Banking Act of 1959, the use of these measures by the Reserve Bank was restricted initially to the privately owned trading banks. State-owned banks, like the Hobart Savings Bank and the Savings Bank of South Australia, and the non-banking intermediaries, like finance companies and life assurance organizations, were exempted. In fact, several of the major trading banks were quick to realize that the purchase of controlling interests in finance companies would serve to place part of their borrowing and lending activities beyond the immediate control of the Reserve Bank.

Over the period 1959-73, there were several relatively minor amendments to the Banking Act, including controls imposed on the types of securities held by life assurance organizations. However, it was not until the Financial Corporations Act of 1974 that an attempt was made to impose on the non-bank intermediaries basically the same controls as are exercised over the banks — that is, control over the types of assets held, lending policies, and the rates of interest paid and charged. Except for the requirement that the non-bank intermediaries provide the Reserve Bank with certain statistics, these powers have not yet been put into effect. Nevertheless, the non-bank intermediaries are well aware of the legislative powers now available to the Reserve Bank. So it is not surprising that the Reserve Bank has since found the co-operation of these intermediaries to be quite satisfactory.

Early in 1979 the Commonwealth government launched a wide-ranging inquiry into the Australian monetary system. Whether this inquiry will result in the implementation of some of the provisions in the 1974 Act or legislation to provide additional powers over the intermediaries remains to be seen. However, it is not at all clear how the powers of the Reserve Bank might be usefully extended. Further controls may result in a search, by the intermediaries, for ways and means of avoiding the additional powers that the government may consider necessary. Furthermore, a greater measure of control over the intermediaries would not serve to overcome all of the problems involved. The larger firms will continue to rely mainly upon their own reserves. If they see profitable opportunities for investment, they will invest. If not, regardless of an increase in the availability of credit and some further (small) reduction in interest rates, they will *not* invest.

Monetary policy is concerned with changes in the supply, cost, and availability of money to assist in regulating the level of economic activity.

Questions

1. Explain how monetary policy may be used to stimulate the economy.

2. List the functions of the Reserve Bank.

3. Explain what is meant by the following terms.
   (*a*) Statutory Reserve Deposit
   (*b*) LGS assets
   (*c*) Free reserves

4. The following is a simplified trading bank balance sheet:

Liabilities	$m.	Assets	$m.
Deposits	100	Cash	10
Other Liabilities	20	Government bonds	20
		SRD account	10
		Advances	80
	120		120

Assume the bank is holding the required amount in the SRD account.

(*a*) What is the SRD ratio?

(*b*) If the LGS requirement is 20 per cent, what is the value of free reserves held by this bank?

(*b*) The bank decides to purchase another $10 million of government bonds. What happens to the LGS ratio?

5. A weapon of monetary policy is open market operations. Describe how open market operations could help to restrain the level of economic activity.

6. How does the holding of free reserves cushion the effect of monetary policy?

7. Suggest reasons why the Commonwealth government may prefer the use of monetary policy to regulate the level of economic activity.

THE USE OF FISCAL AND MONETARY POLICY

Fiscal policy can be selective by varying particular taxes and particular expenditure items. Once introduced, the effects are soon evident. For example, if it is decided to increase personal income tax rates, household disposable income drops at the date of implementation. However, fiscal policy is relatively slow *to implement* because of the political and administrative lags involved. Also there has been a reluctance on the part of successive governments to introduce supplementary budgets. Fiscal policy changes most often occur through changes in the *annual* budgets. Frequently the political problems with certain fiscal measures, such as increased taxation, reduce the willingness of governments to use these weapons.

Monetary policy is politically more acceptable in that it is more subtle. For example, a direction by the Reserve Bank for a reduction in new lending by trading banks will be noticed mainly by potential borrowers, not all members of the public. Also, monetary policy is quick to implement. For example, a call to Statutory Reserve Deposit can be required within a very short time. It is generally accepted that monetary measures are less suitable for stimulating economic activity than restraining economic activity.

Question

1. What are the advantages and disadvantages of using (*a*) fiscal policy, and (*b*) monetary policy to regulate the level of economic activity?

9 The Overseas Sector

As suggested in chapter 4, the levels of production, employment, and income in Australia are not determined in isolation from the rest of the world. For example, our production of wool, wheat, beef, and iron ore is far in excess of our own requirements and is largely in anticipation of sales overseas. If no foreign markets were available for those products, output and employment in our farming and mining industries would be much lower than the present levels. On the other hand, there are some goods, like large aircraft, that we do not produce in Australia and others, like crude oil, that we do not produce in sufficient quantities to meet our own needs. Products like these are imported into Australia and represent part of the total supply of goods and services available in this country. In the same way that our sales of farm products and mineral ores to other countries serve to raise production and employment in Australia, sales *to* Australia by Japan, the United States or the oil-rich countries of the Middle East help to provide job opportunities in *those* countries.

In addition, Australia provides services that are used by foreigners, while other countries provide services that are used by Australians. For example, Qantas and British Airways are both involved in flying passengers between Australia and Britain. Some of those passengers are Australians, paying for their fares in Australian dollars. Others are citizens of Britain or other countries, making payments in their own currencies. Other services of increasing importance in our economic transactions with the rest of the world are those associated with tourism. There are growing numbers of foreign tourists visiting Australia each year. These people make use of our domestic transport services and pay for accommodation and other services provided by Australians. There are also growing numbers of Australians travelling abroad each year, buying similar services in other countries.

Apart from payments for goods and services, both by foreigners to Australia and by Australians to other countries, there are also international flows of funds associated with gifts, loans, the purchase of financial assets, and investment expenditures. For example, the Commonwealth government gives aid, on our behalf, to the developing countries, usually by way of grants, but sometimes in the form of loans. On the other hand, the government periodically raises loans in New York, London, Bonn, or Zurich and must make interest payments on those loans.

Part of the flow of funds between Australia and the rest of the world is accounted for by the sale and purchase of financial assets. There are also inflows and outflows associated with investment expenditures. From time to time, foreign firms from the United States, Britain, and Japan draw upon the reserves of their parent companies to build new plants or increase the capacity of mining ventures in Australia. Likewise, Australian firms must convert reserves held in Australian dollars into foreign currencies in order to undertake investment expenditures in other countries. If and when these Australian firms make profits and have the permission of the governments of those countries to do so, they will return profits to their parent firms in Australia — just as GMH, from time to time, sends back dividends to America.

Of these many types of transaction between Australia and the rest of the world, we will be concerned primarily with commodity exports and commodity imports. These two items are by far the largest among our overseas transactions. Furthermore, because an increase in our exports serves to increase production, employment, and income in Australia, whereas an increase in imports increases production and employment overseas — possibly at the expense of jobs in Australia — fluctuations in commodity trade affect the level of economic activity in Australia.

Transactions take place between Australia and the rest of the world for many reasons, including payments for goods and services, the purchase of financial assets, lending and borrowing, and investment. Concern here will be primarily with the import and export of goods.

FREE TRADE: A PERSISTENT DREAM

In Australia, as in other countries, our land, labour, and capital resources are particularly well suited to the production of some goods but not for others. For example, our soils, climate, and farming know-how in southern Australia lend themselves particularly well to the production of hard wheats and fine wools. On the other hand, the Japanese are able to produce motor vehicles at much lower resource cost than we can produce similar vehicles in Australia. This suggests that we would be better off if we were to concentrate on the production of those commodities in which we have natural advantages, exporting that part of production in excess of our own requirements and importing motor vehicles and other goods produced more efficiently in other countries.

Since the time of Adam Smith, there have been many writers who have pointed to the advantages of **"free trade"** — **that is, a situation in which all countries would have free and ready access to the markets of all other countries**. No country would prohibit the entry of goods from any other country and none would place limits on quantities imported. Nor would any country impose customs duties or any other form of entry tax on imported goods. Regardless of their locations around the world, producers of each commodity would then be free to compete with producers in all other countries. Viewed in another way, producers in each individual country would then face competition from producers of the same (or similar) products in other countries — with only **natural protection** (that is, **the cost of freight and insurance from other countries**) to protect them from their competitors. For example, the cost of producing a certain commodity in Australia may be $10 per unit. The cost of producing the same commodity in some other country may be $9 per unit. If, however, the cost of freight and insurance from that other country to Australia was $2 per unit, this **natural protection** would allow our producers to sell in the Australian market at lower prices than their competitors.

The result, according to those who favour free trade, would be that each country would face competition from the most efficient producers throughout the world. So each would tend to concentrate on the production of those commodities for which its own land, labour, and capital resources were best suited. Each country would specialize, importing from other countries those goods that others could produce at lower cost. As a consequence, consumers everywhere would benefit, because they would be paying the lowest possible prices for each type of commodity.

The force of these arguments lies in the undeniable fact that some countries have particular advantages in the production of certain commodities. It may be that a country has the climatic and soil conditions best suited to the production of rubber or coffee. Alternatively, the combination of low-cost public power supplies, a highly skilled workforce, and advanced production techniques may fit a country particularly well for certain types of manufacturing.

If one country is clearly able to produce a certain commodity at lower cost per unit of output than any other, we would say that country has an **absolute advantage** in the production of that commodity. *However, the* *potential gains from trade do not require that the countries engaged in trade have an absolute advantage in the production of one commodity or another.* Consider two countries, Atlantis and Mythica, each producing wheat and dairy products. Let us assume that the production possibilities curves of Atlantis and Mythica are such that for one unit of input — say, a day of labour — they can produce the following:

a In Atlantis, either 60 kg of wheat or 10 kg of butterfat
b In Mythica, either 40 kg of wheat or 9 kg of butterfat

Atlantis can produce *both* wheat and butterfat at a lower resource cost — that is, more efficiently than Mythica. However, the opportunity cost of producing either more wheat or more butterfat varies in the two countries concerned. At their present positions on their production possibilities curves, Mythica can produce butterfat at relatively less cost than wheat, while Atlantis has a **comparative advantage** in the production of wheat. By giving up the production of 40 kg of wheat, Mythica can produce an extra 9 kg of butterfat. If we ignore the cost of delivery from Mythica to Atlantis, this 9 kg of butterfat is equivalent — in terms of production costs — to 54 kg of wheat in Atlantis ($^9/_{10}$ of 60 kg of wheat). That is, by giving up the production of 40 kg of wheat to produce 9 kg of butterfat, Mythica, if it traded with Atlantis at the rate of 60 kg of wheat for 10 kg of butterfat, would be 14 kg of wheat better off and Atlantis would be no worse off.

In practice, Atlantis might like to be better off from trade as well and may offer less than 60 kg of wheat for each 10 kg of butterfat traded. The "floor" in the trading rate, as far as Mythica is concerned, is when she could produce the wheat at the same relative production cost herself (44.4 kg of wheat for 10 kg of butterfat). The limit to beneficial exchange would also be reduced by the freight and insurance costs of transporting the products between the two countries. The important thing to note is that **both countries can benefit by concentrating on the production of goods in which they have the greatest comparative advantage**.

If countries specialized in the production of goods in which they had a comparative advantage, the world's resources would be allocated in a more efficient way. More production would come from these more efficiently allocated resources. This is the basis of the gains to be made from free trade.

Although the arguments for free trade are very persuasive, there is little evidence of support for these principles in the trading practices of individual countries. Even Adam Smith, a strong advocate of free trade two hundred years ago, admitted that each country would naturally insist on producing its own means of defence. If one country alone produced military hardware, simply because it was the most efficient producer of weapons, it could readily impose its will on all other countries! But with the passage of time, governments have used national defence as an argument to justify assistance to shipbuilders, precision-instrument manufacturers, motor vehicle producers, and many other industries that would have a role to play in the event of war.

There are numerous other reasons why governments intervene to restrict the entry of imports and to encourage growth of domestic industries. Some of these arguments are quite reasonable. For example, Australia has long prohibited the import of certain meat products as a safeguard against the introduction of animal diseases from overseas.

On the surface, the arguments for specialization by individual economies appear to have a great deal of merit. However, those countries choosing to specialize would also face disadvantages — particularly those that concentrated on farm products or industrial raw materials. World demand for products such as these tends to fluctuate more widely than the demand for manufactured goods. So specialization may result in wider fluctuations in total production and employment than could be expected if economic activities were more diversified. The outlook for an individual country that chose to specialize would be even worse if, as a result of technological changes, world demand for its principal product fell steadily and permanently. This has long been a danger facing producers of industrial raw materials like rubber, wool, and tin.

And what of the developing countries? The industrialized countries have had a long start in developing labour skills and production techniques. If the developing countries were to allow low-cost imports to compete freely in their home markets with the products of their own recently established industries, there may be so little demand for the products of those new industries that they would never grow to maturity. These industries are referred to as **infant** industries.

In labour-intensive industries like clothing and footwear, low wage rates *do* give producers a competitive advantage. However, low wage rates paid in the developing countries do not necessarily mean that their products can compete with those of highly paid workers in the industrialized countries. For example, despite much lower wage rates paid to workers in chemical industries in Latin American countries in the 1960s, the cost of production per unit of output was much higher than in the United States — owing to the lower productivity of labour in Latin America. So, if the developing countries are to establish anything other than labour-intensive industries to provide employment for their rapidly growing populations, they must use ways and means of protecting their infant industries against competition from imports.

The need to protect *infant* industries has long been widely accepted. Unfortunately, the industrialized countries also use these *infant* industry arguments when they establish new import-replacing industries and take steps to protect those industries against competition from imports. These "beggar-my-neighbour" policies often serve to generate additional jobs in the industrialized countries at the expense of employment opportunities in the developing countries. Such was the case when the Commonwealth government decided to pay very substantial bounties to Australian cotton producers from early in the 1950s. Whereas we had formerly imported the bulk of our raw cotton requirements, in the space of fifteen years we were growing an exportable surplus.

The major arguments applied in practice against free trade include defence and health considerations, the need for a diversified production base, and the protection of infant industries.

Questions

1. What is meant by the term *free trade*?
   How could free trade benefit Australians?

2. How does "natural protection" benefit Australian producers?

3. Which industries in Australia would be most disadvantaged by free trade?
   What effect would free trade have on Australian production?

4. Some countries are disadvantaged by free trade.
   What type of countries are disadvantaged and what are the disadvantages?

5. A group of twenty people decide to form a communal village. Each person in this village is able to produce 25 kg of potatoes or 50 m of cloth.
   Another twenty people also decide to form a communal village. Each person in this village is able to produce 50 kg of potatoes or 150 m of cloth.
   Specialization may benefit each village. What should each village specialize in producing? Why will specialization benefit each village?

PROTECTION: THE REALITY

What is meant by **"protection"**? In its broadest sense, protection refers to all ways and means by which employment and income in any industry are protected or maintained, whether by barriers erected against competition from other industries at home and abroad or payments made by governments to producers in individual industries.

In international trade, all industries in all countries have *natural* protection against imports from the rest of the world. This being so, we tend to regard *trade* protection as those measures used by governments in attempts to protect home industries against competition from imports. This protection can be provided in a number of ways. **Tariffs** are taxes imposed on imported goods. They are sometimes referred to as **customs duties**.

Until 1921, the Commonwealth government imposed tariffs in a rather haphazard fashion, as much to raise revenue as anything else. In that year, the **Tariff Board** was created and was given powers to investigate and make recommendations concerning the protection of individual industries.

After a few years, the Tariff Board and the government came to accept that all "efficient" Australian industries were entitled to sufficient tariff protection to allow them to make "reasonable" profits. It was never clear what was meant by "an efficient industry". Very few Australians questioned the wisdom of tariff protection. So tariffs came to be set at levels necessary to ensure the survival of individual industries.

One official reason given for raising tariffs against imports was that this would allow higher wage rates to Australian workers. So our workers claimed and received higher wages. In turn, Australian industries pointed to their rising wage costs and were granted still higher levels of tariff protection — in this way avoiding the need to increase their efficiency. This added protection allowed our industries to raise their prices, which then gave workers grounds for claiming higher wage rates.

During the Great Depression of the early 1930s, higher tariffs and other techniques were used in an attempt to prop up industries in Australia that were suffering from reduced demand. Naturally enough, our principal trading partners did the same thing. As protection against imports increased throughout the world, the level of trade declined and our export industries, like those of other countries, suffered very badly. By 1932, about one-third of our workforce was unemployed.

In 1947, in an attempt to prevent a repetition of the beggar-my-neighbour policies of the 1930s, the governments of many countries, including Australia, engaged in negotiations and entered into what is known as the **General Agreement on Tariffs and Trade** (GATT). Under this arrangement, members agreed to limit their tariffs on imports and to avoid discrimination between imports from individual member countries.

However, by the early 1970s, little had changed. Although the Tariff Board had begun to question the wisdom of high tariff protection to some of our less efficient industries, customs duties on imported goods ranged from nothing to well in excess of 50 per cent of the values of some imports at Australian ports of entry.

In contrast to our manufacturing industries, some of our farm industries sell the bulk of their output overseas and do not face competition in the Australian market. Duties on imported substitutes would do little, if anything, to protect employment and income in those industries. On the other hand, tariffs on imports of fencing wire, fertilizers, farm machinery, and other farm inputs serve to raise the costs of farmers above the levels that could be expected if those inputs were allowed to enter Australia free of duties. So employment and income in farm industries have been protected by other means — mainly by subsidies, the payment of bounties on certain farm inputs (like fertilizers and machinery), and government participation in the fixing of some farm product prices in Australia, sometimes at levels in excess of going world prices.

From the beginning of 1974, the Tariff Board was replaced by the **Industries Assistance Commission** (IAC), a statutory authority with powers to investigate and recommend changes, upwards or downwards, in all forms of assistance to Australian industries. Proposed changes are now considered very carefully, and procedures include public hearings of evidence and the issue of draft conclusions and recommendations to allow further discussion with industry representatives before the IAC makes its final submissions to the government. After the government has made its decision, the IAC's final report is published and the necessary administrative changes — for example, changes in customs duties levied on particular imports — are put into effect.

In most instances, duties are calculated as a percentage of the values of goods at ports of entry. The duties payable vary with the nature of the goods and according to the extent of protection which the government considers to be necessary to the industry concerned. For example, some foodstuffs not produced in Australia (like cocoa and some spices) enter duty free. In contrast, yarns containing not less than 50 per cent acrylic fibre incur a duty of 15 per cent, shoes with leather uppers 46.5 per cent, and new motor vehicles 57.5 per cent. People who buy imported goods that would be subject to either sales tax or excise duties if produced in Australia are also subject to those taxes. So, if the value of an imported vehicle at an Australian port was $5,000, the customs duty payable would be $2,875; that is, the price in Australia, *before* sales tax, would be $7,875.

The rates of duty applied are varied, from time to time, according to the assessed need to protect employment in each of the industries concerned. Thus the principal purpose in levying these duties is now the protection of Australian industries, rather than the gathering of tax revenue.

Many of these rates of duty also vary, at any one time, according to the country of origin of the imported goods. Four different rates of duty are widely used — the "general" rate (which applies in all cases except where goods qualify for a lower rate), a "preferential" rate (applied to some imports drawn from British Commonwealth countries), a rate applied to imports from the developing countries, and another rate for imports from Papua New Guinea — a developing country for which Australia feels special responsibility. For some goods these four rates are identical. In other cases the rates vary widely according to the country of origin, but there is no general pattern evident between individual commodities.

On the surface it would seem that our tariff policies are in conflict with the aim that members of GATT should not discriminate between imports from different countries. Preferential treatment of imports from members of the British Commonwealth had its origins in the years of the Great Depression and is in the process of being phased out: in many instances, there is now no difference between the general and preferential rates of duty. On the other hand, the lower rates of duty applied to some imports from the developing countries is a practice that GATT and other international agencies have actively encouraged for many years.

In addition to customs duties, some manufactured imports are also subject to quantitative restrictions — that is, measures by which the total quantities of goods imported are limited, thereby providing greater protection for the industries concerned.

Some goods, such as motor vehicles, steel, chest-type freezers, and some types of footwear, are subject to **import licensing**. People who wish to import these goods must first obtain a licence before they can do so. If such goods are imported without a licence, they are "prohibited imports" and are either confiscated by the Bureau of Customs or are returned to the countries of origin. Import licensing serves to impose a firm ceiling on the quantities of goods imported under these arrangements, leaving the balance of the home market to Australian producers.

Other goods — mainly clothing, footwear, yarns, and fabrics — are subject to what are known as **tariff quotas**. From year to year, depending on the expected ability of the industries concerned to withstand competition, national import quotas are set and individual importers are permitted to import certain quantities. If the national quotas are raised or lowered in the next period, so too are the quotas of individual importers. Each importer is required to pay only the usual rates of duty on such imports — up to the point at which their individual quotas for the period have been filled. In the event that importers *exceed* their quotas — which are constantly monitored by an extensive computer network — they must either pay heavy **penalty rates of duty** or return the excess to the countries of origin. Unlike import licensing, quotas do not impose a rigid upper limit on the quantities of goods imported; however, the penalty duty rates, payable *in addition to* the normal duties, serve as a substantial deterrent to importers.

Tariffs increase the prices at which imported goods are sold, making the prices of similar home-produced goods more attractive to consumers. Consumers pay more than they would if there were no tariff protection and supplies of commodities were drawn from least-cost sources. Quantitative restrictions limit the quantities of certain goods imported so that, no matter how attractive the prices of these imported goods compared with the prices of Australian substitutes, a large part of the market remains available to Australian producers.

Protection encourages greater use of Australian resources in protected industries. Protection therefore results in a less efficient allocation of Australia's resources. Consumers bear the cost in higher prices. The benefits flow to the owners of the resources used by the protected industries.

Most imported foodstuffs are allowed entry at much lower rates of duty than are generally imposed on manufactured goods. Those foodstuffs that enter readily and at low rates of duty are either not produced in Australia or are not produced in sufficient quantities to meet our requirements. However, the import of products that *would* be competing with our major farm export industries, like wheat and livestock products, are subject to the permission of the Department of Primary Industry or quarantine regulations or both and are therefore virtually prohibited imports.

Other countries use similar means of protecting their own industries against imports. Tariffs are used throughout the world, the levels applied to different goods generally reflecting, as in Australia, the ability of industries in those countries to survive competition. For example, subsidies to farmers are commonplace in the industrialized countries, in some cases serving to encourage inefficient producers to produce in excess of national requirements: as a consequence, Australian farmers have at times found themselves competing with surpluses "dumped" in developing countries at less than going world prices. There are also other countries that make use of quotas as additional means of protecting their own industries. For example, both Japan and the United States impose quota restrictions on imports of beef from Australia, as well as from other foreign sources of supply.

In Australia, the Industries Assistance Commission makes recommendations to the government with regard to the protection of industries. Protection against import competition can be given by tariffs, import quotas, import licencing, or subsidies.

Another means of protection that has gained in popularity over the last three decades is the joining together of individual countries to form what is known as a **customs union**. The members agree to allow free trade between themselves. This means they do *not* levy customs duties on imports from member countries. This is done in the belief that each has comparative advantages and that each will benefit by freedom of access to what is, in effect, a larger home market. At the same time, members also agree to levy precisely the same high tariffs on imports from non-member countries, thereby making some of the high-cost products of member countries more attractive than imports to buyers in their domestic markets.

The **European Economic Community** (the EEC) otherwise known as the European Common Market, is an example of a customs union of particular concern to Australia. The EEC was established in 1958 and consisted initially of Belgium, France, Germany, Italy, Luxembourg, and the Netherlands. That arrangement had little immediate effect on our overseas trade while Britain remained our principal trading partner. However, in 1973 Britain joined the EEC and retreated behind the tariff wall common to all member countries. Repeated attempts to recover our former share of the total EEC markets for farm products have failed. So Australia has been forced to seek out and establish alternative markets.

Protection is a two-edged sword, and the attitudes of EEC negotiators are understandable. Like Australia, the countries of the EEC are concerned with employment opportunities available to their own people. They point out that our levels of tariff protection are among the highest in the world and, in response to our requests for more ready access to the EEC markets for farm products, suggest that we reduce our tariffs on manufactured goods.

Similar attitudes are encountered in our trade negotiations with other countries. For example, early in 1979 the Commonwealth government sought an increase in the Japanese quota on Australian beef. The Japanese immediately responded by stating that they would be willing to consider our request provided we were prepared to consider increasing imports of Japanese motor vehicles. Such an arrangement would no doubt prove acceptable to Australian beef producers, but it would not be welcomed by the people in our motor vehicle industry. On balance, a trade-off of that kind would be more likely to result in a reduction, rather than an increase, in job opportunities in Australia.

Questions

1. Why did protection generally increase in the 1930s?
   In the long run, did this increased protection have the desired effect?

2. Protection in Australia takes different forms. What are these forms?

3. What is "dumping"?

4. Discuss the advantages and disadvantages of Australia joining with other countries to form a customs union in "the Pacific Basin".

THE COMPOSITION AND DIRECTION OF AUSTRALIA'S OVERSEAS TRADE

The comparative advantages of individual countries, the extent and forms of protection used, formal trading agreements with other industrial countries, and some purely political considerations are all reflected in our pattern of overseas trade.

Australia's principal commodity exports and imports are indicated in table 12. It would be necessary to examine each of these subdivisions of goods in order to isolate the individual commodities exported and commodities imported. Nevertheless, it is clear that our exports in 1977/78 consisted mainly of mineral ores, metals, coal, grains, wool, and meat. Our major imports were manufactured goods, with machinery for Australian industries and transport equipment accounting for almost one-third of all imports.

Table 12. Composition of Australia's Overseas Trade, 1977/78

Exports (as percentage of total value)	%	Imports (as percentage of total value)	%
Mineral ores and scrap metals	13.6	Machinery (except electrical)	16.7
Coke, coal, briquettes	12.1	Transport equipment	11.7
Cereals and cereal preparations	11.0	Crude oil, petroleum	10.3
Textile fibres (including wool)	9.8	Electrical machinery, appliances	8.5
Meat and meat preparations	9.1	Textile yarns, fabrics, garments	6.1
Chemical elements and compounds	5.9	Miscellaneous manufactures	5.6
Non-ferrous metals	4.7	Chemical elements and compounds	3.5
Sugar, sugar preparations, honey	4.5	Instruments, photo equipment, clocks	3.5
Iron and steel	3.8	Paper and paper products	2.5
Machinery (except electrical)	2.1	Metal manufactures	2.5
All other	23.4	All other	29.1
Total	100.0	Total	100.0

Source: Australian Bureau of Statistics, *Overseas Trade*.

Unfortunately, changes in the Australian system of classification of commodities in the 1960s to conform with the international system make it impossible to compare accurately the composition of our trade in 1977/78 with the composition of our exports and imports in the 1950s. In the 1950s, farm industries accounted for 70 to 80 per cent of all exports by value, and exports of mineral ores and manufactured goods were relatively insignificant. As recently as the period 1963-66, grains, wool, and meat together accounted for almost 56 per cent of our exports, while mineral ores, metals, and coal represented only slightly more than 10 per cent.

Over the last thirty years, rural produce has become less important as part of Australia's exports. Metals and minerals are now a much more important source of export earnings than in the 1950s. The pattern of imports has not changed nearly as much. The largest part of Australian imports is made up of machinery and other inputs used in Australian production.

The major changes in the composition of our exports during the sixties and seventies were very closely associated with changes in the direction of our overseas trade. From the end of the fifties it was apparent that the United Kingdom was seriously considering applying for membership of the EEC. From that time onward it was also evident that we would have to seek out and develop alternative markets for our exports. The principal alternatives proved to be Japan, with its rapidly growing appetite for mineral ores, coal, wool, and to a lesser extent other farm products, and the markets in the United States for beef and sugar. The proportions of our imports drawn from Japan and the United States have grown, while our purchases from Britain have continued to decline in significance. These principal changes in the directions of our trade are indicated in figure 12.

The sharp and continuing decline in our exports to Britain is readily apparent. Fortunately, this has been offset by the growth in our exports to Japan and, to a lesser extent, to the United States. Meanwhile, with the exception of fairly regular exports of wheat to China, growth in our exports to the developing countries in south— and south-east Asia remains little more than a dream of things to come.

Australia's exports and imports by country have exhibited similar patterns of change over the last thirty years. As trading partners, the UK has become much less important, while Japan has become much more important.

Questions:

1. What are Australia's major exports and imports?

2. Which country is the major purchaser of our exports?
   Which one is the largest supplier of our imports?

AUSTRALIA'S BALANCE OF PAYMENTS

The results of all of our overseas transactions are summarized in what is referred to as our **balance of payments**. The costs of freight, insurance and banking services, dividends and gifts paid to and by Australians, and payments made by tourists are included under the so-called **invisible** items. Payments to and by Australia also include substantial flows of funds associated with borrowing by Australian governments, investment overseas by Australian firms and overseas investment in Australia, as well as purchases of shares and other financial assets — such as the purchase of

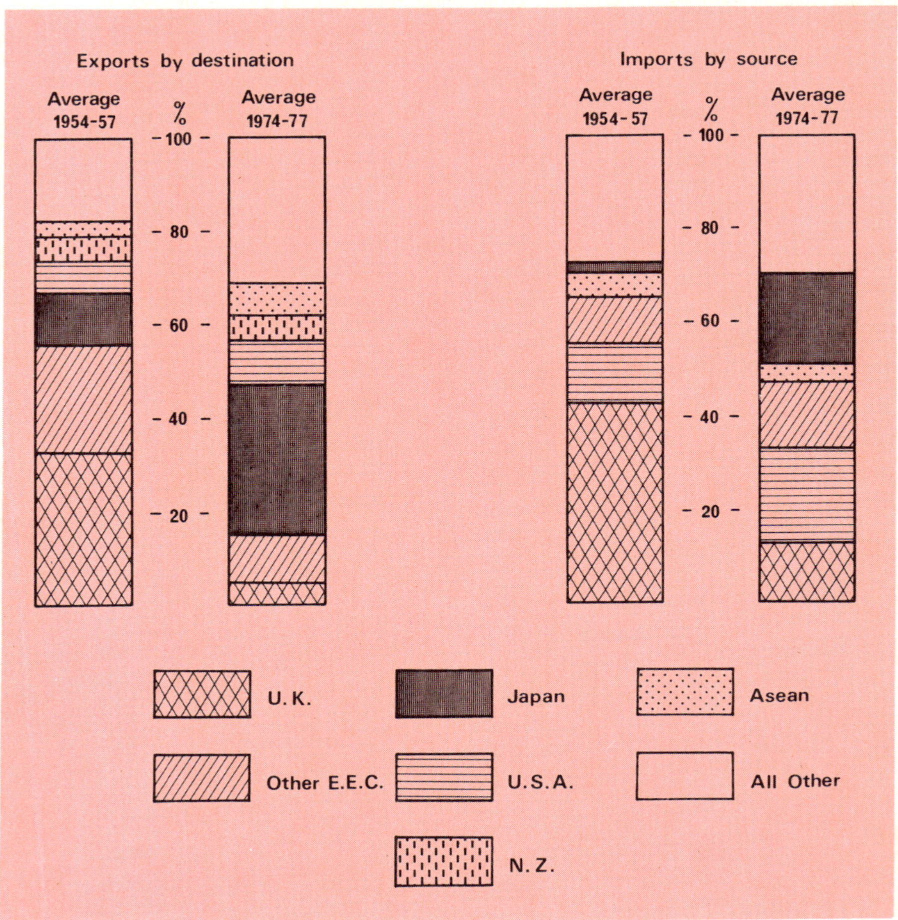

Fig. 12. Direction of overseas trade. (Source: Australian Bureau of Statistics, *Overseas Trade (Part 2): Comparative and Summary Tables*)

shares in BHP by British citizens. All items in this latter group are referred to as **capital account** transactions.

In order to assess our economic relations with the rest of the world, it is necessary to view these different classes of transactions collectively, rather than separately. Our balance of payments for 1977/78, as an example, is set out in table 13.

The **balance of trade** in any period — that is, exports minus imports — is either **favourable** (meaning that the value of exports exceeds the value

Table 13. Australia's Balance of Payments, 1977/78 ($ million)

	Exports	12,043	
−	Imports	−11,203	
=	Balance of Trade		839
+	Net invisibles	−3,249	
	Balance on current account		−2,410
Capital account:			
	Government	1,533	
	Other (private)	335	
+	Balance of capital account		1,868
=	Balance of payments		−542

Source: Budget Speech, 1978—79

of imports) or **unfavourable** (meaning that the value of imports exceeds the value of exports). In 1977/78 we had a favourable balance of trade of $839 million.

However, as table 13 shows, the balance of trade alone would have given a misleading impression of the balance of our external transactions. The item **"net invisibles"** represents payments to Australia for freight, insurance, tourist, and other services *less* our payments to other countries for similar *services*. In 1977/78 our payments overseas for such services far exceeded payments by the rest of the world to us; in fact, the balance of Australia's invisible items has *always* been negative. So, when payments for services are also taken into account, we sold fewer goods and services to other countries than we bought overseas over that period. In other words, our **balance on current account**, representing our sales of goods and services to the rest of the world less our purchases of goods and services from other countries, was strongly negative (-$2,410 million).

The balance of payments records all of Australia's international transactions, and it is composed of three parts:

1. The balance of trade which is concerned with imports and exports of goods.

2. Net invisibles which is concerned with imports and exports of services.

3. The capital account which deals with transactions that have effects beyond the current period. Included here are loans and their repayment and the purchase and sale of assets.

The **capital account** covers foreign exchange transactions not included in our current accounts. For example, the government periodically makes grants to assist the developing countries, borrows funds overseas, and makes payments of interest on those loans. Private capital transactions include foreign investment expenditures in Australia and foreign purchases of Australian financial assets, as well as similar expenditures overseas by Australians. **Net capital inflow** measures the difference between capital inflow to Australia and capital outflow to the rest of the world. Australia's deficit balance on current account has often been offset by net capital inflow — as it was in 1977/78.

It is useful to distinguish between government sector and private capital account transactions. The Commonwealth government borrows and repays substantial sums of money overseas. Following the Loan Council decision in the late 1970s to give the states power to borrow money from overseas for specific projects, it seems likely that government sector borrowing will grow.

Private capital inflow is the term used to describe transactions by firms and persons resident in other countries. These transactions involve the purchase of assets and are often called **foreign investment.** When an overseas firm establishes or expands a subsidiary in Australia, this is known as **direct** foreign investment. This is the most common source of private capital inflow for Australia. The subsidiary acquires assets in Australia, but it is financed by an inflow of funds from overseas. In return, the subsidiary is expected to remit profits to the owners living overseas.

Portfolio investment refers to the purchase of shares in *existing* Australian companies by overseas purchasers. The shareholding is not large enough for the foreign owners to control the company concerned. As a source of capital inflow, this is less significant than direct foreign investment.

The Commonwealth government, mainly through the Reserve Bank, carefully monitors and controls capital flows. This is necessary because of the importance of capital flows in the total balance of payments and also because of the direct effect on the Australian economy. For example, if the government decides to increase interest rates in line with general economic policy, it may be that foreign capital inflow will be attracted by these increased rates. This increase in the money supply may destroy the effectiveness of the particular policy objective. That is, private capital inflows during boom conditions and outflows when business prospects in Australia look bleak tend to have a destabilizing influence upon the Australian economy.

Foreign investment is a contentious issue. Foreign investment brings with it technical know-how and more rapid development of industry than would exist if Australia had to rely exclusively on domestic capital. However, the costs are in terms of the loss of control over Australia's resources as well as the ultimate interest and dividend payments that have to be made in the currency of the owners living overseas.

The Commonwealth government's objective of **external balance** refers to the overall result of our overseas economic transactions over any period. At any time, Australia holds foreign currencies, gold, and either credits or drawing rights with foreign and international banks. Collectively, these means of making payments to other countries are referred to as our **foreign exchange reserves**. The effect of our balance of payments deficit of $542 million in 1977/78 was to reduce our foreign reserves to that extent. Had there been a surplus in our balance of payments, this would have *added* to our foreign reserves.

Changes in international reserves reflect the overall surplus or deficit in our balance of payments.

By the end of 1977/78, our reserves amounted to $3,225 million. Had the deficit in that year followed periodic surpluses and deficits in the preceding years, there would have been no reason for concern. On the other hand, either a repeated balance of payments surplus or a repeated deficit, year after year, would result in progressive growth or reduction in our foreign exchange reserves. Neither situation could be regarded as being consistent with the objective of external balance. In fact, in either situation, the Commonwealth government would be expected to take action to correct such an imbalance.

Consider, for example, a situation in which Australia has a deficit in her balance of payments year after year, threatening to wipe out the means of settlement with other countries. What could the government do in such circumstances? Much would depend on whether aggregate demand for Australian-produced goods and services was less than or in excess of our capacity to produce. **The internal economic situation will determine the policies adopted towards external imbalance.**

In the shorter run, the government could borrow overseas and take steps to encourage private capital inflow in an attempt to prop up our dwindling reserves of foreign exchange — meanwhile hoping, perhaps, for increases in prices received for our exports, such as wheat and wool, or increases in quantities exported or both. In an endeavour to increase exports in the longer run, the government could perhaps offer export industries some form of incentive payments and loans at low rates of interest designed to encourage investment and increased production in those industries. However, there would be little point to such measures if there were not additional market outlets available overseas. Alternatively, the government may choose to concentrate on cutting back imports, either by extending import licensing to other products or by increasing the severity of its tariff quotas.

If measures such as these failed to halt the running down of our foreign exchange reserves, it may be necessary to change the rate at which the

Australian dollar is exchanged against other currencies — in this case, by **devaluation** of the Australian dollar.

In order to illustrate the effects of devaluation, let us assume that the Australian economy is initially operating at less than its capacity. That is, there are workers unemployed and machines idle or working at less than their designed capacity. In these circumstances, steps designed to increase demand for Australian-produced goods and services would generally be appropriate.

Immediately before devaluation, assume that one Australian dollar bought 250 Japanese yen. That is, the official rate of exchange was $A1 = Y250. The government then devalues the Australian dollar by 20 per cent. What this would mean is that one Australian dollar would then buy only 80 per cent as much of each foreign currency (including Japanese yen) as it did before devaluation. So one Australian dollar would then buy only 200 yen and anyone holding 250 yen could then buy $A1.25.

The effects of these new exchange rates would be that Japanese (and other overseas) importers could then buy 25 per cent more Australian currency for any specified amount of their own currency. Put another way, the cost of a unit of Australian exports (for example, a kilogram of wool or a tonne of iron ore) would be *less in terms of Japanese currency* than it was formerly. For example, a tonne of iron ore, sold in Australia at $20, formerly cost Japanese buyers 5,000 yen. After devaluation, if iron ore continued to be offered at $20 per tonne, the cost to Japanese buyers would be only 4,000 yen. In other words, **from the viewpoint of Japanese and other buyers overseas, the price of Australian goods, measured in terms of their own currencies, would have fallen as a result of devaluation of the Australian dollar.**

At these lower prices, relative to the exports of other countries, the Commonwealth government would be hoping that foreign buyers would increase their purchases of Australian goods and services. Increases in our sales would presumably result in an increase in production and employment in Australia. However, the quantities sold would, in this particular case, have to increase by more than 25 per cent if we were to increase our earnings of foreign exchange.

There is, however, another aspect of devaluation that also needs to be considered. After devaluation, one Australian dollar would buy only 200 yen, rather than 250 as formerly. Looked at in another way, a manufactured item selling in Japan for 2,500 yen per unit would formerly have cost Australian importers $10 plus freight, insurance, and customs duties payable at an Australian port. After devaluation, the cost to Australian importers would be $12.50 plus the charges associated with importing. So **devaluation would also serve to increase the cost per unit of imports in terms of Australian dollars**.

This would have two important effects. Since imported goods would then be more expensive relative to Australian-produced substitutes, there would be a switch away from imported goods towards goods produced in Australia. This would result in an increase in job opportunities in Australia and a reduction in employment in the countries formerly supplying those imports. Since we assumed excess capacity in the Australian economy before devaluation, this would clearly represent a bonus. On the other hand, there are some imports for which substitutes are difficult to find. Since the price of *all* imported goods would rise in terms of the Australian dollar, the costs of industries using imported goods would also rise. For example, the higher cost of imported crude oil would add to the transport costs of all Australian industries. Higher prices in Australia would lead workers to press for higher wages, adding further to the increase in costs faced by Australian industries. To some extent, the competitive edge given to exports by devaluation would then be reduced.

Devaluation of the Australian dollar would make Australian exports cheaper in terms of foreign currencies and could be expected to result in some increase in overseas demand for Australian products. It would make our imports more expensive, to some extent diverting demand in Australia away from imports and towards home-produced goods and services. At the same time, since some imports have few substitutes, this would serve to increase production costs and prices in Australia.

In the shorter run, devaluation appears to offer a solution to a persistent balance of payments deficit and domestic unemployment. In the longer run, however, the expected benefits may not be realized — not only because devaluation results in higher domestic costs, but also because foreign buyers may not respond by increasing their purchases of Australian goods and services to the extent expected.

Now briefly consider the reverse situation. Assume that Australia has had a balance of payments surplus year after year, so that our foreign exchange reserves have been growing. Assume also that aggregate demand for Australian-produced goods and services is in excess of our capacity to produce. In those circumstances, the government could consider a number of alternative measures, including a reduction in tariff protection given to Australian industries and removal of quantitative restrictions on imports. It may also consider **revaluation** of the Australian dollar relative to all other currencies.

If our currency was revalued by 20 per cent, this would mean that the Australian dollar would then buy 20 per cent more of each foreign currency. Our exports would then be more expensive in terms of foreign currencies, and because our prices would be raised relative to those of our competitors, the quantities exported could be expected to fall. On the other hand, Japanese and other foreign goods would then be cheaper in terms of the Australian dollar. Since the landed prices of imported goods would fall relative to the prices of Australian-produced goods, we could expect a switch from home-produced goods to imported substitutes. So revaluation of the Australian dollar could be expected to cause a decline in our export sales as well as a switch in the preferences of Australians towards imported goods. However, as a consequence of the reduction in import prices, the initial disadvantage suffered by exporters would be offset, to some extent, by lower production costs.

Revaluation would make our imports cheaper and our exports dearer. Demand would switch towards foreign goods. Revaluation is most appropriate when a country is experiencing large balance of payments surpluses as well as excess demand on its resources.

An economy's international operations and its internal activity are closely related. For example, increased exports may boost economic activity in Australia, while increases in imports may decrease the demand for Australian resources. This suggests that there are likely to be occasions when the government will need to manipulate external economic affairs in an attempt to influence internal economic activity. As well as fiscal policy and monetary policy, the two arms of government policy explained in chapter 8, **we can now identify a third arm of policy, external policy**. By manipulating such instruments as the exchange rate, tariffs, import quotas, and restrictions on foreign investment, the government can help steer the economy in the direction of its economic objectives of price stability, full employment, and external balance.

Questions

1. What are "invisible" items in our balance of payments? Why has the Australian balance of invisible items always been negative?
2. What is meant by a "favourable balance of trade"?
3. What is meant by the term *devaluation*?
   What effects would devaluation of the Australian dollar have on (*a*) exports; (*b*) imports?
4. Why is a persistent balance of payments surplus sometimes undesirable?
5. How could the government use trade policies to reduce the level of economic activity in Australia?
6. Assume the exchange rate was initially at $A1 = Y250. The Australian government revalues the dollar by 20 per cent. If a tonne of iron ore was offered both before and after revaluation at $20 per tonne, what would be the new price to Japanese importers in yen?

CONCLUSION

It is apparent that governments have at their disposal numerous ways and means by which to influence our balance of payments. For example, exports can be encouraged by incentive payments and other forms of direct assistance to export industries. Imports can be reduced by increasing the severity of our tariff quotas or increased by a reduction in tariff protection given to Australian industries. Governments can borrow overseas, encourage overseas firms to invest in Australian industries, or change the rate at which the Australian dollar is exchanged for other currencies.

What this suggests is that the government has adequate means by which to achieve and maintain external balance. However, some of the changes that occur in our balance of payments are hard to predict. For example, throughout 1971 the demand for Australian wool was very weak. At that time the United States was experiencing a deep recession and Japanese buyers faced restrictions on the use of foreign exchange. Manufacturers overseas were holding very small inventories of wool in anticipation that wool prices would fall still further. Wool prices fell to the lowest level in many years and sales prospects for 1972 looked very bleak. Late in 1971 the prices of the principal synthetic fibres in competition with wool increased by 5 to 7 per cent. From early in 1972 the American economy showed signs of recovery and the Japanese government lifted its restrictions on the use of foreign exchange.

In Europe, the new fashions gave emphasis to what was referred to as "the natural fibre look". Quite suddenly, in the space of a few months, both the quantities of wool sold and the prices received increased sharply as buyers from overseas scrambled for the available supplies.

In view of the many quite complex factors that have a bearing on our balance of payments, it is understandable that sharp changes in export earnings, imports, and capital inflows have occurred periodically over the last three decades. For these reasons, maintenance of external balance is not as simple as it would seem, and governments have generally been reluctant to undertake major changes, of the kind described earlier, until convinced that surpluses or deficits have reached intolerable magnitudes and are likely to persist.

10 The Australian National Accounts

So far, we have considered the various sectors and the role of money in the economy. A principal purpose of this book is to explain changes in the level of economic activity in Australia. In order to do this we must, in some way, *measure* the activity that takes place.

This chapter is concerned with accounting for the economic activity that takes place in each period. As such, the total level of production is recorded in what are generally referred to as the **National Accounts**. These accounts are a detailed and complex record of total production and expenditure in Australia. In this respect they tend to be like the books of account of a firm, that is, a record of *past* events. For the economy as a whole, these activities are recorded by the Bureau of Statistics in **the Australian National Accounts.**

THE VALUE OF AUSTRALIAN PRODUCTION

In general, we will assume that employment in Australia varies with total Australian production of goods and services. In some periods in the past, changes in total output have been associated with changes in the amount of overtime worked by the existing workforce, rather than with changes in the number of people employed. In the longer run, some increases in output are brought about by the use of new machines, improved technology, and better organization of the resources available. *In the short run* we can safely assume that a change in the level of production will be associated with some change in total employment. Provided we have the means of measuring total output in each period, we can then attempt to relate changes in production, from period to period, to changes in total employment.

It would be meaningless simply to add together the quantities of all goods and services produced in each period. Adding together tonnes of wheat, numbers of houses built, numbers of passengers carried by our Australian airlines and so on is not useful. So the answer lies in adding together the *market values* of all goods and services produced in each period, including goods produced and added to inventories.

Although this would seem to be a straightforward task, the value of production in any period is not simply the sum of *all* sales plus the change in the value of inventories. Most trading enterprises buy raw materials, components, and services from other firms and use up these **intermediate goods** in their own production processes. Bakers use intermediate goods, such as flour, in making bread. Flour millers use up wheat in making their flour. The prices that bakers charge for bread are intended to cover all purchases from other firms, as well as payments to their own employees engaged in baking, packing, and delivering the bread, and a margin for profits. Likewise, the prices that millers charge for flour include, among other things, the cost of wheat. **Since the prices at which goods and services are sold include the costs of intermediate goods bought from other firms and used up completely in production processes, the adding together of all sales by trading enterprises would involve "double counting"**; that is, the value of some goods, like wheat, would be counted more than once.

How can double counting be avoided? What we must do is to deduct from the sales of each firm the value of intermediate goods and services bought in from all other firms.

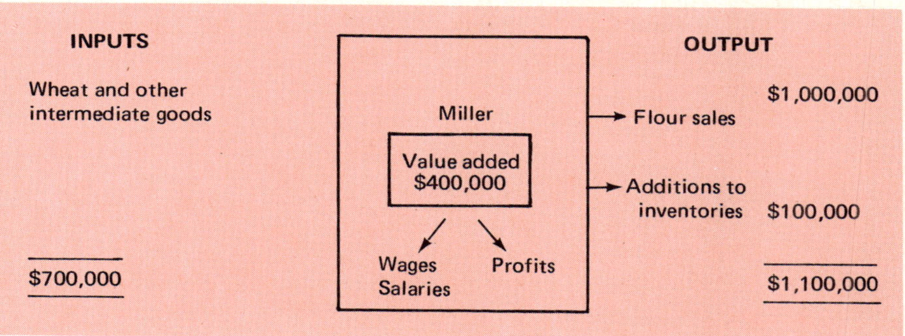

Fig. 13.   Value added by the flour miller

Consider the case of the flour miller in figure 13. Assuming for convenience that flour is the only commodity produced by a flour mill, the **value added** by the miller is then the total value of flour sales (say, $1 million) *plus* the value of flour added to the mill's inventories over the period considered (say, $100,000) *less* the value of wheat and other intermediate goods and services (such as sacks for the packaging of flour and electricity used in operating the mill) purchased from other firms over the same period (say, $700,000). The miller's value added (the $400,000) is equal to the wages and salaries paid to people employed in the mill *plus* gross profits. Put another way, the gross profits of the mill (in part set aside as depreciation allowances and undistributed profits, in part used in the payment of company taxes and dividends to shareholders) are equal to value added *less* wages and salaries paid to the employees of the mill.

For the trading enterprises sector as a whole, the value of production (or the sum of value added) over any period is given by:

	(1)	sales to persons (households),
plus	(2)	sales to other trading enterprises —
		(*a*) of fixed capital equipment,
		(*b*) of intermediate goods,
plus	(3)	sales to governments,
plus	(4)	additions to inventories,
less	(5)	purchases of intermediate goods from other firms.

Since sales of intermediate goods by all firms are necessarily equal to all purchases of intermediate goods, items (2) (*b*) and (5) are equal and therefore cancel out. Thus the value of production by the trading enterprises sector over any period is given by sales to persons *plus* sales of capital equipment *plus* sales to governments *plus* additions to inventories. In this way, sales and purchases of intermediate goods are eliminated and the problem of double counting is avoided.

The other production sector within the Australian economy consists of our Commonwealth, state, and local governments. Since government-operated trading enterprises are already included in the trading enterprises sector, production in the government sector is confined to the provision of various services, like defence and education. These services are not sold in the same way as goods and services supplied by the trading enterprises sector; that is, government services do not carry "price tags". So we have no direct means of assessing the market value of these services. On the other hand, we *do* know the cost of providing these services — which is the cost of all goods and services purchased *plus* the sum of wages and salaries paid to public servants.

Sales to governments by trading enterprises have already been taken into account as part of the value of production in the trading enterprises sector. Since we would be double counting if we were to include these purchases again as part of the value of government services, the value of production by the government sector is entered in our *National Accounts* as the sum of wages and salaries paid by our governments.

If we were to ignore our transactions with the rest of the world, the value of production in the Australian economy over any period would be given by sales to persons *plus* sales of capital equipment to trading enterprises *plus* sales to governments *plus* additions to inventories *plus* the sum of wages and salaries paid to public servants.

However, many of our trading enterprises sell part of their output to other countries: so the sum of sales to economic units within Australia would understate our total sales in any period. At the same time, we buy raw materials, components, and finished goods from the rest of the world. If no allowance were made for foreign goods sold in Australia, the value of Australian production would be overstated.

Sales to other countries represent part of the total demand for Australian-produced goods and services and must be added to the value of sales made by our trading enterprises to other economic units within Australia. Imported goods are either used up in the production of goods and services by Australian firms or are finished goods (like clothing and footwear) and sold directly in local markets. Either way, the value of imports must be deducted from the total sales of Australian firms to give a measure of the value of goods and services produced in Australia in any period. *That is, we must add the value of exports but deduct the value of imports.*

The total value of goods and services produced in Australia in any period is therefore given by:

> sales by trading enterprises to other economic units in Australia (excluding sales of intermediate goods),

plus   additions to inventories,

plus   wages and salaries paid to public servants,

plus   exports of goods and services,

less   imports of goods and services.

The sum of these items — that is, the total value of Australia's production in any period — is referred to as our **gross domestic product (GDP)**. But why *gross* product? The measure is gross because it refers to the total value of production before allowance is made for the depreciation of fixed capital equipment in the process of producing output in each period. So GDP includes the value of all buildings, plant, and equipment produced in each period, whether added to our stock of capital or used as replacements for buildings demolished or plant sold as scrap metal.

Gross domestic product is the total market value of goods and services produced in Australia within a given period, after deduction of the cost of goods and services used up in the process of production but before deducting allowances for the consumption (depreciation) of fixed capital.

Since it is the total demand for Australian-produced goods and services that generates production and employment in Australia, and changes in that demand that account for changes in production and employment, we will be concerned with gross domestic product rather than any alternative measure of production or income.

Questions

1. Why is it more useful to add together the market value of goods and services rather than to add physical quantities?

2. In a small forestry settlement, there are self-employed timber cutters, the sawmiller, and the timber buyer who purchases the total output of the settlement. The following transactions occurred in a period of one year in this settlement.
   Timber cutters produced 100 logs from wild bushland.
   The logs were all sold to the miller for $10,000.
   The miller sawed the logs into timber, which was both sold to the timber buyer for $30,000 and stockpiled as planks worth $5,000. The miller did not have any other purchases in this period, but employed two men who were paid $5,000 each.
   What is the value of output of this settlement for this year?
   What is the total value of incomes paid to people in this settlement?
   What is the value added by the sawmiller?

3. What measure do we use to determine the value added by the government sector?

4. Wheat and flour are intermediate goods in the production of flour and bread respectively. Give examples of intermediate goods used in the car industry, in farming, and in the transport industry.

5. We can refer to changes in inventories of goods, but not inventories of services. Why?

6. Why must the value of imports be deducted from total sales when calculating the value of goods and services produced in Australia in any period?

THE EQUALITY OF PRODUCTION, INCOME, AND EXPENDITURE

Apart from the valuation of government services at cost and additions to the inventories of trading enterprises, the measurement of GDP is based entirely on sales made within and between the various sectors. Sales made by one economic unit are necessarily the purchases of other economic units. Provided we assume that all services produced by governments over any period are "purchased" by the Australian public and additions to inventories are "purchased" by each of the firms concerned, **the value of total production will be equal to the sum of the expenditures of all sectors of the economy over the same period**.

This becomes evident if we consider again the component parts of GDP. For example, the sales of trading enterprises to persons, viewed from the opposite direction, are the consumption expenditures of households (C). Sales of capital equipment plus additions to inventories together represent the investment expenditures of trading enterprises (I). Sales by trading enterprises to governments *plus* wages and salaries paid to public servants together equal government sector expenditure (G). Our export of goods and services to other countries (X) are added, and our imports from the rest of the world (M) are deducted. Now we have accounted for the expenditures of all sectors of the economy.

The sum of all expenditures — that is, $C + I + G + X - M$ — is equal in value to our gross domestic product. In the financial year 1977/78, GDP and expenditure on gross domestic product were estimated at $90,220 million and included the items and amounts shown in table 14.

Table 14. The Composition of Production and Expenditure, 1977/78

Production Items	Expenditure Items	Symbols Designating Expenditures	Value in 1977/78 ($m)
Sales to persons	Consumption	C	53,628
Sales of capital equipment *plus* additions to inventories	Investment	I	16,984
Sales to governments *plus* wages and salaries paid to public servants	Government sector expenditure	G	18,785
Exports of goods and services	Exports	X	13,900
Statistical discrepancy	—	—	1,276
			104,573
Imports of goods and services	Imports	M	−14,353
	GDP = $C + I + G + X - M$		= 90,220

Source: Australian Bureau of Statistics, *National Income and Expenditure, 1977–78*

Since we assumed that additions to inventories are purchased by the producers themselves and that government services are purchased at cost by the Australian public, it follows that production is necessarily equal in value to expenditure. However, some items of production and expenditure — for example, the values of goods added to inventories — are simply estimates that cannot be checked by reference to sales. These estimates are subject to error. Hence the need for a balancing item (referred to in table 14 as a "statistical discrepancy") in order that the total value of GDP may be equal to the sum of expenditures over that period.

GDP in any financial year is also equal to total income received over the same period. For example, the value added by each trading enterprise is equal to its total sales *plus* additions to its inventories *less* all purchases of intermediate goods from other firms. That is, value added is what remains after meeting all day-to-day production costs other than wages and salaries paid to the firm's own employees. Looked at in another way, value added by each firm is equal to wages and salaries paid *plus* the firm's gross profits. These gross profits are distributed in various forms — in payments of interest on debts, in taxes paid to governments (including indirect taxes if included in the prices charged for a firm's products) and dividends paid to shareholders, as well as depreciation allowances and undistributed profits set aside on behalf of the owners of the firm. The value added by governments is distributed to public servants in the form of wages and salaries. Exports are part of the sales of trading enterprises and are therefore included in the value added of Australian firms. In contrast, imports must be deducted from sales made in Australia because the sale of these goods and services serves to produce income in other countries.

GDP can be estimated by measuring total value of production, total income, or total expenditure. That is, production (GDP) = expenditure = income.

Questions

1. There are three ways of estimating gross domestic product. What are these ways? Which ways are used to calculate Australian GDP?

2. Income tax statistics are used to calculate total income and hence gross domestic product. Suggest why this may understate the level of total income and hence GDP.

3. Explain why income, production, and expenditure are equal.

4. By using table 14, calculate approximate percentages that each expenditure component comprises of GDP.

THE LIMITATIONS AND USES OF GROSS DOMESTIC PRODUCT

Gross domestic product is not a precise measure. In part, it is based on actual sales values. However, some components of GDP are not valued in the market. Government services are not sold in formal markets and do not carry price tags. The convention used in our *National Accounts* is that production in the government sector is valued as the cost of wages and salaries paid to public servants.

On the other hand, there are some goods and services produced which are *not* taken into account in GDP. For example, fruit and vegetables produced by home gardeners in urban areas are not considered; nor are the housekeeping services of housewives. Yet such goods and services *do* have a value — as we know when it is necessary to buy fruit and vegetables or hire domestic help.

Nor does GDP distinguish between the production of goods and the production of what American economists refer to as "bads". For example, if a tanker loaded with crude oil were to break up outside Sydney Harbour or Port Phillip Bay, the cost of ships, materials, and people used in cleaning up the mess would *add* to the value of GDP in that financial year. So it would be questionable to argue that each and every source of increase in our GDP necessarily means an increase in the welfare of the Australian people.

In any particular financial year, the value of Australia's GDP tells us the estimated value of all Australian-produced goods and services taken into consideration for the purposes of our *National Accounts*. It tells us nothing concerning the *distribution* of income between individuals or households. Nor does it suggest anything concerning the quality of our diets, the quality of housing, infant mortality, the level of literacy, and so on. We must therefore resist the temptation to rely solely on GDP or GDP per head of population as a measure of the welfare of Australians in general, particularly in relation to similar measures calculated for other countries.

In fact, our estimates of GDP were never intended to be used for such purposes. The principal purpose of these estimates is to allow comparison of the level of economic activity in one period with the levels of activity in other periods. Admittedly, some items in our GDP cannot be measured precisely and some economic activities are not taken into account. However, since the items included and the methods of estimation are the same, period after period, the consistency in methods of estimation make our estimates of GDP in one financial year comparable with estimates of GDP in other periods. As an indicator of changes in the level of economic activity from period to period, GDP is the most comprehensive measure available and serves its intended purpose quite well.

GDP is a comprehensive measure of economic activity, but it has limitations:
1. Some items are estimated, rather than measured.
2. Some output is not marketed and is not included.
3. Preparation of the national accounts is a complex and time-consuming task. So there is a considerable time lag before these figures are made available.

Both the government and firms require **economic indicators** which will give them a ready appreciation of how the economy is performing and likely to fare in the near future. Many decision-makers prefer to base their judgements upon information on the *present* (and possible future) state of the economy rather than an accurate but lagged account of the economy in the *past.* In return for the speed in measurement, those who use these indicators must be prepared to accept a degree of imprecision and therefore the risk of inaccurate predictions concerning future events. Be that as it may, there are some economic activities that *can* be readily measured and have proved a useful guide to the level of activity. For example, movements in the level of approvals for house construction and the amount of overtime worked in manufacturing industries have been found to be very sensitive to changes in the state of the economy and therefore quick and fairly reliable indicators of changes in economic activity.

Questions

1. Why is GDP not a precise measure?

2. Why is GDP per head not a very helpful measure of standard of living and welfare?

3. Why do businessmen and governments find it necessary to make predictions about future levels of economic activity? How useful are GDP measures in making their predictions?

THE MEASUREMENT OF CHANGES IN GROSS DOMESTIC PRODUCT

The principal purpose behind estimates of GDP is to allow comparison of production in one period with production in another. If all prices remained constant (that is, never rising or falling) period after period, an increase in GDP in one period over the last would indicate an overall increase in the quantities of goods and services produced. Given that we assume no changes in technology, labour skills, or the quality of management in the short run, employment will vary with the level of production. So an overall increase in the quantities of goods and services produced would be associated with an increase in employment.

Assume, for example, that we produce only four commodities: *A, B, C,* and *D;* further, that the prices of these commodities were precisely the same in period 2 as they were in period 1. For simplicity, assuming no purchases of intermediate goods between individual firms, changes in the value of production may have been as in table 15.

Although there was no change in the production of *A* and a fall in production of *C,* there were increases in the output of both *B* and *D.* In aggregate, the value of production increased from $50,000 to $55,000.

Table 15. Changes in Quantities Produced with Constant Prices

| Commodity | Price per Unit ($) | Period 1 | | Period 2 | |
		Quantity Produced (Units)	Value of Production ($)	Quantity Produced (Units)	Value of Production ($)
A	2.00	4,000	8,000	4,000	8,000
B	5.00	1,400	7,000	2,000	10,000
C	10.00	1,500	15,000	1,300	13,000
D	20.00	1,000	20,000	1,200	24,000
Total Value			50,000		55,000

Since all prices were the same in period 2 as in period 1, we could conclude that total production was higher by 10 per cent in the second period. Furthermore, we could assume that this increase in production would have been associated with an increase in employment — either an increase in the average number of hours worked per week by those who were already employed in period 1, or an increase in the numbers of people employed, or both.

Employment can be expected to vary with the quantities produced, but not with the money value of production. If, in one period, all prices were 10 per cent higher but output was precisely the same as in the immediately preceding period, then the aggregate values of production, income, and expenditure would all be 10 per cent higher. But we would not expect any change in the level of employment between these two periods.

However, it would be quite remarkable if all prices were to remain unchanged period after period, or were to change by precisely the same percentages. Changes in products available, tastes, and incomes result in changes in demand for individual products. Changes in the prices of raw materials, labour, machines, and other factors of production result in changes in production costs. So it is more likely that there would have been changes in prices as well as changes in quantities between periods 1 and 2.

In table 16 the prices and quantities assumed for period 1 are the same as in table 15. However, in period 2 both the prices and the quantities have been changed. For example, the prices of *A* and *D* are higher, but the prices of *B* and *C* are lower. Yet the total value of production in period 2 is again $55,000.

What can we conclude with regard to the *total* change in quantities of goods produced? Is the overall effect the same as indicated in table 15? It is apparent that the quantities produced of *A* and *D* have fallen, while the quantities of *B* and *C* have increased. But how can we add together these

Table 16. Changes in Quantities Produced and Changes in Prices

		Period 1			Period 2	
Commodity	Price per Unit ($)	Quantity Produced (Units)	Value of Production ($)	Price per Unit ($)	Quantity Produced (Units)	Value of Production ($)
A	2.00	4,000	8,000	3.00	3,000	9,000
B	5.00	1,400	7,000	4.00	2,500	10,000
C	10.00	1,500	15,000	8.00	2,000	16,000
D	20.00	1,000	20,000	25.00	800	20,000
Total value			50,000			55,000

changes to obtain some measure of the *total* change in production? Is it likely that these changes, taken together, would have resulted in some alteration in the level of employment?

A change in employment can be expected only if there is a change in the total quantities of goods and services produced. Where production is valued at **current market prices**, that is, at the actual prices received for each of the goods and services in each period, changes in the total value of production from period to period *reflect changes in prices as well as changes in quantities.* The level of employment can be expected to change only if there is a change in **"real" production**, that is, a change in the **actual quantities of goods and services produced**, rather than a change in the *money* value of production. These real changes can be established only by eliminating the changes in prices that have occurred between the two periods being considered.

Consider, again, the prices and quantities set out in table 16. This time, instead of the actual prices at which these goods were sold in period 2, we will substitute in period 2, the prices received in period 1. That is, goods

Table 17. Changes in Quantities Produced, Valued at Constant (Period 1) Prices

		Period 1		Period 2	
Commodity	Price per Unit ($)	Quantity Produced (Units)	Value of Production ($)	Quantity Produced (Units)	Value of Production ($)
A	2.00	4,000	8,000	3,000	6,000
B	5.00	1,400	7,000	2,500	12,500
C	10.00	1,500	15,000	2,000	20,000
D	20.00	1,000	20,000	800	16,000
Total value			50,000		54,500

produced in both periods are valued at the same prices and the quantities actually produced in period 2 are *valued at constant (period 1) prices.*

Having applied the prices of period 1 to actual output in each period, we have now eliminated the change in the value of production that was due to changes in prices. With production in period 2 now valued at constant (period 1) prices, we are now in a position to assess the aggregate change in quantities produced. Despite the decline in output of both *A* and *D*, real production in period 2 was 9 per cent higher than in period 1. Presumably, that increase in production would have required a marked increase in total employment.

As an alternative, we could have applied period 2 prices to actual quantities produced in period 1 — that is, output in both periods could have been valued at constant (period 2) prices. That would likewise have served to eliminate changes in prices between the two periods.

Changes in the value of production may be due to changes in prices, changes in actual production, or a combination of both. To identify changes in actual production, there is a need to adjust the figures to eliminate the effect of price changes.

Questions

A simple economy produces only three goods, *A*, *B*, and *C*. The following table shows the output and prices of these goods in three consecutive periods, I, II, and III.

Commodity	I Price	I Quantity	II Price	II Quantity	III Price	III Quantity
A	$1.00	250	$1.00	300	$1.20	300
B	$2.00	400	$2.00	300	$2.50	300
C	$10.00	50	$10.00	100	$9.00	100

1. What is the total value of production in each of the periods I, II, and III?

2. Why did the value of production increase between period I and period II?

3. Why did the value of production increase between period II and III?

4. In terms of period I prices, did the value of production in period III increase compared with period I value of production? What about period III compared with period II when measured in period I prices?

5. Explain the difference between GDP measured in *constant* prices and GDP measured in *current* prices. Which one of these measures is more useful and why?

THE CONSUMER PRICE INDEX: LIMITATIONS AND USES

In order to calculate changes from period to period in our real GDP — using a method such as that used in table 17 — it would be necessary to know the prices of each of the thousands of different goods and services produced in each period. Such information is not available. Even if it were, it would be a long and tedious job to apply the prices of each of the goods and services in one period to the quantities produced in another.

Our task is greatly simplified if we can use some widely accepted **index of prices** — that is, a series of numbers that summarize the prices of goods and services in general in each period compared with the prices of the same goods and services in some specified **base period**. This base period is conventionally given a value of 100 and may be either a single financial year (for example, 1966/67) or an average of, say, three years (for example, 1964-67).

If 1966/67 is chosen as the base year and, despite a decline in the prices of *some* goods, prices *in general* (or on average), were 3 per cent higher in the following year, then the price index for 1967/68 would be 103. If, in the following year, prices in general were 2 per cent *less* than in the base period, the index number for 1968/69 would be 98. That is, the change is calculated in relation to the base year, 1966/67, and not in relation to the immediately preceding year. In this particular case, we would be using constant 1966/67 prices.

One important feature of such an index is the **weight** given to each of the individual goods and services. If *all* prices were to increase by 3 per cent between one period and the next, there would be no problem. But prices tend to change at different rates and sometimes in different directions. It could be, for example, that the prices of milk and bread increased by 3 per cent over a particular period, while the prices of motor vehicles and houses increased by 2 per cent. Should we simply average these changes in prices or, because motor vehicle and housing expenses generally account for much larger proportions of household expenditure, somehow weight the changes in prices of each commodity and service according to some notion of its importance? Most price indexes are weighted according to either the quantities sold or the proportions of total expenditure on each of the items included. If, for example, housing was given ten times the weight of bread in an overall index of prices, a 2 per cent increase in the cost of housing would then have a much greater effect on that index than a 3 per cent increase in the cost of bread.

The Australian Bureau of Statistics has available several price indexes, each covering a particular group of goods and services. For example, the bureau produces separate indexes of export prices and import prices, as well as an index of wholesale prices. However, the most widely used index of prices in Australia is the **Consumer Price Index** (or CPI) — intended primarily as a guide to changes in the living costs of Australian households, but also widely regarded as a guide to changes in the level of prices in general.

The CPI does *not* cover *all* goods and services produced or sold in Australia. It covers what is considered to be a representative "basket" of goods and services — the selection of the individual items and the weights given to each being based on periodic surveys of Australian households. This index covers eight major groups of goods and services — food, clothing, housing, household equipment and operation, transportation, tobacco and alcohol, health and personal care, and recreation. Within each of these major groups are sub-groups. For example, food is subdivided under dairy produce; cereal products; meat and seafoods; fruit and vegetables; soft drinks; ice cream, and confectionery; meals out, take-away food, and other food. These sub-groups are further subdivided into "expenditure classes", so that there are thirty-four classes of foodstuffs, fourteen classes of clothing, and many other goods and services covered by this index.

It is quite possible that the prices of some goods and services *not* included in the CPI do not change in ways suggested by recorded changes in the index. In some periods, these prices may change to a greater extent; in others, to a lesser extent. But one important reason why the bureau makes no attempt to record the prices of *all* goods and services is that concentration of its resources on a representative selection allows the change in the CPI from month to month to be calculated within a few days of the end of each month. **The CPI is an important economic indicator.** If we are to expect the government to counter undesirable trends in the economy almost as quickly as they emerge, it is important that such indicators be available at frequent intervals and with the least possible delay.

A price index indicates the extent of price changes. It is constructed by selecting a sample "basket" of goods to be priced, weighting each item to reflect its relative importance, and measuring the change in value of this weighted basket. These changes are represented as index numbers by giving a selected base period a value of 100 and relating the value of the weighted basket to that in the base period. The Consumer Price Index is the most widely used price index in Australia.

For how long is the bureau's basket of goods and services likely to remain representative of the expenditures of Australian households? It is apparent — for example, from table 6 — that people *do* change their consumption habits from time to time. The bureau also changes the composition and weighting of the items included in the CPI, although only at very infrequent intervals. For example, for a number of years up to June 1976 the total weight given to expenditures on foodstuffs was 28.3 per cent of total expenditure. From September 1976 the weight given to foodstuffs was reduced to 21.0 per cent. Such changes in consumption habits do not occur overnight, or even in the space of a few years. This suggests that the composition and weighting of the index should be revised more frequently. On the other hand, frequent revisions in the composition and weighting of the CPI would then cast doubt on the accuracy of changes in prices based on different sets of goods.

Admittedly, there are also problems involved in comparing prices from one year to the next. For example, the *quality* of individual fruits, vegetables, and meats may be higher or lower in one period than in the last, owing to poorer or better seasonal conditions experienced by the producers. Quality changes are also evident in some consumer durables. Motor vehicles, for example, change in styling, motors, lighting, and other ways from year to year. "Optional extras" in one period tend to be included as standard equipment in a later period. This is not intended to suggest that the later models are necessarily better products, but simply that changes in prices have been accompanied by changes in the *nature* of the products. **So changes in prices may also reflect changes in quality.**

In contrast, some changes in prices are due to changes in the *rates of indirect tax* imposed by the Commonwealth government. Since motor vehicles, petrol, tobacco, and other products subject to sales tax or excise duties are included in the CPI, increases or decreases in such taxes are reflected in the overall changes in the index.

Some of the limitations of the Consumer Price Index are:
1. The composition of the weighted basket needs periodic revision to reflect changes in consumer spending patterns.
2. Changes in prices may reflect changes in quality.
3. The CPI covers only a sample of all goods and services available.

Although the Bureau of Statistics uses specially designed "deflators" to separate changes in prices and changes in the quantities of goods and services produced, we can use the CPI to illustrate the principles involved. For example, GDP *at current market prices* was estimated at $22,571 million in 1966/67 and at $24,068 million in 1967/68. Measured in the prices current in each of those periods, GDP increased by 6.6 per cent from 1966/67 to 1967/68. Over the same period, there was an increase in the general level of prices. The Consumer Price Index (base 1952/53 = 100) rose from an average of 138.8 in 1966/67 to an average of 143.4 in 1967/68, indicating an increase in prices of 3.3 per cent.

In order to separate the change in prices from the change in quantities produced — that is, to calculate the change in real GDP — it is first necessary to revalue GDP in each of these years in terms of prices in the base period. Since the general level of prices in 1966/67 was higher than in the base period, we must multiply GDP estimated in 1966/67 prices by the ratio of the price index in the base period to the price index in 1966/67; that is, GDP measured in the prices of 1952/53 was equal to:

$$\$22,571\text{m} \times \frac{100}{138.8} = \$16,261.5\text{m}$$

Likewise, GDP in 1967/68, valued at 1952/53 prices, was equal to:

$$\$24,068\text{m} \times \frac{100}{143.4} = \$16,783.8\text{m}$$

In each case, we have **deflated** GDP at current market prices to allow for the increase in the general level of prices after 1952/53. Had prices *decreased* over that period, it would have been necessary to **inflate** the estimates of GDP at current market prices, again by multiplying the estimated values of GDP in each of those years by the ratio of the price index in the base period to the price index in each of the years under consideration. Either way, the result of this process is that we have measured GDP in constant (1952/53) prices.

The measurement of GDP in constant (1952/53) prices shows an increase from $16,261.5 million in 1966/67 to $16,783.8 million in 1967/68. This indicates an increase in real GDP of only 3.2 per cent compared with the increase of 6.6 per cent suggested by our initial comparison of GDP at current market prices. In contrast, data published by the Australian Bureau of Statistics — using constant 1968/69 prices and modified by checks on actual changes in output that occurred in some industries — suggest that real GDP increased by 4.6 per cent over that period.

Over the period from June 1967 to June 1968, the numbers of civilian employees in Australia increased from 3.775 million to 3.903 million, representing an increase of 3.4 per cent in the numbers employed. Although evidence based on observations in only two successive years is in no way conclusive, this does suggest some kind of relation between changes in the quantities of goods and services produced and changes in employment. In this case, the change in the real GDP of something in the range of 3.2 to 4.6 per cent was associated with an increase in persons employed of 3.4 per cent.

Changes in GDP at current market prices include changes in prices as well as changes in quantities. In order to isolate changes in quantities produced (and to relate changes in real GDP to changes in the level of employment) there is first a need to eliminate the effects of changes in the general level of prices.

Questions

1. Why is it important to "weight" items when constructing a price index?

2. Give some reasons why household consumption patterns change in the course of time.

3. How is an index such as the CPI constructed?

4. Explain some of the difficulties experienced in using the CPI as a measure of the cost of living?

5. Complete this table:

	GDP Current Prices	GDP Constant Year 1 Prices	Price Index
Year 1	1,000	?	100
Year 2	?	1,250	150
Year 3	1,500	1,000	?

11 | Models of the Australian Economy

The purpose of this chapter is to explain what determines the level of economic activity, and hence the level of employment, in the Australian economy. In addition, the effect of changes in planned spending on production and employment will be considered.

A year-by-year study of the *National Accounts* reveals changes in GDP and changes in the individual income and expenditure components. Although these year-to-year changes can be measured, either at current market prices or in constant prices, this contributes little to our understanding of the way in which the economy operates. For example, what could we say about the likely effects on production and employment of a decision by households in general to save less and consume more? What would be the effects of an increase in the investment expenditures of trading enterprises? Would the effects be the same, regardless of whether the economy was already operating at full capacity or at less than full capacity?

To answer questions such as these, we must first understand the relationships between the various parts of the economy. However, the real world is extremely complex and there are *thousands* of variables that have a bearing on production and employment in Australia in any period. For example, the production of fertilizers, fencing materials, and other farm inputs in any period depends *in part* on the immediate past prices received by our woolgrowers, which depend in part on purchases of wool by Japanese textile manufacturers, which are heavily influenced by current and expected future sales of these textiles in North America and Western Europe.

In view of the complex nature of the real world, economists rely heavily on **models** of the economy as a means of isolating and better understanding some of the more important causal relationships.

What is an economic model? It is an attempt to represent the real world in a simplified form, eliminating all variables other than those considered to be immediately relevant to the questions we seek to answer. Having selected what we regard as the essential components and necessary linkages, we can then proceed to manipulate this theoretical structure in an attempt to understand how it works.

Such a model cannot be expected to provide us with precise answers to many of the urgent problems of our times. On the other hand, a model that serves to reproduce features that closely approximate to economic behaviour in the real world can add greatly to our understanding.

We have already made use of one particularly simple model — namely, the production possibilities curve used in chapter 1. For that purpose, we assumed that only two commodities were produced — even though each economy produces many different goods and services. Nevertheless, that model was useful in that it showed, for example, that any economy operating at full capacity cannot, in the short run, increase production of one commodity without a reduction in production of the other.

Economic models are established to aid the understanding of economic relationships. It is often difficult to examine the relationships clearly in the complexity of the real world.

Some economic models, like the production possibilities curve, are geometric in form; others are expressed mathematically. With the aid of sophisticated computers, mathematical models have grown in popularity. In Norway, for example, one mathematical model designed to predict changes in that economy includes more than two thousand variables.

Our models will be much less complex. The variables we will be concerned with are those that we have already considered — in particular, the components of expenditure on *gross domestic product.* We will begin with a simple two-sector model of the economy, consisting of the household and trading enterprises sectors. Later, we will add in the government and overseas sectors as we seek to approximate more closely to the real world.

SOME GENERAL ASSUMPTIONS

In each of the models considered in this chapter, we will be concerned only with changes *in the short run* — that is, over a period so short that we will assume population, the size of the workforce, labour skills, technology, the quality of management, and the stock of fixed capital equipment to remain unchanged. This is not an unrealistic assumption, since a significant change in any one of these variables takes time.

Within each short-run period we will assume that producers are able to vary their levels of production. For this to be possible it is necessary to assume that the economy is operating at something less than full capacity. As a consequence, **the level of production can be varied** simply by combining different quantities of labour, raw materials, and components with the existing stock of fixed capital equipment. If the economy is already operating at full capacity, there is no way in which output can be increased in the short run.

Further, we assume that businessmen have already made their investment plans by the beginning of each short period. That is, they have already decided what fixed capital equipment they will buy and the changes they intend to make in their inventories. We will assume that these investment plans remain unchanged throughout the following period.

We will assume throughout that **output is measured in constant prices**, so that changes in GDP represent real changes in the quantities of goods and services produced; further, that changes in output are assumed to be related to changes in the level of employment.

General assumptions:
1. Some variables remain constant in the short-run.
2. There is more than one production period in the short run.
3. The economy is operating at less than full capacity.
4. Output is measured in constant prices.
5. Changes in output are related to changes in employment.

Questions

1. Why is it important to make the assumption that the economy is operating at less than full capacity?
2. What is an economic model? What value is there in using models to explain economic relationships?
3. Explain the link between changes in output and changes in employment.
4. What is meant by the "short run"?

A TWO-SECTOR MODEL

A two-sector model of the economy consists of *households* **and** *trading enterprises.* There is no government sector; so no taxes are imposed and there is no government sector expenditure. There are no transactions with the rest of the world. This simple model clearly falls far short of reality; nevertheless, it serves as a useful starting point.

The Equality of Production, Expenditure, and Income

In this two-sector economy the value of production is equal to the value of expenditure. All goods and services produced in any period but not consumed represent the gross investment expenditure of trading enterprises in that period — either in fixed capital equipment or additions to inventories. *Any goods produced but not sold are assumed to be added to inventories, whether or not the firms concerned had intended to build up their inventories.* Since inventories are assumed to be purchased by the firms accumulating unsold goods, the value of production in this two-sector economy would necessarily equal the sum of consumption and investment expenditures.

The value of production is also equal to the incomes paid in return for resources used in the production process. *In this two-sector model we make the simplifying assumption that all income is distributed to households.* Hence, total value of production is equal to total income. This simplification differs from the real world, where firms hold undistributed profits and depreciation allowances, but it allows us to concentrate on the essentials of the two-sector model.

Since the scale on each axis is the same, this equality of production and expenditure is represented by points along the 45-degree line shown in figure 14.

In period 1, total production (= total income) is indicated by $0Y_1$. Since total expenditure is equal to total income, it can also be represented by $0E_1$, where $0Y_1 = 0E_1$. In period 2, output is indicated by $0Y_2$ and expenditure by $0E_2$ (where $0Y_2 = 0E_2$). Since $0Y_1 = 0E_1 = Y_1a$ and $0Y_2 = 0E_2 = Y_2b$, the points a and b lie on a line drawn at 45 degrees to each axis from the origin at 0.

For the purposes of our *National Accounts*, which provide us with a backward-looking view at the end of each financial year, changes in inventories represent part of total expenditure in any period — **whether or not such changes in inventories were intended**. So, *by definition*, production is equal to expenditure. In this sense, production and expenditure in any period are equal and can be represented by a point on this 45-degree line.

The 45-degree line joins all points where total expenditure equals total production (which equals total income).

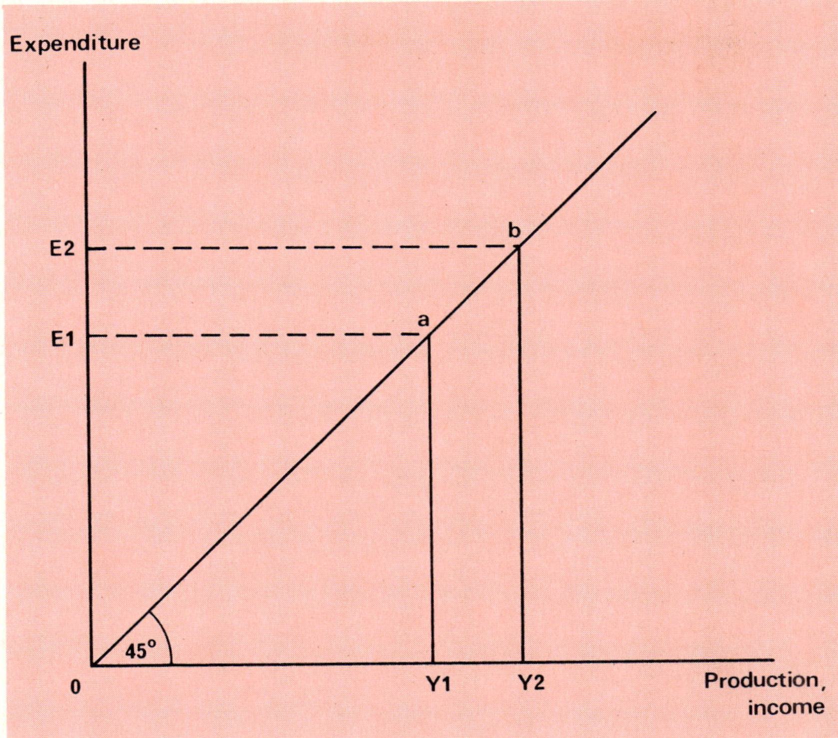

Fig. 14.   Equality of production, income and expenditure

Household Consumption Expenditure

A number of factors influence household consumption expenditure, but the most important is household disposable income. Considering all households in aggregate, a certain level of total consumption expenditure is associated with a given level of total household disposable income. In the two-sector model, with all income distributed to households, total income is equal to total household disposable income. The relationship between total consumption expenditure and the level of total income is known as the **aggregate consumption function**. Total household consumption is an aggregation of all household consumption expenditure in a particular period.

Figure 15 shows an aggregate consumption function, labelled *C.* From figure 15 it can be seen that a given increase in total income will lead to a smaller increase in consumption expenditure. A similar relationship, known as the *marginal propensity to consume*, was discussed in chapter 5;

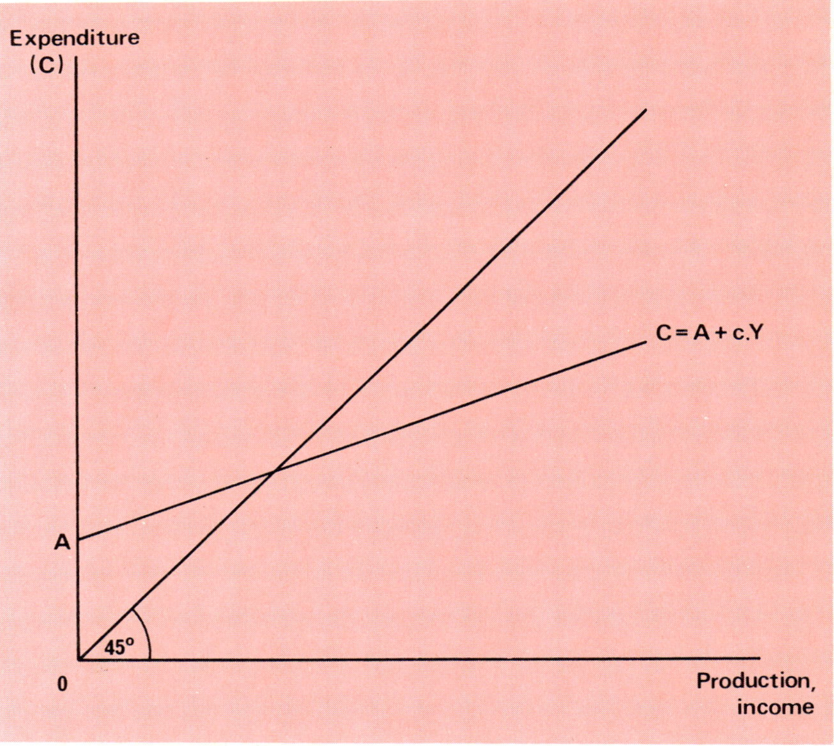

Fig. 15. The consumption function

but that referred to households. In this case, the marginal propensity to consume refers to the change in total consumption expenditure caused by a change in total income. The slope of the consumption function is the m.p.c. The consumption function is drawn as a straight line. This shows that the marginal propensity to consume is assumed to be the same at all levels of total income.

Also, it will be noticed that at zero level of total income, some consumption expenditure has been assumed. This expenditure is said to be independent of the level of total income. Hence the relationship between total household consumption expenditure and total income consists of a constant amount, plus a fraction of total income. This may be expressed as

$$C = A + cY$$

where C = total consumption expenditure

A = a constant amount, independent of the level of income
c = m.p.c.
Y = household disposable income (= total income in the two-sector model).

Hence *planned* values of consumption spending are largely determined by the level of total income in the period being considered. At the same time, this level of planned consumption expenditure is always satisfied, because firms are willing to draw upon their inventories if sales exceed current production.

Total consumption expenditure depends upon the level of total household disposable income. This relationship is expressed in the consumption function which takes the form $C = A + cY$.

Investment Expenditure by Trading Enterprises

The investment expenditure of trading enterprises represents another expenditure component in our two-sector model. *It is important, for the purposes of the model, to distinguish between investment in fixed capital equipment and investment in inventories.*

We will assume that, at the beginning of each short run period, trading enterprises plan to buy fixed capital equipment of various kinds as well as to make changes in their inventories. **We will also assume that all items of fixed capital equipment, such as buildings and machines, are made to order and that all orders placed at the beginning of any short period are filled during that period.**

On the other hand, since individual firms set production at levels intended to meet expected sales *plus* their intended changes in inventories, their *planned changes in inventories will be realized only if they have correctly forecast demand for their products.* If trading enterprises, in aggregate, sell less in any period than they expected at the beginning of that period, they will experience an unplanned increase in inventories. In that event, total investment actually realized will be greater than the level of investment expenditure planned for that period. In contrast, if sales prove to be greater than expected, it will be necessary for firms to run down their inventories in order to meet demand. In that case, both inventory and total investment expenditure will be less than was intended.

Since it is assumed that all plans regarding the purchase of fixed capital equipment are realized, any difference between total investment planned at the beginning of any short period and investment expenditures actually realized over that period will be due to unintended changes in inventories.

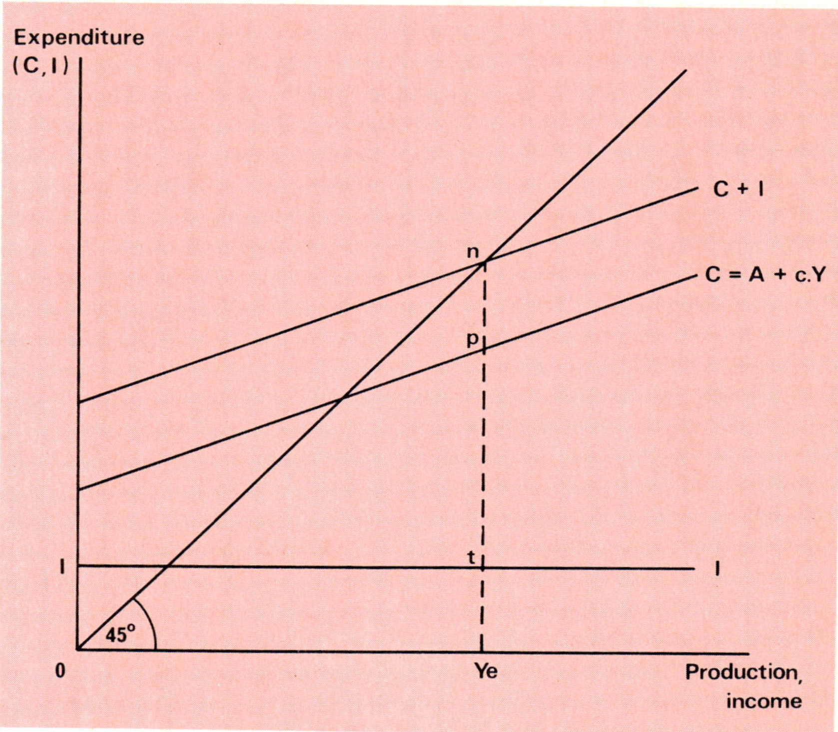

Fig. 16.   Equilibrium output in the two-sector model

The Equilibrium Level of Output

The two expenditure components in a two-sector model of the economy are the consumption expenditures of households and the planned investment expenditures of trading enterprises.

Investment expenditure is planned at the beginning of each short period and can be assumed to be of some given magnitude and independent of the level of production. This is represented in figure 16 by a straight line drawn parallel to the production axis at a distance $0I$. Consumption expenditure varies with the level of output and is represented in figure 16 by C. The aggregate demand for goods and services in this two-sector economy is represented by adding these two components — that is, by $C + I$.

By inspection of figure 16, it can be seen that total planned expenditure $(C + I)$ is equal to production at only one level of real output — namely, at $0\,Y_e$. At that level of production, households consume the quantities of goods and services that the consumption function suggests they *would* consume at that level of output, that is, pY_e. The remaining part of output (np) is equal to investment planned for this period (tY_e). That is, the investment plans of trading enterprises are realized at this level of production.

This level of output, $0Y_e$, is known as the **equilibrium level of output.** At this level of production, the sum of sales to households *plus* sales of fixed capital equipment by trading enterprises *plus* planned additions to inventories is equal to total output. In other words, the level of production chosen by trading enterprises in aggregate was precisely right in the sense that all plans and expectations were realized. Provided trading enterprises do not intend either to increase or to decrease their planned investment expenditures in the next period and do not expect any change in total consumption expenditures, they will have no incentive to change the total level of production in the next period. Hence, the notion of *equilibrium* — meaning no tendency to change.

An economy will only stabilize at an equilibrium level of output when total planned expenditure equals total output and therefore there are no unplanned changes in inventories. Economic activity will increase or decrease in accordance with planned expenditures.

However, it should be noted that this **equilibrium level of economic activity does not necessarily coincide with the capacity or full employment level of output**. Equilibrium may, *by chance*, correspond to something like the capacity of the economy, in which case there would be only a very small part of the workforce left unemployed. On the other hand, the equilibrium level of production may be well below capacity and associated with a high level of unemployment. Since the equilibrium level of output means that there are no forces tending either to increase or to decrease production, the economy will continue at that level of output, period after period, until there is a change in one of the components of total planned expenditure.

The Attainment of Equilibrium

We have so far considered a situation in which total production, the level of which is set by trading enterprises at the *beginning* of each period, proved to be equal to the sum of planned investment and consumption expenditures *during* a particular period. That is, the total output of goods and services was equal to total planned expenditure. However, despite attempts by businessmen to estimate future sales at the beginning of each period, it is unlikely that total production *would* be such as to allow all consumption and investment plans to be realized.

Consider, for example, a situation in which firms estimate likely sales in the next period and, after allowing for their intended changes in inventories, set total production at the level $0Y_1$ indicated in figure 17. Total planned expenditure would be aY_1, consisting of dY_1, which households intend to consume at this level of production and income, and planned investment expenditure amounting to ad ($= eY_1$). Since $0Y_1 = bY_1$, the total demand for goods and services (aY_1) is clearly in excess of total production in this period. In other words, trading enterprises underestimated demand for their products in setting their levels of output.

The consumption plans of households would be realized, but not the investment plans of trading enterprises. Investment actually realized by trading enterprises would be equal to the remaining part of production in that period, namely, bd. This is clearly less than the level of investment planned ($ad = eY_1$).

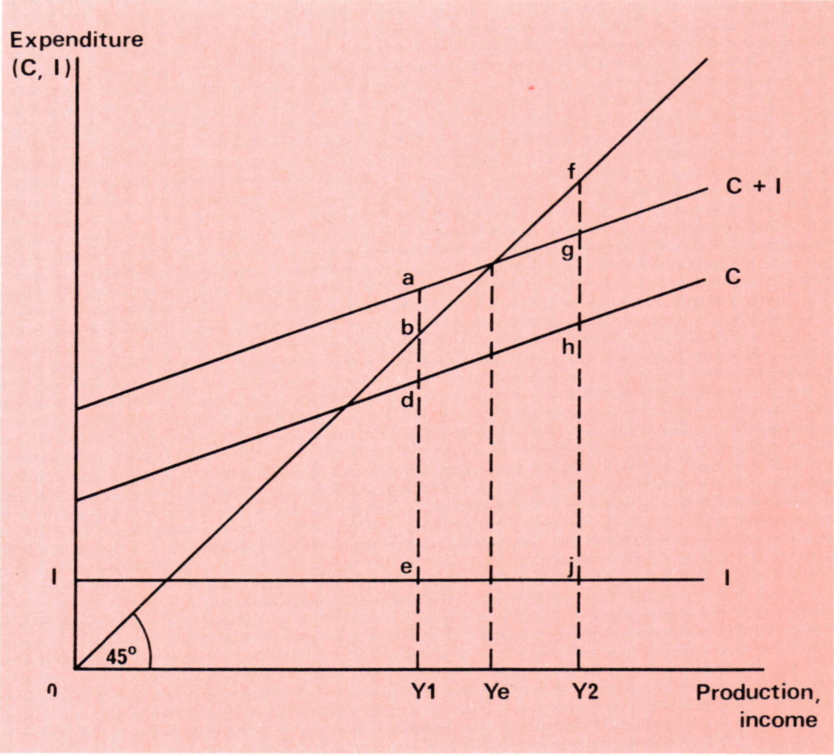

Fig. 17.   The attainment of equilibrium

Orders for fixed capital equipment are assumed to have been filled. Therefore the shortfall in planned investment expenditure would be evident in inventory investment. Hence inventories held at the end of the period would be less than the level intended. This failure to realize inventory investment plans would, in turn, serve as a signal to firms that they had underestimated demand for their products. Provided there were no other actual or expected changes, trading enterprises would then tend to raise their levels of output in the next production period, serving to lift output towards $0Y_e$.

An unintended rundown of inventories, or failure to build up inventories to the extent intended, serves as a signal to businessmen to raise their levels of production in the next period.

What would have happened if trading enterprises had set production at $0Y_2$ in this period? At that level of production, planned expenditure would have been gY_2, consisting of consumption expenditure amounting to hY_2 and planned investment of gh. Total production $(0Y_2 = fY_2)$ would have exceeded aggregate expenditure by fg. Since unsold goods must be added to inventories, there would have been unintended inventory accumulation to that extent.

Total saving would then be the difference between total production and consumption expenditure — that is, fh. This would be equal to *actual* investment expenditure in this period, but would not be equal to investment *planned* for this period (gh).

Whereas firms had planned investment amounting to jY_2, investment actually realized over that period would have been fg (unintended inventory accumulation) *plus* jY_2. That unintended build-up of inventories would serve as a signal that firms had overestimated demand for goods and services. In the absence of any other change or expected change, trading enterprises would then cut back total production in the next production period, moving back towards $0Y_e$.

Unintended inventory accumulation, all other things equal, serves as a signal to businessmen to reduce their levels of production in the next production period.

As a consequence of unintended changes in their inventories in any period, trading enterprises tend to increase or decrease their levels of production in the following period. In this way, total production adjusts towards the equilibrium level of output. So unintended changes in inventories serve to signal that a change in output is necessary.

Changes in Planned Investment Expenditure

Discussion of the equilibrium level of production and the way in which a two-sector economy would move towards equilibrium has so far assumed no change in the investment plans of trading enterprises. Such changes can and do occur. How would a change in investment expenditure plans affect the level of economic activity?

Consider a situation in which our two-sector economy is operating at less than its capacity. This means it is operating at less than the full employment level of output. It is initially in equilibrium at $0Y_e$ in figure 18.

Initially, planned investment expenditure is $0I$ and the equilibrium level of output is $0Y_e$. $0Y_{fe}$ represents the full employment level of output. At the beginning of the next short period, businessmen, for some reason not explained by the model itself, plan to increase investment expenditure from $0I$ to $0I^*$. This is known as *an autonomous increase* in investment. Aggregate demand would now be $C + I^*$.

The most immediate effect of this increase in planned investment expenditure would show up in an increase in demand for investment goods. The former level of production, $0Y_e$, would not be sufficient to allow consumption and investment plans to be realized. So there would be

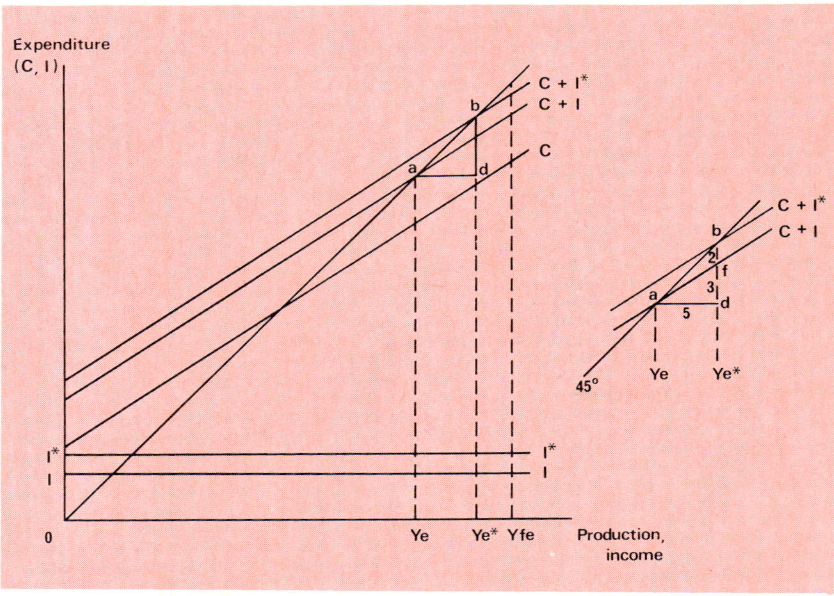

Fig. 18.   The effect of changes in planned investment expenditure

an increase in production and this two-sector economy would move towards a higher equilibrium at $0Y_e^*$.

If planned investment expenditure changes, the economy will move to a new equilibrium level of production.

As a result of this increase in aggregate expenditure, the level of production will be higher than it was previously. But how much higher? In figure 18 the increase in output is indicated by $0Y_e^* - 0Y_e$. This is *greater* than the initial increase in planned investment expenditure, $0I^* - 0I$. Why would this be so?

The immediate result of an increase in planned investment expenditure would be an increase in production and employment in the industries producing investment goods, including those industries aiming to build up their inventories. As a result of this increase in production, incomes would rise and households would spend more on consumption. This is, after all, what the consumption function suggests (namely, the consumption expenditure increases as household disposable income increases). This increase in consumption expenditure would in turn lead to an increase in production and employment in consumer goods industries. So, in general terms, what determines the increase in output? Firstly, the increase in investment expenditure; secondly, the **induced** increase in consumption expenditure that *follows* the initial increase in production. In other words, the initial change in planned investment expenditure would be *multiplied* in some way, so that the final change in output is greater than the initial change in expenditure.

An increase in planned investment expenditure will generate a much larger increase in output because of the increases in consumption expenditure that are induced.

Once some initial increase in expenditure has triggered these induced increases in consumption expenditure, why is it that output fails to increase *beyond* $0Y_e^*$? Why does it not continue to grow, in effect, feeding upon round after round of induced increases in consumption?

The extent of the change in output, following some initial change in expenditure, is determined by the marginal propensity to consume.

If the marginal propensity to consume (m.p.c.) of households in aggregate was equal to 1, then the whole of each dollar increase in income would be spent on consumption and a small initial increase in expenditure would result in an *endless* chain reaction that would tend to increase output indefinitely. In contrast, if the m.p.c. of households was zero, then the initial increase in household disposable income would not result in any increase in consumption expenditure. If that had been the case, there would have been no induced increases in consumption expenditure and the increase in production would have been *equal to* the initial increase in investment expenditure. So the change in output depends upon the marginal propensity to consume.

The extent of induced consumption depends upon the fraction of any increase in income that is spent on consumption. The greater the m.p.c., the greater will be the changes in consumption induced by a change in investment.

The fact that an autonomous change in expenditure, such as II^* $(=bf)$ in figure 18 generates a change in output of $Y_e\,Y_e^*$ $(=ad)$ can also be explained in terms of the triangle *abd* (and its enlargement). The change in output, *ad*, because of the 45-degree line, is equal to *bd*. But *bd* is made up of two components: *bf*, which is the *initial* change in investment expenditure, and *fd*, the *induced* change in consumption expenditure resulting from the extra disposable income generated by the initial increase in output (and income).

The higher the value of the m.p.c., the greater the increase in consumption expenditure — and therefore induced increase in output generated by some autonomous increase in expenditure. In terms of the triangle *abd*, the *steeper* the consumption function, the larger will be *fd*. Since *bf* remains constant, $bf + fd$ will be greater the steeper the slope of the consumption function. That is, the higher the m.p.c., the larger will be the induced change in output (ad).

This relationship between an autonomous change in expenditure and the total change in output is called the multiplier effect.

We can also illustrate the multiplier effect in simple mathematical form. If $\triangle I$ is the autonomous change in expenditure (such as II^* in figure 18), $\triangle Y_e$ the change of output that results, and c the m.p.c., then:

$$\triangle Y_e = Y_e^* - Y_e$$
$$= ad$$
$$\text{but } ad = bd$$
$$= bf + fd$$
$$\text{but } fd = c.ad$$
$$\therefore ad = c.ad + bf$$
$$\text{i.e., } ad - c.ad = bf$$
$$\therefore ad\,(1-c) = bf$$
$$\therefore ad = bf.\ \frac{1}{1-c}$$

And since $ad = \triangle Y_e$ and $bf = \triangle I$

$$\therefore \triangle Y_e = \triangle I . \frac{1}{1-c}$$

Generalizing so that $\triangle E$ is any autonomous change in expenditure,

$$\triangle Y_e = \triangle E . \frac{1}{1-c}$$

The term $\frac{1}{1-c}$ is called the **income multiplier** and it follows from our explanation above that the closer c approaches to unity (1), the larger is the value of the multiplier. That is, the greater the m.p.c., the larger the effect of an autonomous change in expenditure upon output. Since the marginal propensity to save (m.p.s.) is what remains after consumption from each extra dollar of household disposable income; the lower the m.p.s., the larger the multiplier effect.

As an illustration, assume that the increase in investment expenditure in figure 18 (bf) was $3 million. If we assume the m.p.c. is 3/5, the multiplier in this two-sector model would be $\frac{1}{1-3/5} = 2.5$.

That is,

$$\triangle Y_e = \triangle I \times \frac{1}{1-c}$$
$$= 3 \times 2.5$$
$$= \$7.5 \text{ million}$$

It would be wrong to assume that the process of change which results from the multiplier effect is *instantaneous*. There are time lags between the initial change in expenditure and reactions to that change. For example, there would be lags between the initial increase in production of investment goods, the increase in household disposable income, the increase in demand by households, and the increase in production of consumer goods. However, provided there are no other intervening changes in expenditure plans, the initial change in expenditure will, after these time lags, result in a change in output of the magnitude suggested by the multiplier.

The income multiplier indicates the number of times the final change in production is greater than the initial increase in expenditure.

The income multiplier formula for a two-sector economy is $\frac{1}{1-c}$

Changes in Planned Consumption Expenditure

An initial change in expenditure that leads to a change in the equilibrium level of production is not necessarily initiated by businessmen. It may be brought about by an autonomous change in the consumption behaviour of households. That is, a change in consumption expenditure brought about by some reason *other than* a change in income.

Consider a situation in which planned investment expenditure at the beginning of a short period is given and remains unchanged. Initially, as shown in figure 19 aggregate expenditure is given by $C + I$ and the economy is in equilibrium at OY_e. That is, an economy is operating at less than capacity, OY_{fe}. Households are initially consuming Oc.

Households then decide — for some reason not explained by the model, perhaps fear of rising unemployment — to save more and consume less out of their current incomes. This is represented by a downward shift in the consumption function to C^*. While production remains at $0Y_e$, the intentions of households to save more would be realized:

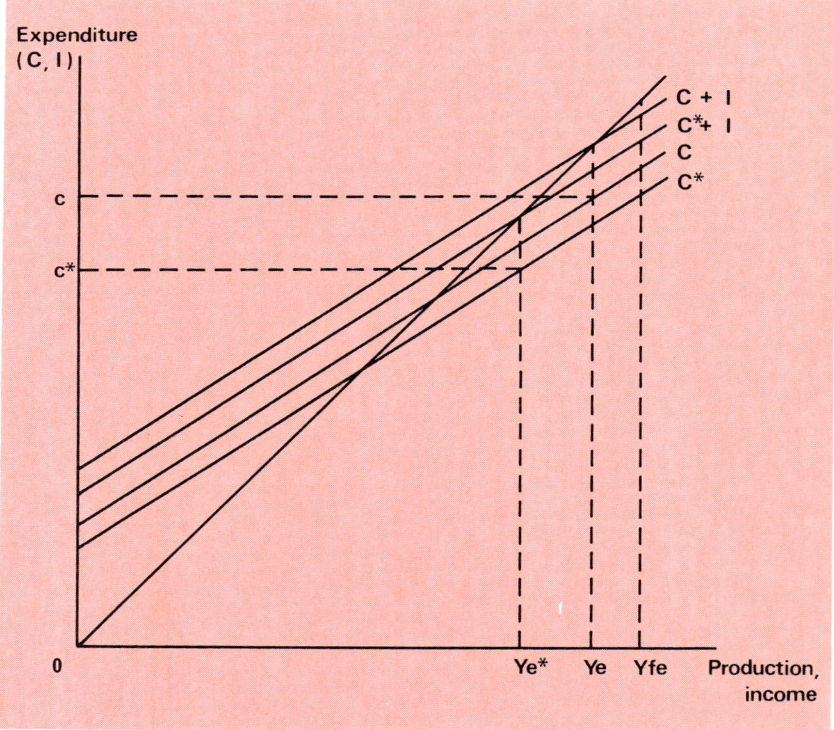

Fig. 19.   The effect of changes in planned consumption expenditure

saving would rise. Meanwhile, aggregate demand would have fallen by the extent of the downward shift in the consumption function, that is, to C^* + I. Trading enterprises would find that their sales were less than expected. That is, the reduction in consumption would serve as a signal to businessmen that they had overestimated market demand. From the beginning of the next production period, they would reduce output. Provided there were no other changes or expected changes in expenditure, the economy would finally settle at a new (lower) equilibrium $0Y_e^*$, where consumption and investment expenditure plans would be realized.

In these circumstances, how would we calculate the change in output? The answer to that question is the same as in the case of an increase in investment expenditure. When the consumption function shifts, either upwards or downwards, we assume that the slope remains unchanged. Hence the magnitude of the multiplier, $\frac{1}{1-c}$ would also remain unchanged. If the initial reduction in consumption expenditure was $6 million, the final change in output would be $(-\$6m \times \frac{1}{2/5}) = -\$15m$. That is, the new equilibrium level of output would be $15 million lower than it was at $0Y_e$.

The change in the equilibrium level of output following an initial change in either planned investment or consumption expenditure, whether an increase or decrease in expenditure, is given by $\triangle Y_e = \triangle E . \frac{1}{1-c}$ where $\triangle E$ represents the initial change in expenditure. That is, any autonomous change in planned expenditure will have a multiplier effect upon the equilibrium level of production.

In passing, it is important to note the final effect of the attempt by households to increase their saving. Initially, before any change in the level of production, households would have been able to increase their saving out of current income. However, as a result of that increase in saving and the associated reduction in consumption expenditure, trading enterprises reduced the level of production. Although households would have continued to save a greater *proportion* of disposable income at the lower level of output, total saving by households would have finally been no greater than it was formerly. This sequence of events is referred to as **"the paradox of thrift"**, because an attempt by households to save more out of current income finally results in no change in actual saving.

Questions

1. Explain why total production = total expenditure = total income in the two-sector model.

2. What does the 45-degree line show on an expenditure-income diagram?

3. Calculate the m.p.c. for the economy given this information:

Total Income	Total consumption expenditure
$1,000	$800
$1,200	$950

4. Express the consumption function in the form $A + cY$, given the following information:

Total Income	Total Consumption Expenditure
0	$500
$1,000	$1,100
$2,000	$1,700

At each level of income, calculate the level of saving or dissaving.

5. What is meant by the terms *saving* and *consuming*?

6. If firms incorrectly forecast consumer expenditure on their products to be higher than it actually turns out to be, actual investment turns out to be higher than planned. Explain why this is so.

7. What is meant by the terms *equilibrium* and *disequilibrium*?

8. In the two-sector model, what is the signal to businessmen to change their levels of production? Explain the reaction of businessmen to this signal.

9. Explain why the change in total income will be greater than an initial autonomous change in planned investment.

10. Explain what determines the size of the income multiplier.

11. For the following, state which are autonomous changes and which are induced changes:
    a. Businessmen plan to increase investment.
    b. There has been an increase in total income leading to an increase in consumption expenditure.
    c. There has been a decision to consume less at all levels of income.

12. Calculate the final change in total income in a two-sector economy when—
    (a) m.p.c. = 0.6 and an autonomous increase in planned investment is $10 million;
    (b) m.p.c. = 0.8 and an autonomous decrease in consumption expenditure is $50 million;
    (c) m.p.s. = 0.2 and an autonomous decrease in planned investment is $15 million.

13. Use the information that $C = 100 + 0.7Y$ and planned $I = \$50$ million to answer the following questions:
    a. What is the constant component of consumption?
    b. What is the m.p.c.?
    c. What is the equilibrium level of income?
    d. If planned investment increases by $10 million, what will be the new equilibrium level of total income?

14. As a simplifying assumption, our two-sector model assumed that all income was distributed to households. If we had assumed instead that firms hold a constant proportion of income as undistributed profits and as depreciation allowance, what effect would this have had on the position and slope of the consumption function?

A THREE-SECTOR MODEL

A three-sector model of the economy includes households, trading enterprises, and government. The overseas sector is excluded. So this may be described as a model of **"a closed economy"** — that is, one assumed to be closed to transactions with the rest of the world.

The same general assumptions will apply as were used in the two-sector model.

One consequence of adding in the government sector is that we must now make allowance for the effect of direct taxes. Direct taxes will decrease household disposable income. Thus there will be less consumption expenditure associated with any level of total income. The fraction of any *extra* income paid in direct taxation is termed the **marginal rate of taxation (t)**. For the purpose of this model, we assume that taxation is a constant proportion of total income. In this case the marginal rate of tax and the average rate of tax are the same and do not change as income changes. The effect of the inclusion of taxation in the model is to decrease the slope of the consumption function, as shown in figure 20.

Another effect of adding in the government sector is that we now have

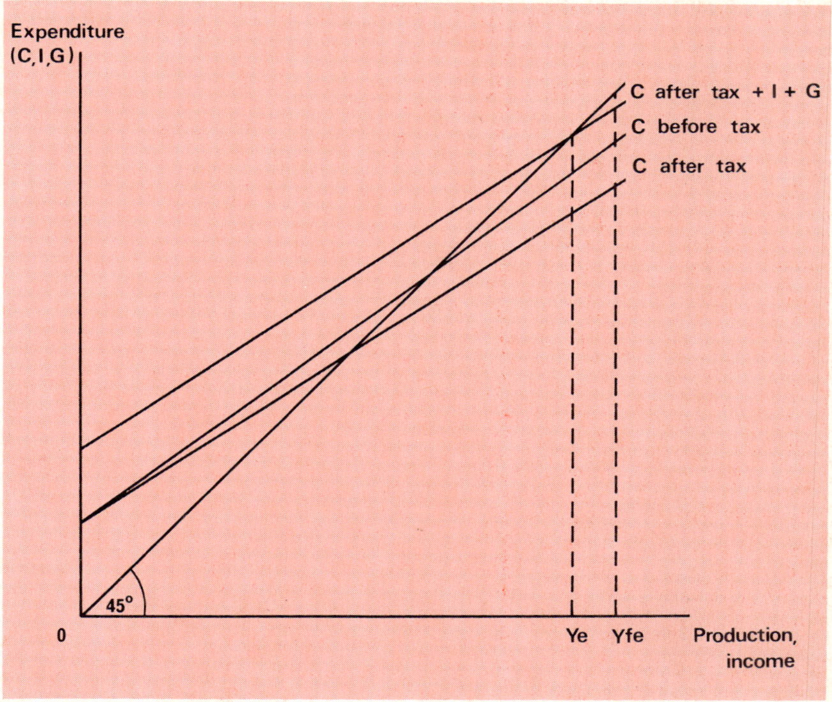

Fig. 20.   The three-sector model

a third expenditure component, namely, government sector expenditure (represented by G). We will assume, for the purposes of the model, that the expenditure plans of government are always realized — even though evidence suggests that a perfect match between plans and actual expenditure would be improbable. So we now have three expenditure components — C, I, and G — which, taken together, account for aggregate demand in this three-sector economy.

Initially, this three-sector economy is in equilibrium with production at $0Y_e$ as indicated in figure 21. All expenditure plans are being realized and there is no reason for businessmen to change the level of production. At the beginning of the next short period, businessmen decide to increase planned investment expenditure from $0I$ to $0I^*$. Provided there are no other changes, this increase in planned investment expenditure will lead to a new (higher) equilibrium level of production at $0Y_e^*$.

As in the two-sector model, the final increase in production will be greater than the initial increase in planned investment expenditure. But how much greater? In other words, what will be the relationship between

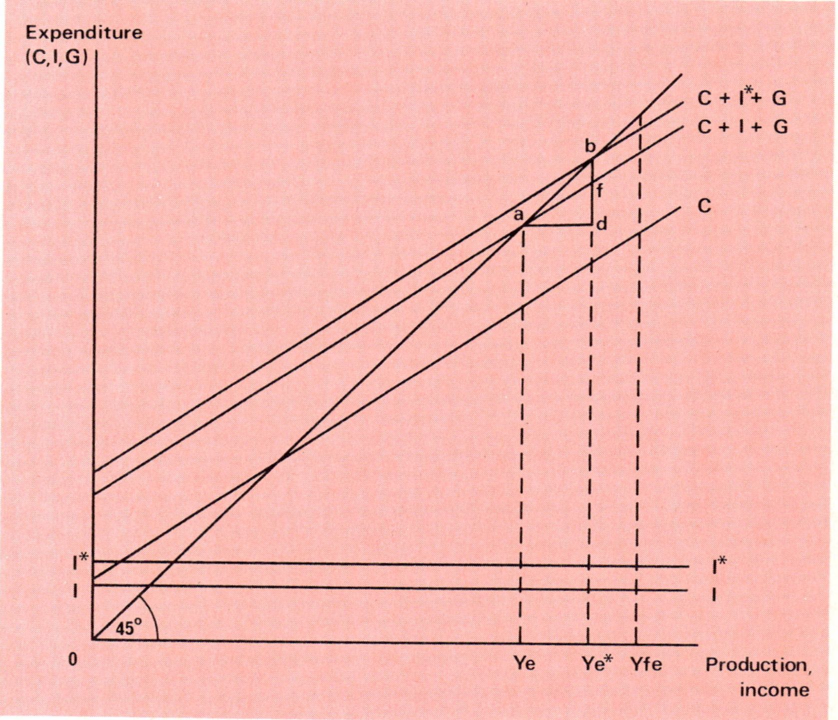

Fig. 21.   Changes in production plans in the three-sector model

the change in the equilibrium level of real GDP (that is $0Y_e^* - 0Y_e$) and the initial change in investment expenditure $(0I^* - 0I)$?

Unlike the two-sector model, the slope of both the consumption function and the aggregate expenditure function now take into account not only the leakage into saving, but also the leakage into direct taxation. As production and the incomes of households rise, part of the increase in income is lost by way of taxation. Of the remainder — that is, the increase in income after tax — part finds its way into additional consumption and part is saved. So the income multiplier in a three-sector economy must allow for *both* the leakage into taxation *and* the leakage into saving.

Changes in government spending have a multiplier effect in the same way as changes in consumption or investment. Taxation reduces the size of the income multiplier.

The Three-Sector Multiplier

The magnitude of the three-sector income multiplier depends on *two* variables, the m.p.c. (c) *and* the marginal rate of tax (t). A change in either of these variables will result in a change in the size of the multiplier. In the three-sector model, the multiplier is dampened by the effect of taxation on the incomes of households. Thus the new multiplier becomes $\frac{1}{1-[c(1-t)]}$ (The square brackets are retained to remind us that it is the slope of the household consumption function net of taxation that is relevant in terms of changes in output.) Figure 20 showed that an *increase* in t, for example, has the effect of *reducing* the slope of the consumption function and therefore the value of the multiplier.

Given this new three-sector multiplier, we can now conclude that, regardless of the source of the initial change in expenditure ($\triangle E$), whether from a change in consumption ($\triangle C$) investment ($\triangle I$), or government sector expenditure ($\triangle G$), the final change in the equilibrium level of output ($\triangle Y_e$) is given by

$$\triangle Y_e = \triangle E \times \frac{1}{1 - [c(1 - t)]}$$

In the case of the increase in planned investment expenditure from $0I$ to $0I^*$ in figure 21, if we let $\triangle I$ be $8 million, the m.p.c. remain as before as 3/5, and assume the marginal rate of tax (t) is 1/6, then the income multiplier would be:

$$\frac{1}{1 - [3/5\,(1 - 1/6)]} = \frac{1}{1 - 3/5 \times 5/6} = \frac{1}{1 - 1/2} = 2$$

The change in the equilibrium level of output ($\triangle Y_e$) would then be $8 million x 2 = $16 million.

It will be noticed that, while keeping the same value for the m.p.c. in the three-sector example as was used in the two-sector illustration, the value of the income multiplier has fallen from 2.5 to 2.0 as a result of the leakage into direct taxation.

The multiplier formula for a three-sector model is $\dfrac{1}{1 - [\, c\,(1 - t)\,]}.$

Questions

1. What are the components of expenditure in the three-sector model?

2. What effect does taxation have on (*a*) household disposable income; (*b*) household consumption expenditure?

3. Suppose that total tax revenue is equal to government expenditure. This is a balanced budget situation. Both taxation and government spending are then increased by an equal amount so that there is still a balanced budget. Explain the effect that this will have on the equilibrium level of income.

4. What is the multiplier for the three-sector model?
   For the following situations, calculate the change in the equilibrium level of total income:
   (*a*) m.p.c. = 0.6 $t = 0.2$ $\triangle I = +50$
   (*b*) m.p.c. = 0.8 $t = 0.1$ $\triangle G = -10$

A FOUR-SECTOR MODEL

Addition of the overseas sector serves to complete a full (or "*open*") model of the economy. In addition to the components in the three-sector model, what this requires is that we also take into consideration expenditure by the rest of the world on Australian-produced goods and services (our exports) and expenditure by Australia on goods and services produced overseas (our imports).

Foreign demand for our exports is *not* dependent on the level of Australia's real GDP. That component in aggregate expenditure is determined by factors outside of the Australian economy — such as those referred to in connection with the demand for wool in chapter 9. For the purposes of our model, the demand for our exports in any short period will be regarded as given; it is simply another component in aggregate demand. However, in this regard *changes* in the level of exports will induce changes in the level of income just like other autonomous changes in expenditure.

Total demand for goods and services in any period is given by $C + I +$

$G + X$, as indicated in figure 22. However, the values of C, I, G, and X each include imported raw materials, components, and finished goods. For example, consumption expenditures in Australia include clothing and footwear imported from Taiwan and Hong Kong. Investment includes the cost of machines imported from Japan, the United States, and other countries; and virtually all production in Australia relies to some extent on imported crude oil. Since we are concerned with *Australian* production and employment, we must deduct the value of imports from $C + I + G + X$ in order to represent the demand for Australian-produced goods and services.

In order to include import expenditures in the model, we will assume that Australia's demand for imports increases in step with total demand; further, that the ratio of imports to total demand — that is, $\frac{M}{C + I + G + X}$ — remains constant. This is, at best, a rough approximation to reality. There have been times when aggregate demand has exceeded the capacity of the economy and this demand has spilled over increasingly into imports. At other times, quantitative restrictions have resulted in a sharp

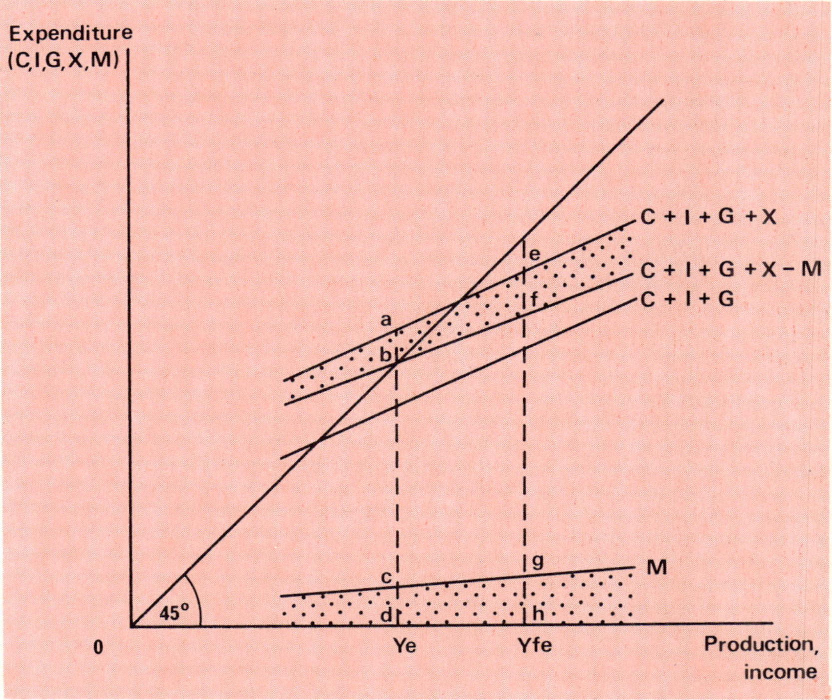

Fig. 22. The four-sector model

reduction in imports. However, this assumption serves to simplify the model.

The assumed relationship between imports (M) and the total demand for goods and services in Australia ($C + I + G + X$) is represented in figure 22. The line $C + I + G + X$ represents the total demand for goods and services in the Australian economy. Because the demand for exports is assumed to be given, the line $C + I + G + X$ is drawn above and parallel to $C + I + G$, in the same way that the given level of planned investment expenditure was drawn above and parallel to the consumption function.

To represent the demand for Australian-produced goods and services, we must deduct the value of imports from $C + I + G + X$. At output $0Y_e$, the demand for imports would be $cd = ab$. At a higher level of production, $0Y_{fe}$, the demand for imports would be higher at $gh = ef$. A line drawn through b and f ($C + I + G + X - M$) thus represents the aggregate demand for Australian-produced goods and services. In figure 22, the equilibrium level of production is indicated by $0Y_e$.

In our three-sector model we saw that the extent of the change in the equilibrium level of production, following some initial change in expenditure ($\triangle C$, $\triangle I$ or $\triangle G$), was dampened by leakages both to saving and to direct taxes. This was reflected in the income multiplier. Now that we have expanded the model to take into account our overseas transactions, the total demand for goods and services is given by $C + I + G + X$. As total demand grows, so too does the demand for imports. In other words, as total expenditure on $C + I + G + X$ rises, there is an *increasing* leakage into imports.

This leakage into imports is designated as **the marginal propensity to import and is defined as the ratio of the change in imports to some small change in total expenditure** and is represented by the symbol m.

The Four-Sector Multiplier

Given the additional leakage into imports from any change in expenditure, the size of the four-sector multiplier is less than it was in our three-sector model, assuming c and t are of the same magnitudes. Whatever the source of the initial change in expenditure, some of the *initial* as well as *induced* expenditure will be on imports. This differs from the two- and three-sector models where the leakages were confined to household saving and government taxes.

Imports reduce the size of the multiplier.

We therefore have the situation where the propensity to import reduces the slope of $C + I + G + X$ *and* part of the initial as well as subsequent expenditure is "leaked" to imports. That is, the four-sector income multiplier when applied to an autonomous change in expenditure ($\triangle E$) now results in a change in the equilibrium level of output of the order of:

$$\triangle Y_e = \triangle E \times \frac{1}{1 - [c(1-t)(1-m)]} - \frac{m.\triangle E}{1 - [c(1-t)(1-m)]}$$

$$= \triangle E \times \frac{1-m}{1 - [c(1-t)(1-m)]}$$

Again we can illustrate with an example in which $\triangle E$ is an increase of $8 million, c remains at 3/5 and t at 1/6, and let m be 1/5. The four sector multiplier becomes:

$$\frac{1 - 1/5}{1 - [3/5(1 - 1/6)(1 - 1/5)]}$$

$$= \frac{4/5}{1 - [3/5 \times 5/6 \times 4/5]} = \frac{4/5}{1 - 2/5} = \frac{4/5}{3/5} = 1\ 1/3$$

The change in the equilibrium level of output will then be:

$$\$8 \text{ million} \times 1\ 1/3 = \$10\ 2/3 \text{ million}$$

Again it will be noticed that in terms of the three-sector model illustration, the multiplier has been reduced; this time from 2 to $1^{1}/3$, while the value of c and t was held constant.

The multiplier formula for a four-sector model is $\dfrac{1-m}{1 - [c(1-t)(1-m)]}$.

Questions

1. In the open economy, what are the components of total expenditure?

2. What is the multiplier for the open economy?

3. What is meant by the term *marginal propensity to import*?

4. For the following situations, calculate the change in the equibrium level of total income:
   (a) m.p.c. = 0.6 $t = 0.2$ $m = 0.1$ $\triangle I = +10$
   (b) m.p.c. = 0.8 $t = 0.1$ $m = 0.2$ $\triangle I = +10$

5. What determines the equilibrium level of income in the open economy?

DEFLATIONARY AND INFLATIONARY GAPS

In considering changes in production brought about by changes in expenditure in our two-sector, three-sector, and four-sector models, we have in each case assumed that the economy was initially in equilibrium at less than its full capacity. We have identified this capacity production with full employment of the workforce — in effect suggesting that, *in the short run*, there would be no further increase in real GDP once all people who want employment have found jobs.

When the economy is in equilibrium at less than the full employment level of production, the economy may be described as having a "deflationary gap". Up to the time of the Great Depression, such a situation was expected to result in a decline in prices and money wage rates. These lower prices, in turn, were believed to act as a stimulus to aggregate demand. However, if all prices and incomes fell in the same proportions, this *in itself* would do nothing to change real GDP. However, since prices and money wage rates are no longer believed to be flexible downwards, there is nothing to be gained by further questioning former macroeconomic theories.

The term "deflationary gap" is now used to describe any situation in which aggregate demand is less than sufficient to generate the full employment level of production.

In figure 23, the economy is in equilibrium at $0Y_e$. That is, the level of output is less than that necessary for full employment of the workforce $(0Y_{fe})$.

The size of the deflationary gap is measured by reference to the extent to which total planned expenditure for Australian-produced goods and services falls short of the level necessary to generate full employment. That is, the "gap" measures the deficiency in aggregate demand at the full employment level of output and is indicated, in figure 23, by the vertical distance *ab*.

It is apparent that an increase in total expenditure to the extent indicated by *ab* would serve to close the deflationary gap and, through the income multiplier, to increase production to the full employment level of output.

A deflationary gap exists whenever total planned expenditure is insufficient to generate the full employment level of production. It is always measured at the full employment level of GDP and is the additional expenditure needed to ensure demand for the total output of the economy at full employment.

Given the equilibrium level of output indicated in figure 23 and no changes or expected changes in any of the expenditure components (*C*, *I*,

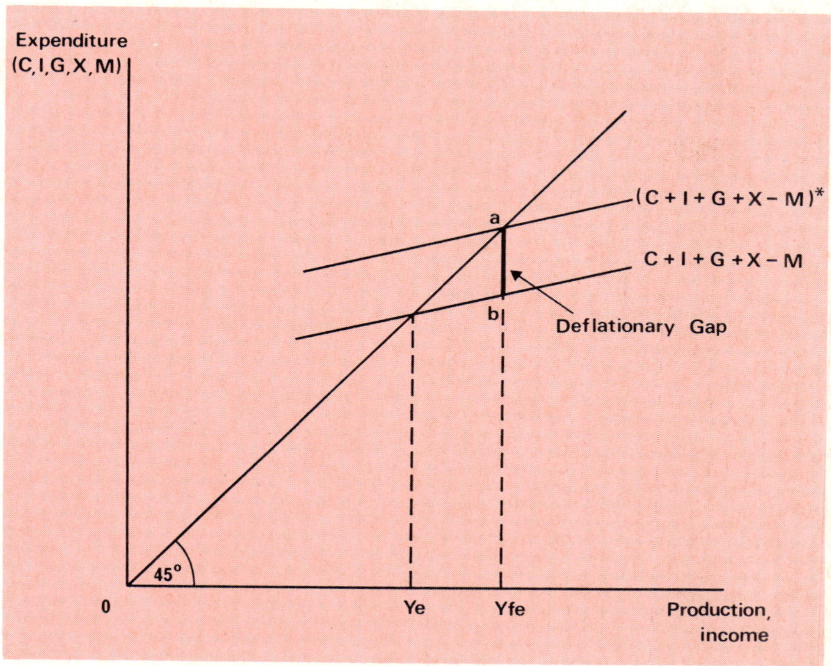

Fig. 23.   A deflationary gap

G, or X), there would be no incentive for businessmen to change the level of production in the next period. That is, there would be no forces at work that would tend to lift production towards the full employment level of economic activity — where aggregate expenditure would be $(C + I + G + X - M)^*$.

The main thrust of the arguments advanced by John Maynard Keynes was that when an economy like Australia's is operating well below capacity, period after period, the government must intervene. It is now widely accepted that government has the responsibility for stabilizing the level of economic activity at something close to the full employment level of output. For example, when the economy is experiencing a recession and market forces tending to raise production are either weak or absent, it is now expected that the government will introduce measures designed to stimulate production.

What measures might government use in these circumstances? The government may choose to use its *fiscal* weapons, either increasing government sector expenditure or reducing taxation or both. An increase in government sector expenditure would have the same effect on output as an increase in consumption, investment, or exports. But it's unlikely that the government would need to increase expenditure sufficiently to close the gap completely. Clear signs of recovery and growing business confidence in the future growth in sales would probably lead to an increase in planned investment expenditure. A reduction in direct tax on personal income would result in an increase in household disposable income. This could be expected to result in an increase in consumption expenditure. It would also serve to increase the size of the income multiplier.

Alternatively, or in addition to these fiscal measures, the government might make use of *monetary* measures, relying on a reduction in interest rates and an increase in the availability of credit to stimulate both sales of consumer durables and investment expenditure.

Other options may be open to the government through *external policy measures*. The government may be able to stimulate exports through the introduction of incentive payments to exporters. At the same time, it might impose quantitative restrictions on imports, in this way forcing Australians to substitute home-produced goods and services. Since this would reduce the leakage into imports, it would also increase the size of the multiplier.

The Keynesian model suggests that a deflationary gap calls for government action to stimulate total planned expenditure. This could be done by means of fiscal, monetary, or external policy measures.

In direct contrast to a deflationary gap, **an inflationary gap exists when aggregate demand is more than sufficient to generate the full employment level of production.** In figure 24, the full employment level of output is indicated by $0\,Y_{fe}$, but aggregate demand for Australian-produced goods and services is initially $C + I + G + X - M$. The inflationary gap is indicated by de, which measures the excess of aggregate demand above the level necessary to ensure full employment. The level of aggregate demand required for full employment is indicated by $(C + I + G + X - M)^*$.

In a situation such as this, the demand for goods and services cannot be met by the existing capacity to produce. Buyers would be scrambling for the limited supplies available, and sellers, realizing that they could sell more if they could produce more, would raise their prices. Money wage rates would rise, in part because the available supply of labour would have already been absorbed and workers would then be in a stronger position to bargain for higher wage rates; in part because employers, realizing that they would sell more if only they could increase output, would offer higher wage rates in an attempt to attract labour away from other firms. As money wage rates rise, trading enterprises find that they can add this increase in costs to the prices of their products and still continue to sell all

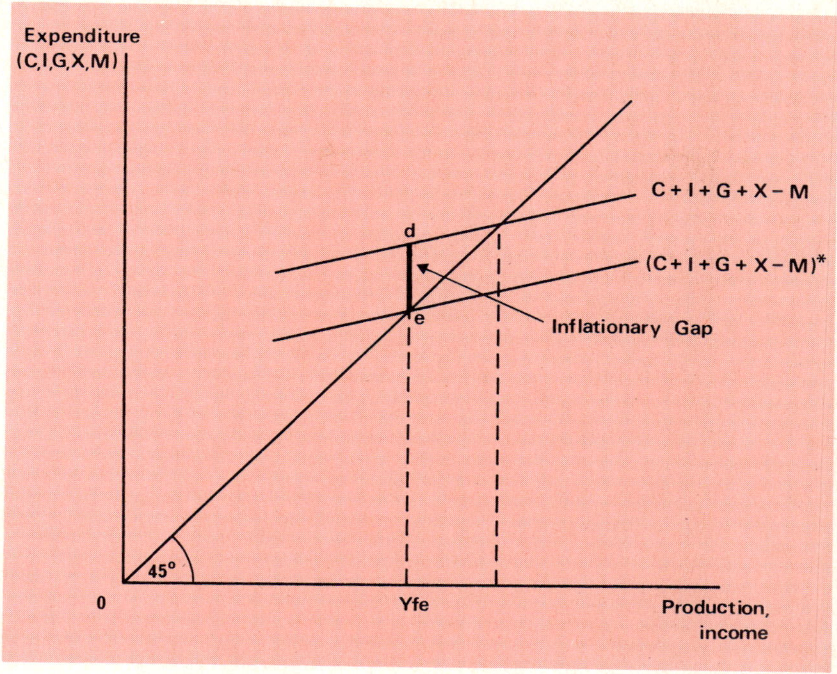

Fig. 24.   An inflationary gap

that they can produce. As prices continue to rise, there would be an increasing tendency for demand to spill over into imports — particularly if import prices had remained unchanged. In that event, there would be a reduction in our foreign exchange reserves.

Such a situation would be *unstable*. For example, businessmen would find it difficult, if not impossible, to foresee the costs and prices likely to be associated with planned investment projects. They would also *expect* government to intervene with measures designed to dampen aggregate demand. So businessmen would be likely to adopt a "wait and see" attitude towards long-term investment projects. For reasons such as these, we cannot describe the level of output that would correspond to $C + I + G + X - M$ in figure 24 as an equilibrium level of production.

An inflationary gap is measured at the full employment level of output. It is the excess demand that cannot be satisfied by the economy operating at full capacity. An inflationary gap generates upward pressure on prices, wages, and imports.

Over the period 1945-74, Australia *did* experience excess aggregate demand on several occasions. In each instance this was accompanied by an increase in the general level of prices. Bearing in mind the source of this problem, namely, excess aggregate demand, and the responsibility of the government for price stability, what measures could the government take in these circumstances?

To strike at the root of this problem, the government would need to adopt measures designed to cut back expenditure on Australian-produced goods and services. It might reduce government sector expenditure, increase direct taxation (reducing household disposable income and consumption expenditure), raise interest rates, and reduce the availability of credit. The government might also take steps to encourage the substitution of imports for Australian-produced goods and services — for example, by reducing tariffs on imported goods and eliminating quantitative restrictions, or revaluing the Australian dollar.

Although it would be necessary to pursue measures such as these until aggregate demand dropped to $(C + I + G + X - M)^*$, the introduction of such measures would probably be sufficient to cause households and trading enterprises to revise their expectations about the future. That is, given resolute pursuit of such policies by the government, we could also expect some reduction in planned consumption and investment expenditures that would tend to reinforce the government's initiatives.

Keynesian theory suggests that the existence of an inflationary gap calls for government action to reduce total planned expenditure.

Although excess aggregate demand was evident in some periods between 1945 and 1974 and did explain increases in the general level of prices in those periods, we cannot explain rising prices during the latter half of the 1970s by reference to excess demand. Clearly, the evidence around us — including the highest level of unemployment since the Great Depression — indicates that the Australian economy has been operating far below capacity. So it will be necessary to look for alternative explanations.

In chapter 12 we will review macroeconomic features of the Australian economy over the period from 1950 to the mid 1970s. This will involve an evaluation of the fiscal and monetary policies adopted by the government in attempts to realize the principal economic policy objectives of full employment, price stability, and external balance. In chapter 13 we will concentrate on the events of the 1970s, when inflation *together with* a very high level of unemployment presented problems which our models are less well equipped to handle.

Questions

1. (*a*) What is meant by a deflationary gap?
   (*b*) What is meant by an inflationary gap?
   Sketch diagrams to illustrate each of these situations.
2. (*a*) Describe the measures that may be taken to remove a deflationary gap.
   (*b*) What factors might influence the selection of particular measures?

12 | Policy Objectives and Past Performance

In chapter 8, reference was made to three principal economic policy objectives of the Commonwealth govenment — namely, *full employment, price stability*, and *external balance*. We have now considered various fiscal, monetary, and external weapons available to the government in its pursuit of these objectives. But what is the *meaning* of each of these objectives? For example, what is meant by full employment? Probably most people would suggest that this means that all people who wish to work are able to find jobs. For our purposes so far, that definition would have been adequate. However, for practical purposes, should we suggest that full employment has been attained *only* when there is not one person in Australia who is seeking employment left unemployed? Some people would say that full employment has been attained when only 1 or 2 per cent of the workforce is unemployed. Would that assessment be clearly wrong?

Likewise, we need to be clear as to the meaning of "price stability" and "external balance". Again, opinions differ — even between economists. So these questions need to be considered before any attempt is made either to assess the need for government intervention in the economy or to judge the consequences of economic policy measures introduced in past periods.

THE FULL EMPLOYMENT OBJECTIVE

At any time there are always *some* members of the workforce unemployed — even under boom conditions, when the overall demand for labour exceeds the available supply. This can be understood if we attempt to categorize the types of individuals who will remain unemployed.

1. Frictional unemployment. The term *frictional unemployment* is used to describe people who are in the process of changing jobs, re-entering the workforce, or entering the labour force for the first time. These people are unemployed because of the time involved in their job search. For any of a number of reasons, such as lack of opportunities for advancement, lack of interest, or conflict with the management, individuals decide to give up their jobs and search for some alternative. In fact, there are very few people who remain in the same occupation and with the same firm throughout their working lives. The time taken to find alternative employment is likely to reflect the skills of the individual, the availability of information concerning job vacancies, and the overall demand for labour. When the demand for labour is strong, there are likely to be large numbers of frictionally unemployed; but the time taken to find other employment is generally likely to be very short. In contrast, when there is a high level of unemployment, people are less willing to give up their jobs and to risk searching for alternatives.

2. Structural unemployment. Some people will be unemployed owing to a mismatch of the supply and demand of labour with regard to skills or location. There may be a demand for certain types of skills in certain locations within Australia. At the same time there may be unemployed persons possessing different skills in different locations. Some people lose their jobs as a result of either once-for-all changes in market demand or changes in technology. For example, in the 1950s a switch to alternative sources of supply and to alternative fuels resulted in a reduction of 40 per cent in the numbers of coalminers employed in New South Wales. The combination of rising costs and falling farm product prices forced many farmers to seek alternative jobs in the late sixties and early seventies. More recently, there has been a reduction in the demand for certain types of labour as a result of capital deepening, such as the introduction of computers and self-service petrol retailing.

Many of the structurally unemployed have great difficulty in finding alternative employment, particularly if they are middle-aged and have no other skills. When the overall demand for labour is very strong, these people can usually find semi-skilled work. However, if the demand for labour is weak and there are already many thousands of skilled workers seeking employment, their prospects are very bleak.

The rate of structural change appears to be quickening and it seems likely that the structurally unemployed will account for an increasing proportion of the total numbers unemployed. This in turn suggests a need for manpower planning and increasing attention to retraining for the types of employment likely to be available in the future.

3. Hard-core unemployment. Some people may have difficulty finding employment owing to certain personal characteristics. Such things as minor mental or physical disabilities, a criminal record, alcoholism or other drug problems, untidy appearance, and the inability to work under supervision could hinder a person's employment prospects. As with frictional and structural unemployment, the extent of hard-core unemployment is influenced by the total demand for labour. When total planned expenditure is high, the demand for labour is correspondingly high. At such a time employers are not in a position to be too choosy, and hard-core unemployment tends to drop.

Even at full employment there will always be some unemployed owing to the existence of frictional, structural, and hard-core unemployment.

Taken together, the existence of hard-core, frictional, and structural unemployment necessarily means that there are always *some* members of the workforce who are unemployed. So full employment, or the fullest possible level of employment, is always something less than 100 per cent of the workforce. How much less we cannot say. We have no means of knowing how many of the unemployed fit each of these categories at any time.

The remaining category of unemployment is that which results from a deficiency in aggregate demand — that is, arising from a situation in which aggregate demand is less than sufficient to employ all people seeking employment other than those included in the three categories already considered. We will refer to unemployment that results from a deficiency in aggregate demand as "*general unemployment*".

If hard-core, frictional, and structural unemployment together always accounted for 1 per cent of the workforce, there would be no point in the government taking measures designed to stimulate production when unemployment amounted to 1 per cent of the workforce. Very few of the unemployed would have skills of the types sought by the firms that would then be aiming to increase their output. Employers would be much more likely to respond to an increase in demand for their products by increasing the amount of overtime worked by their employees. Because of the higher wage rates paid for overtime, this would result in higher labour costs per unit of output. An increase in the demand for labour would increase the power of workers to bargain for higher wage rates. Also, the increase in the demand for output would make employers more willing to offer higher wage rates in an attempt to attract labour away from other firms. Rising wage rates would feed higher prices. So a stimulus to production when the economy is operating close to the full employment level of output is likely to endanger the *price stability* objective. In these circumstances, it is also likely that demand will spill over increasingly into imports, posing a threat to *external balance*.

Attainment of the full employment objective may result in a threat to the objective of price stability and external balance.

In contrast, if unemployment rose to, say, 3 per cent of the workforce, this would suggest a deficiency in aggregate demand and unemployment of a "general" kind. In those circumstances, assuming an absence of market forces that seemed likely to close the deflationary gap, we would expect the government to intervene with measures designed to stimulate production.

The level of unemployment indicates the extent to which output in the economy is falling short of its capacity to produce. But how is unemployment *measured*?

Unemployment statistics provide a measure of the number of people who wish to work for an income but don't have a job. A measure of all people not earning incomes would be of little use. Many of these could not be regarded as a likely source of labour services in the short run. Some would be at school, some retired, and some would be engaged in home duties.

At any time the population can be split into those who are employed and earning incomes and all others. Those not employed can be split further into those not actively seeking employment and those who are. It is the people in this last group that we refer to as the unemployed.

The total workforce at any time is defined as all people currently employed and earning incomes plus all who are currently seeking employment.

Each month, there are two sets of unemployment statistics published, one prepared by the Australian Bureau of Statistics (ABS) and the other by the Commonwealth Employment Service (CES). Neither set of statistics can be regarded as a precise or infallible measure of unemployment.

The ABS figures are derived from a monthly sample survey of households and, because they do not cover a large number of households, are subject to sampling errors. In addition, some households probably supply false information to the interviewers. However, the ABS surveys are specifically designed to measure unemployment and also provide useful information about the unemployed, such as the duration of their unemployment and the size of their families.

In contrast, the CES figures are to a large extent a by-product of their job placement activities. The CES publishes the numbers of people registered as unemployed on the last Friday of each month. They also publish additional information concerning the age, sex, and regional distribution of the registered unemployed. People register with the CES for two reasons: they seek the assistance of the CES in their search for employment, and they *must* register in order to qualify for the payment of unemployment benefits.

However, there are always some people who are unemployed but not registered with the CES. Some prefer to search for employment in their own ways. Others are not eligible for unemployment benefits or wish to avoid what they regard as a stigma attaching to unemployment benefits. There are some people, particularly in times of very high unemployment, who fail to renew their registration with the CES. For these reasons, the CES figures understate the extent of unemployment.

Although less than perfect, these two measures of unemployment in Australia are the best available. Given the different means of estimation, we would not expect these two estimates to coincide closely. On the other hand, each serves as a useful indicator of *changes* in unemployment from period to period.

Both the Australian Bureau of Statistics and the Commonwealth Employment Service release monthly figures on unemployment. However, these statistics have limitations owing to the methods used to collect the data.

Questions

1. At any time there is some unemployment. What are the reasons for this unemployment?

2. Some of the unemployed are frictionally unemployed. What is frictional unemployment?

3. What is meant by general unemployment?

4. (*a*) How is unemployment measured in Australia?
   (*b*) How may unemployment be (i) overstated and (ii) understated by these measures?

THE PRICE STABILITY OBJECTIVE

From period to period, the prices of individual goods and services change in response to different market forces. For example, the prices of many farm products reflect changes in seasonal conditions as well as changes in local and overseas demand. In any period there are some prices that rise and others that fall.

When we refer to "price stability" in a macroeconomic sense, we refer to prices in general — for example, by reference to overall changes in the

Consumer Price Index — as distinct from the prices of individual commodities and services.

Although changes in the prices of individual commodities play an important part in the longer-run allocation of resources between industries — in that rising prices for particular products can be expected to attract resources into those industries, while falling prices have the reverse effect — stable prices, period after period, serve to simplify the tasks of businessmen in planning their investment decisions. The same can be said about prices in general. However, it would be quite remarkable if all increases in prices over any period were nicely offset by decreases in the prices of other products, so that the general level of prices remained unchanged. If this were so, we would have *absolute* price stability. In practice, however, the general level of prices can be expected to change and the best we can hope for is *relative* price stability.

How should we define relative price stability? In Australia, as in similar economies elsewhere, full employment has long been a major economic policy objective. However, as suggested earlier, the attainment of full employment tends to generate upward pressures on money wage rates and prices. In the latter half of the 1960s, it was generally accepted that proximity to full employment necessarily involved an upward movement in the general level of prices — that is, **inflation** — perhaps at an annual rate of 2 or 3 per cent. Some economists in Western Europe went so far as to suggest that a mild rate of inflation served as a useful stimulus to business investment and economic activity. On the other hand, while governments seemed willing to accept inflation at an annual rate of 2 or 3 per cent as a "trade-off" for low levels of unemployment, it soon became clear that they were not prepared to accept annual increases in the general level of prices of the order of 5 per cent or upwards.

In practice, an annual rate of increase in the general level of prices of 2 or possibly 3 per cent can be accepted as consistent with the government's objective of price stability. If, on the other hand, aggregate demand was seen to be clearly pressing hard against the capacity of the economy and the rate of inflation was higher, we would expect the government to introduce measures designed to reduce the demand for output in an attempt to reduce the upward pressures on prices.

In the past, the price stability objective has been seen to have been achieved at inflation rates of 3 per cent or less. Pursuit of an even lower rate of price increase was likely to conflict with the full employment objective.

Questions

1. What is the "price stability" objective?

2. Explain how the objective of full employment may conflict with the price stability objective.

THE EXTERNAL BALANCE OBJECTIVE

What is meant by "external balance"? Although commodity trade and invisible transactions are important elements in our balance of payments, it would be an unnecessarily restrictive view to suggest that we should aim for balance in our transactions on current account. There are frequent changes in both the prices and volumes of exports and imports. So external balance is viewed in the broader sense of our overall balance of payments position.

Proximity to overall balance on a year-to-year basis is not necessary. In the event of running an occasional deficit, we can always draw on our foreign exchange reserves. It is for such circumstances that foreign reserves are held. What this means is that, in practice, external balance is a fairly flexible concept. However, if we were persistently running a surplus or persistently running a deficit in our balance of payments, year after year, then it would be reasonable to suggest that we no longer had external balance.

What the government should do to correct that imbalance depends, as we suggested in chapter 9, on the domestic economic circumstances. If, for example, the Australian economy was operating well below capacity and we found a persistent balance of payments deficit, the government might take steps to stimulate exports and to restrict imports. In contrast, a balance of payments deficit would be no cause for concern if we held more than adequate foreign reserves and faced excess aggregate demand in the Australian economy. In fact, if an increasing proportion of aggregate demand was being met by imports, this might serve to ease the pressures on domestic prices until measures designed to dampen demand had time to take effect.

In other words, the external balance objective is in part dependent on the level of aggregate demand relative to the capacity of the Australian economy. Aggregate demand above the level necessary to ensure full employment can be satisfied only by a sharp increase in the volume of imports. This in turn may threaten external balance.

The *prices* of Australian-produced goods and services compared with those of imports also have effects on our balance of payments. For example, if the rate of increase in prices in the rest of the world was greater than in Australia, we would expect Australians to be substituting home-produced goods for imports — provided, of course, that we had excess capacity available to meet this growing demand. In the reverse situation — that is, where prices in Australia were rising more rapidly than overseas — we would expect a switch from home-produced goods to imports — provided there was no tightening of import restrictions. At the same time, our exporters would find it increasingly difficult to pass on their rising costs to foreign buyers.

So there is a natural conflict between the objectives of full employment, price stability, and external balance. The attainment of one objective is likely to make it increasingly difficult to realize another.

The external balance objective has the function of maintaining a desired level of international reserves. The Reserve Bank of Australia's holding of international reserves is intended to accommodate short-term balance of payments deficits or surpluses. Corrective action to assist the attainment of external balance may be at the cost of the full employment or price stability objectives.

Questions

1. Explain what is meant by the external balance objective.

2. Why may the external balance objective be difficult to attain when there is an inflationary gap?

INDICATORS OF PERFORMANCE

For the purpose of assessing past performance in the Australian economy, there are numerous economic indicators available. For the sake of simplicity, and bearing in mind the major policy objectives of full employment, price stability, and external balance, we have used the following indicators:

1. *The numbers registered for employment and the numbers of job vacancies registered with the CES.* During the first two periods considered, 1950-53 and 1960-63, there were no ABS surveys designed to measure the extent of unemployment. Despite reservations that must be attached to the CES data, we assumed that full employment had been achieved when the numbers of job vacancies were equal to the numbers registered for employment. In those circumstances, we have assumed that there was no "general" unemployment and that those registered for employment were either seasonally, frictionally, or structurally unemployed.

2. *The Consumer Price Index.* Although there are other price indicators available, the CPI is the most widely used indicator of changes in the

general level of prices. It is frequently the basis for union claims, Conciliation and Arbitration Commission wage decisions, and government economic policy judgments.

3. *The values of exports and imports of goods and services.* The value of exports is independent of the level of economic activity in Australia. Imports, on the other hand, are related to the level of production and employment in Australia — except to the extent that restrictions on competition from imports have been deliberately tightened or eased from time to time. Although telling us nothing about Australia's balance of payments, changes in the relationship between exports and imports indicate changes in our balance on current account.

4. *New houses commenced and new motor vehicle registrations.* There are a number of alternative indicators available to show changes in production or sales, including indexes of industrial output and the value of retail sales in different groups of industries. The two indicators selected here were chosen primarily for three reasons. Firstly, the housing and motor vehicle industries are particularly large employers of labour and tend to lead the way in any major downturn or recovery in the demand for labour. Secondly, these two industries have often been singled out by governments for fiscal or monetary action designed to restrain or stimulate the level of economic activity. Thirdly, expenditure on houses and motor vehicles relies heavily on borrowed funds and is therefore strongly influenced by monetary policy.

In the case of the CPI, we have used the value of the index at the end of each quarter. All other data are quarterly averages. These data have been represented in the form of "*time series*" over each of the periods to be considered, with the variables in each case plotted against vertical axes and time represented on the horizontal axis.

THE PERIOD 1950 TO 1953

During World War II, the diversion of many Australians into the armed forces and the production of munitions forced a cutback in production of many consumer goods. Some goods were rationed and others were not available. As a result, households were unable to consume the same proportions of their incomes as they did before the war. So savings accumulated more rapidly in those years.

After the war, most people were looking forward to using those savings to buy goods that had not been available during the war years. However, both time and investment were needed to switch production back to meet peacetime requirements. Realizing that the backlog of demand for consumer and investment goods was likely to drive up prices, the Commonwealth government extended its emergency wartime powers to include price controls on some goods and the issue of permits for the purchase of others.

At the same time, the government's monetary and fiscal policies were contributing further to aggregate demand. The government was intent on a "cheap-money" policy — that is, holding down interest rates — in order to stimulate investment in fixed capital equipment and housing. In each of the years up to 1949, taxation was reduced. For example, tax cuts in the last three years of the 1940s added 3.0, 1.9, and 2.4 per cent respectively to household disposable income.

Following the return of ex-service personnel, there was a sharp increase in the numbers of marriages, adding to the unsatisfied demand for housing. Population was growing rapidly, owing to increasing numbers of immigrants from Western Europe as well as natural increase. During 1950, for example, total population increased by 3.3 per cent. This rapid growth in population not only added to the demand for consumer goods; it also added to the pressures on governments to provide more schools, roads, and other basic services.

Through this period, a strong inflow of foreign capital was boosting Australia's foreign exchange reserves. It was also serving to swell the growing supply of money, the ability of the banks to lend, and the aggregate demand for goods and services.

Nor did overseas trade provide Australia with the means of relieving excess demand by increasing reliance on imports. Our traditional principal source of imports, Western Europe, had suffered widespread destruction of its industrial capacity. Furthermore, merchant shipping losses during the war were so great that freight services betwen Europe and Australia were infrequent and uncertain. On the other hand, Australian farm products like wheat and wool, which had been stockpiled during the war for want of markets and shipping, were quickly snapped up by foreign buyers at rising prices. This led to a further growth in our foreign reserves; but it also added to the demand for goods and services by farmers and their families.

By 1949 an *inflationary gap* was clearly evident and prices were rising. Most of the immediate post-war controls had been removed. However, goods were still in short supply and permits were still required for the purchase of building materials. A coalition of opposition parties promised to remove the last of these controls, as well as to fight the growing inflation. On these promises, the Labor Party government was swept from office.

The situation faced in 1950 by the newly elected government is reflected in the economic indicators shown in figure 25. The extent of the excess demand can be judged by the numbers of registered job vacancies

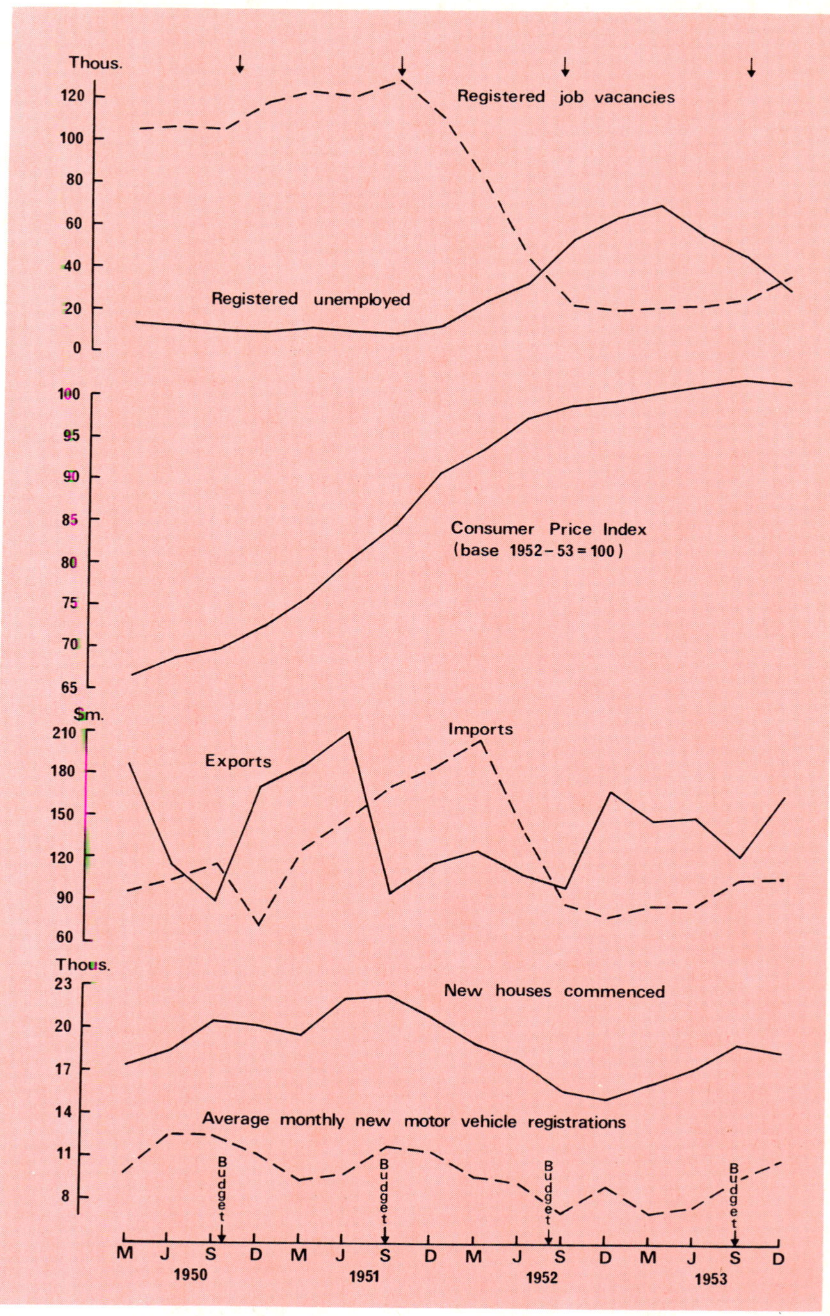

Fig. 25. Economic indicators, 1950-53. (Source: Australian Bureau of Statistics, *Monthly Review of Business Statistics*)

in relation to the registered unemployed. The general level of prices, as indicated by the CPI, was rising at an annual rate of about 9 per cent.

During 1950 the M3 supply of money continued to grow, and the Commonwealth Bank, which at that time carried out the government's central banking functions, attempted to restrict the ability of the banks to lend by requiring sharp increase in Special Account deposits — today's equivalent of SRDs. The government continued to pursue a cheap-money policy. Meanwhile, sales of government securities had grown to such an extent that the central bank found it necessary to engage in large-scale open market purchases to hold up prices and hold down yields. This added further to the supply of money and deposits held by the trading banks, requiring still further calls into Special Accounts. Different monetary policy weapons were therefore working in opposite directions.

Before 1950, sales tax was applied at a uniform rate of 8½ per cent. In its *budget of October 1950*, the government raised the rate of tax on motor vehicles to 10 per cent and the rate on some luxury goods, such as furs and jewellery, to 33⅓ per cent. Strangely enough, the rate of tax on income was reduced still further. In effect, the increase in indirect taxes and reduction in direct taxation cancelled each other out, leaving no overall influence on the demand for consumer goods. Meanwhile, the government increased its own real expenditures. Not surprisingly, the inflationary gap continued to grow, along with money wage rates and prices in general.

Finally, it was the changes in wool prices during the Korean War that forced the government to adopt measures designed to reduce the level of aggregate demand. In July 1950 the index of wool prices (base 1939 = 100) stood at 592. By March 1951 the wool price index had soared to 1437. Combined with an increase in the volume of exports, our export earnings in 1950/51 rose significantly and boosted our foreign reserves. These higher wool prices also served to increase the incomes and spending of woolgrowers, adding further to aggregate demand.

An inflationary gap existed in Australia by 1949 and grew to a peak around August 1951. Various elements had boosted total planned expenditure:

1. **The spending of savings accumulated during World War II**
2. **Government "cheap-money" policies**
3. **A series of reductions in income tax**
4. **Post-war marriages and growing population**
5. **Large capital inflows**
6. **Growing export demand**
7. **Supply problems restricting imports.**
8. **A dramatic surge in wool prices caused by demands associated with the Korean War**

The money supply was growing even more rapidly, despite a further sharp increase in deposits required to be lodged in the Special Accounts held by the central bank. By the third quarter of 1951, excess demand was at a peak and prices were rising at an annual rate in excess of 20 per cent. Clearly, the coalition government's promise to bring a halt to inflation had not been realized. Worse still, wool prices had fallen sharply to a level lower than a year earlier, while imports were beginning to grow — presenting a threat to the objective of external balance.

Early in the second quarter of 1951, the government faced a general election. This helps to explain the delay in the introduction of restrictive and politically unpalatable measures earlier in that year. However, by the time of its budget in 1951, the rate of inflation was very high and foreign exchange reserves were falling rapidly. A "touch on the tiller" would have achieved very little; by that time, what was required was a sharp change in direction.

The *budget of September 1951*, sometimes referred to as the "horror budget", was a remarkable event in several ways. The treasurer, for the first time, suggested that the government could and should use fiscal policy as a means of stabilizing the level of economic activity. He stated that while in times of high unemployment the government must be prepared to spend in excess of its revenue, when faced with excess demand there was, in contrast, a need to increase taxes and to run a budget surplus. That is, the government indicated its agreement with the basic prescriptions of John Maynard Keynes.

Having said this, the treasurer then announced increases in both direct and indirect taxes. For example, the general rate of sales tax was raised from 8½ to 12½ per cent, the rate on new motor vehicles was raised to 20 per cent, and the rate on some luxury goods was raised to 66⅔ per cent. The overall increase in taxation was equivalent to about 6 per cent of household income before tax during the 1951/52 financial year. Not surprisingly, consumption expenditure in real terms fell by about 2½ per cent in that year.

At the same time, the government increased the rate of company tax and introduced the requirement that companies pay part of their expected tax liability *in advance*. Special depreciation allowances for tax purposes, introduced in 1946 in an attempt to stimulate investment in fixed capital equipment, were withdrawn. Taken together, these measures were clearly intended to dampen investment in fixed equipment and did, in part, have that effect. Meanwhile, however, government sector expenditure was planned to *rise* in real terms — a strategy strongly in conflict with the treasurer's view of the government's responsibilities in these circumstances.

These fiscal measures resulted in an immediate decline in aggregate demand — as indicated in figure 25 by the demand for new houses and motor vehicles as well as by the numbers of job vacancies. In addition, import orders that had been placed before the September budget continued to flow in. These imports presented serious competition to domestic producers in the weakening Australian market and resulted in further cuts in production and employment.

As demand dropped, Australian firms were faced with unintended inventory accumulation. With falling sales and growing liquidity problems, they turned to the banks to borrow funds to finance this inventory investment. Public deposits with the banks were falling and the liquid assets of the banks fell to dangerously low levels — one reason being the absence of an LGS convention such as we have to day. The central bank responded by releasing deposits from its Special Accounts. It also stepped up its purchases of government securities with the object of increasing deposits and cash held by the banks. Even so, the banks faced such a shortage of cash that by January 1952 they had borrowed $136 million from the central bank at penalty rates of interest. In these circumstances, there was widespread and growing uncertainty concerning future business prospects.

At the time of the budget in September 1951, the government was not particularly concerned with the growing inflow of imports. Given the excess demand that existed at that time, imports were seen as a means of relieving the pressures of demand on the general level of prices. However, the government had not allowed for the growing volume of imports in response to orders placed before its September budget. Our balance of payments deficit continued to grow, and in March 1952 the government announced severe quantitative restrictions on imports from all sources. The effect of those restrictions on the value of imports can be seen in figure 25. During the financial year 1951/52, our export earnings fell to $1,334 million. Despite import restrictions, our balance of payments on current account fell from a surplus of $466 million in 1950/51 to a deficit of $766 million in 1951/52. Our foreign reserves slumped to $724 million.

In March 1952 import quotas were introduced. The balance of payments had moved into deficit owing to a turn-around of wool prices and substantial imports. Many of these imports had been ordered in mid 1951, when the economy was booming, but arrived, after some time lag, when demand had dropped.

In an attempt to improve our balance of payments position, the government gave high priority to a number of incentives designed to encourage farm investment, production, and exports. Owing to lags between investment decisions and the following growth in production, these measures had no immediate effect on the volume of exports. However, they did contribute substantially to the growth in farm production and exports in later years.

The *budget of August 1952* was introduced several weeks earlier than usual, apparently in response to growing concern about the slump in economic activity. The excess demand for labour had been eliminated and unemployment had grown to 1.9 per cent of the workforce. In contrast to the years since 1948, the M3 supply of money had fallen and the rate of growth in the CPI was slowing down. As a result of the import restrictions and an improvement in export prices, our foreign reserves were beginning to show signs of recovery.

In an attempt to counter the effects of its 1951 budget, the government introduced slight reductions in both indirect and direct taxes. On the other hand, after steady growth, year after year, the government *reduced* its own real expenditures. Real consumption expenditure continued to fall and the former steady growth in fixed capital expenditure was temporarily put into reverse — despite further releases from Special Accounts in an attempt to stimulate lending. By March 1953, unemployment had grown to 2.7 per cent of the workforce.

During the second and third quarters of 1953, consumption and investment expenditures showed signs of recovery. This was due, in part, to the effects of import restrictions, which diverted demand to home-produced goods and allowed trading enterprises to dispose of their unwanted inventories. It was also due to rising export prices and incomes, growing farm investment, and a recovery in public confidence.

This period is of particular interest in that it was marked by the Commonwealth government's first attempts to use *fiscal policy* to stabilize the level of economic activity. The "sharp shock" treatment handed out in the budget of 1951 was certainly effective in eliminating excess demand. But it also served to undermine public confidence. It could be argued that the government should have introduced milder ("touch on the tiller") restraints on the economy a year earlier; further, that the government itself contributed to the inflationary gap in the early fifties because it continued to increase its own expenditures long after excess aggregate demand was evident.

Admittedly, it is not always easy *at the time* to be certain of either the need for action or the severity of the measures required. Yet it is clear that the government was slow to act in the early fifties. When it did finally intervene, the time for moderate restrictive measures was already past. The boom was quickly brought to an end. But in the process, business confidence was dealt a severe blow. Then, when the economy seemed in need of a mild stimulus, late in 1952, the government decided to cut back its own expenditures. On the whole then, fiscal policy in this period was to some extent destabilizing in its effects.

Although the government action contained in the September 1951 "horror budget" was too late and too heavy handed, this first important exercise in fiscal policy demonstrated that fiscal policy can be a very powerful weapon. The inflation rate fell dramatically following reductions in total planned expenditure.

Question

1. Describe the economic conditions in the period 1950-52, under the following headings:
   a. Inflation
   b. Money supply — monetary policy
   c. Fiscal policy
   d. Employment
   e. External balance

THE PERIOD 1960 TO 1963

During the latter half of 1959, aggregate demand was growing strongly. In November of that year, the central bank, in an attempt to restrict new lending, called an additional $30 million into Special Accounts, increasing the SRD ratio to 15.5 per cent.

In 1959 the central banking functions of the Commonwealth Bank were transferred to a new institution, the Reserve Bank. In principle, the means of restricting credit seemed quite clear. The Reserve Bank could request the trading banks to restrict new lending and cut back their total advances outstanding. If the banks failed to heed such a request, an increase in the SRD ratio would force the banks to take the required action.

However, one of the major problems faced by the Reserve Bank at that time was the wide difference in free reserves held by the individual banks — ranging from as little as 5 per cent of deposit liabilities to almost 20 per cent. An increase in the SRD ratio to about 20 per cent would have wiped out the free reserves of some banks, while leaving others able to greatly increase their lending.

In February 1960 the Reserve Bank reached agreement with the banks to raise the LGS convention from 14 to 16 per cent. The SRD ratio was raised to 16.9 per cent in that month and was lifted further to 17.4 per cent in March. However, after a slight reduction in their lending early in 1960, bank advances continued to grow — even though three of the eight major trading banks had found it necessary to borrow from the Reserve Bank in order to maintain the required LGS convention.

At that time, the maximum rate of interest on advances was 6 per cent, but this was much higher than the rates of interest available on government securities. So lending by way of overdraft was a more attractive alternative. Furthermore, the government faced a general election in the following year and there was a widespread belief that it would not risk imposing really severe credit restrictions. So bank lending continued to grow.

Meanwhile, in the first quarter of 1960, the Commonwealth government removed the last remaining restrictions on imports, argued for restraint by the **Conciliation and Arbitration Commission** in the fixing of minimum wage rates — at that time referred to as the **Basic Wage** — and indicated its intention to tighten up on government sector expenditure. Each of these actions was intended to dampen the rate of inflation.

By the third quarter of 1960, as indicated in figure 26, employment had fallen almost to the point of matching the registered numbers of job vacancies. The CPI was rising at an annual rate of almost 6 per cent. The demand for new houses and new motor vehicles was growing rapidly and, as we would expect in a full employment situation, so too was the demand for imports.

The growing inflationary gap of 1959/60 caused problems for price stability. Government action to dampen demand before November 1960 included credit restrictions, the lifting of import restrictions, and submissions to the Conciliation and Arbitration Commission for wage restraint.

The *budget of August 1960* was very mild in these circumstances and did little to suggest that the government was aiming to sharply reduce aggregate demand. Company tax was raised by 2½ per cent, a 5 per cent rebate on personal income tax during 1959/60 was withdrawn, and very minor changes were made in the structure of indirect taxes. On the other hand, the government planned to increase its own real expenditure by 7 per cent. Overall, what this amounted to was a slight reallocation of resources away from households and trading enterprises towards the government sector.

Only three months later, on 15 November 1960, the government introduced a **supplementary budget.** The government was concerned with the increasing volume of imports and the growing deficit in our balance of trade on current account — by that time having reached an annual rate in excess of $600 million. The treasurer claimed that excess demand, *particularly in the building and motor vehicle industries*, had created ''serious shortages of labour'' that were forcing up costs and prices; further, that the materials and components used in these industries were

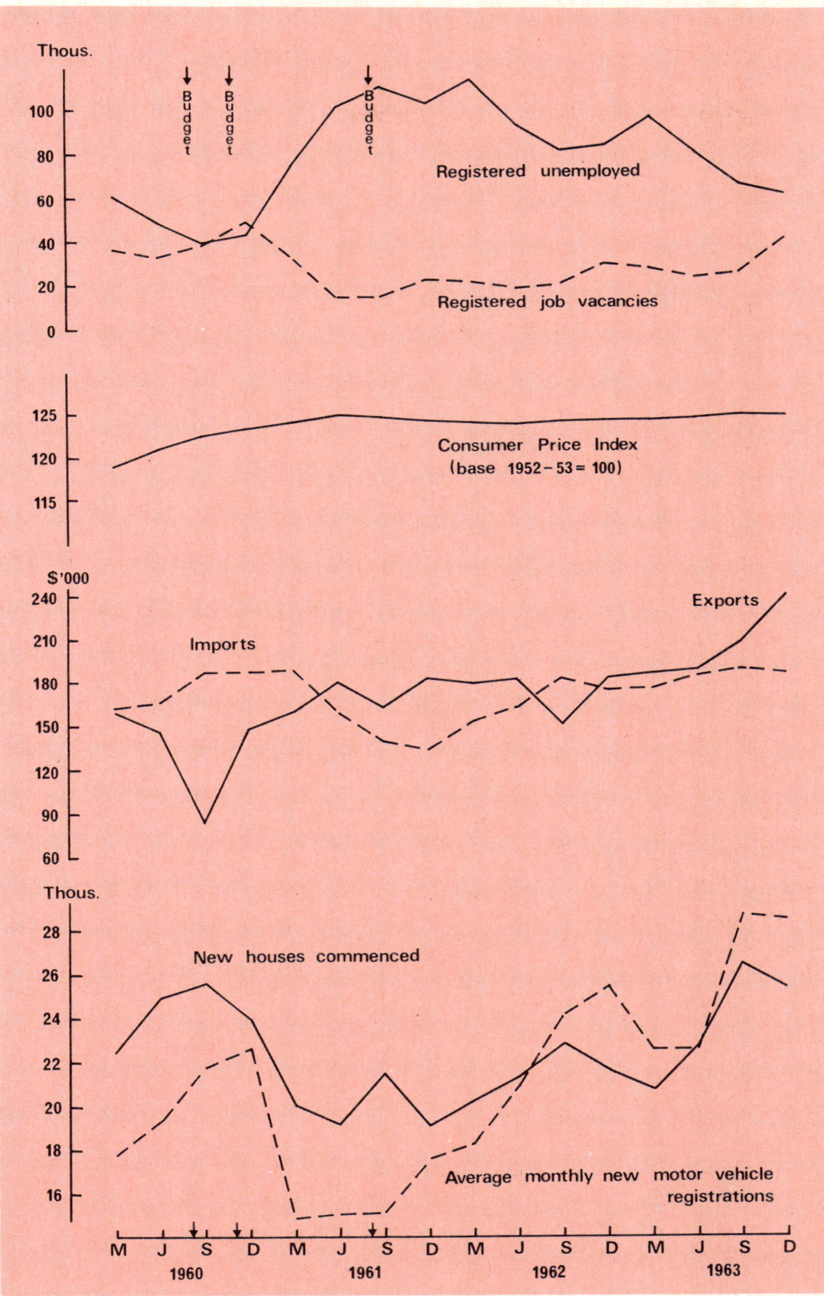

Fig. 26.   Economic indicators, 1960-63. (Source: Australian Bureau of Statistics, *Monthly Review of Business Statistics*)

THE AUSTRALIAN CONCILIATION AND ARBITRATION COMMISSION

Following many major industrial disputes during the Depression of the 1890s, the Constitution provided for a Commonwealth court to assist in the settlement of disputes regarding wage rates and working conditions. The first court was established soon after Federation and was succeeded in 1956 by what is now known as the Australian Conciliation and Arbitration Commission. This industrial court has jurisdiction to act in industrial disputes which extend beyond the boundaries of any one state. Disputes affecting only workers in any one state are handled by individual state tribunals.

Over the years, the commission has assumed a leading role in the fixing of wage rates—not only through its decisions concerning disputes that extend across state borders, but also because state tribunals tend automatically to grant "flow-on" increases to workers operating under state awards following increases in wage rates granted by the commission to workers subject to federal awards.

The commission has frequently argued that it has a responsibility to reach wage decisions that are in the best interests of the economy as a whole. On the other hand, it is well aware that its powers to restrain increases in money wage rates are limited. Employers and unions often negotiate directly and reach agreement without consultation with the commission. As a consequence, the commission must periodically determine increases in wage rates for *all* Australian workers, bearing in mind that some workers must rely on these decisions as the only means of catching up with rising prices, while others who have independently negotiated increases in wage rates will *also* benefit to the same extent from such decisions.

In his 1977 Annual Report, the president of the commission indicated that 5,559 matters had been lodged with the commission for consideration. Of these, only 161 were heard by the Full Bench of the court. The remaining matters were dealt with by individual commissioners, frequently serving to assist disputing parties to reach voluntary agreement—that is, in the "conciliation" role of the commissioners.

Source: *Annual Report*, the president of the Australian Conciliation and Arbitration Commission, various issues.

contributing to the growth in imports and serving to reduce exports of steel — thereby contributing to our balance of payments problems.

Despite a tight rein held on SRDs and repeated requests by the Reserve Bank that the banks restrict their lending activities, bank advances during 1960 had grown by 15 per cent over 1959. The government indicated that it intended to take immediate steps to reduce liquidity in the economy and suggested that monetary conditions would be tightened still further in the second quarter of 1961. The Reserve Bank would give much more specific guidance to the banks concerning the direction of their lending, with a view to cutting back on funds available for hire purchase and other forms of consumer credit, share market and other speculative activities, and the financing of inventory accumulation. Such restrictions on credit were *not* to be applied to export industries.

The government was also aware of the part played by non-bank intermediaries in the expansion of credit for consumption purposes and speculative purchases of shares and land. The treasurer admitted that the government could see no immediate means of controlling the activities of non-bank intermediaries. However, in an attempt to restrict their funds and lending activities, the government introduced three measures: an increase in the rates of interest paid by the banks on fixed deposits, designed to make such deposits more attractive than financial assets offered by the non-bank intermediaries; the introduction of limits on tax deductibility of interest paid on loans; and legislation to force life insurance, superannuation, and provident fund organizations to hold at least 30 per cent of their assets in the form of government securities. At the same time, the maximum bank overdraft rate was raised to 7 per cent, the only exception being that the banks were directed to offer preferential rates to export industries.

Finally, in this supplementary budget, the government raised the rate of sales tax on new cars and station wagons from 30 to 40 per cent in a deliberate attempt to cut back sales and production in the motor vehicle industry.

In conclusion, the treasurer stated: "We judge these [measures] to be no less and no more than necessary to make stability real in terms of costs and prices, and to achieve internal balance between demand and supply and external balance between overseas receipts and expenditures. . . . The test will lie with events."

In the second half of 1961 there were signs of excess aggregate demand. But the magnitude of the inflationary gap was quite small compared with the situation in the early 1950s. The events that followed the government's supplementary budget of November 1960 suggest that the government over-reacted to the circumstances at that time.

During the four months following this supplementary budget, SRDs were raised further and the trading banks put into reverse the former steady growth in advances outstanding. By February 1961, advances had dropped by 6.3 per cent below the level a year earlier. New motor vehicle registrations, hit by both the increase in sales tax and restrictions on consumer credit, fell by 32.5 per cent in December. In January there was a further sharp fall in the numbers of new vehicles registered. The numbers of new houses commenced during the first quarter of 1961 was down by 16 per cent on commencements in the December quarter of 1960. As unemployment and pessimism spread to other industries, retail sales fell much further than usually expected in the first quarter seasonal trough.

The outcome of the November 1960 measures demonstrated the powerful effect that strong monetary measures can have on economic activity.

The government was clearly worried by the extent of the reaction to the measures introduced in its supplementary budget. From 22 February 1961 the former 30 per cent sales tax on cars and station wagons was restored, but the sales of motor vehicles were slow to respond. New house commencements were consistently about 18 per cent lower than in 1960, and retail sales, instead of following the seasonal pattern and recovering in the June quarter, fell even further. Inventories piled up, and the stage was set for a sharp cutback in production.

By June 1961, registered unemployment had grown to 111,700. Registered job vacancies had slumped from 52,700 in November 1960 to 12,300. As the deflationary gap opened up, the increase in the general level of prices was brought to a halt and imports shared the effects of the decline in aggregate demand.

At the time of the *budget in August 1961*, the unemployed represented almost 3.6 per cent of the workforce. Price stability had been restored, and the former unfavourable balance of trade had been reversed: in fact, our foreign reserves had grown steadily in each month after February.

In these circumstances, some fiscal stimulus to economic activity was widely expected. However, tax relief was very limited. Sales tax on household furniture and appliances was reduced by 2½ per cent, and income tax concessions were restricted to primary producers, miners, and relatively small disadvantaged groups in the community. These concessions together were expected to result in a cost of total tax revenue equivalent to only 0.8 per cent of that revenue. At the same time, the government planned to raise its own expenditure by 3.5 per cent, planning for a small deficit.

The government apparently believed that this evidence of easing fiscal restraint on economic activity would prove sufficient to start a recovery. But it had seriously underestimated the effects on business confidence of the events of 1960/61, and its budget did very little to change expectations about the future. At the end of 1961 the government faced a general election and, not surprisingly, lost many seats and was returned with the barest possible majority.

Early in 1962 unemployment reached a new peak as school leavers sought to join the workforce. In February the government reduced the rate of sales tax on new cars and station wagons to 22½ per cent and re-introduced the 5 per cent rebate on personal income tax. From March onwards the Reserve Bank rapidly reduced the SRD ratio, and the banks quickly responded by increasing their advances. But retail sales (other than motor vehicles) during the first half of 1962 were 3 per cent lower than in the first half of 1961. Furthermore, trading enterprises were meeting part of the demand for consumer goods by running down inventories accumulated during 1961 and not entirely from current production. Inventory disinvestment, combined with a reduction in fixed capital expenditures, resulted in a fall of 28 per cent in private investment expenditure in the financial year 1961/62 compared with the preceding year.

Despite the government's attempts to stimulate economic activity by reducing both direct and indirect taxes and a sharp reversal in credit conditions, recovery was very slow. At regular intevals, members of the government claimed that future business prospects had never looked brighter. However, businessmen preferred to base their decisions on tangible evidence — namely, their current sales and the levels of their inventories. It was not until the middle of 1963 that there were clear signs of recovery, and it was only in the last quarter of that year that Australia was again approaching the full employment level of production.

What emerged from the experience of the early 1960s is that governments need to closely monitor business expectations as well as all economic indicators available, to use more frequent but much milder changes in monetary and fiscal policies — in effect, as "touches on the tiller" — and to avoid sharply restrictive measures that serve to shatter business confidence. Once expectations about the future have been revised sharply downwards, it requires much more than the oratory of government members to restore business confidence. Meanwhile, the cost of "sharp shock" treatment, in terms of jobs lost and production forgone, can be very high.

The events of the 1960s emphasize the importance of timing and decisive action in managing the economy.

Question

1. Describe the Australian economy in the period 1960 to 1963 under the following headings:
   a. Inflation
   b. Money supply — monetary policy
   c. Fiscal policy
   d. Employment
   e. External balance

THE PERIOD 1972 TO 1975

During 1971 there were already signs of problems that were to grow in severity in the latter half of the 1970s. The CPI (base 1966/67 = 100) had increased by 7.2 per cent. Unemployment was growing and by the March quarter of 1972 represented 2.1 per cent of the workforce. There was also a growing deficit in our balance of payments on current account, due in part to the lowest wool prices in many years. Consistent with its previous approach to management of the economy, the coalition government had been keeping a tight rein on fiscal and monetary policies.

From early in 1972 the level of economic activity showed signs of recovery. Wool prices increased very sharply, as did the prices received for wheat and beef. The balance of payments on current account swung sharply from a deficit in 1971 to a surplus that grew throughout 1972. The demand for new houses and motor vehicles began to rise quickly, and there was moderate growth in demand for most other consumer goods. This recovery in demand was assisted by easier credit conditions and lower interest rates. However, as in the early sixties, this recovery in demand was at first met in part by a running down of inventories accumulated during 1971. For this reason, the demand for labour tended to lag behind the recovery in the demand for output.

In its *budget in August 1972*, the government expressed concern about two features of the economy — the level of unemployment and the rate of inflation. Referring to the level of unemployment at the end of July, the treasurer stated: "This figure . . . is too high for us and we are determined to reduce it." Speaking of "the evils of inflation", he admitted that prices were rising more rapidly than at any time since the Korean War boom. "This process has to be stopped and reversed," he stated.

The budget was intended to stimulate activity, in part perhaps in response to widespread discontent with what was then regarded as a high level of unemployment and mindful of the approaching general election in December 1972. The government planned to increase its expenditure by 11.6 per cent in money terms or about 5 per cent in real terms — raising its allocation for education by 20 per cent, increasing home savings grants, and again raising age and invalid pensions. Apart from a slight increase in excise duties on petroleum products, there were no changes in indirect taxes. On the other hand, the government raised the minimum level of income subject to tax, increased concessional allowances for dependants, and cut rates of personal income tax by an average of 10 per cent. The cost to revenue of these reductions in taxation was estimated at $565 million. In all, the government budgeted for a deficit of $630 million.

There was no doubt that this budget would serve to stimulate economic activity. How the government proposed to restrain inflation was not at all

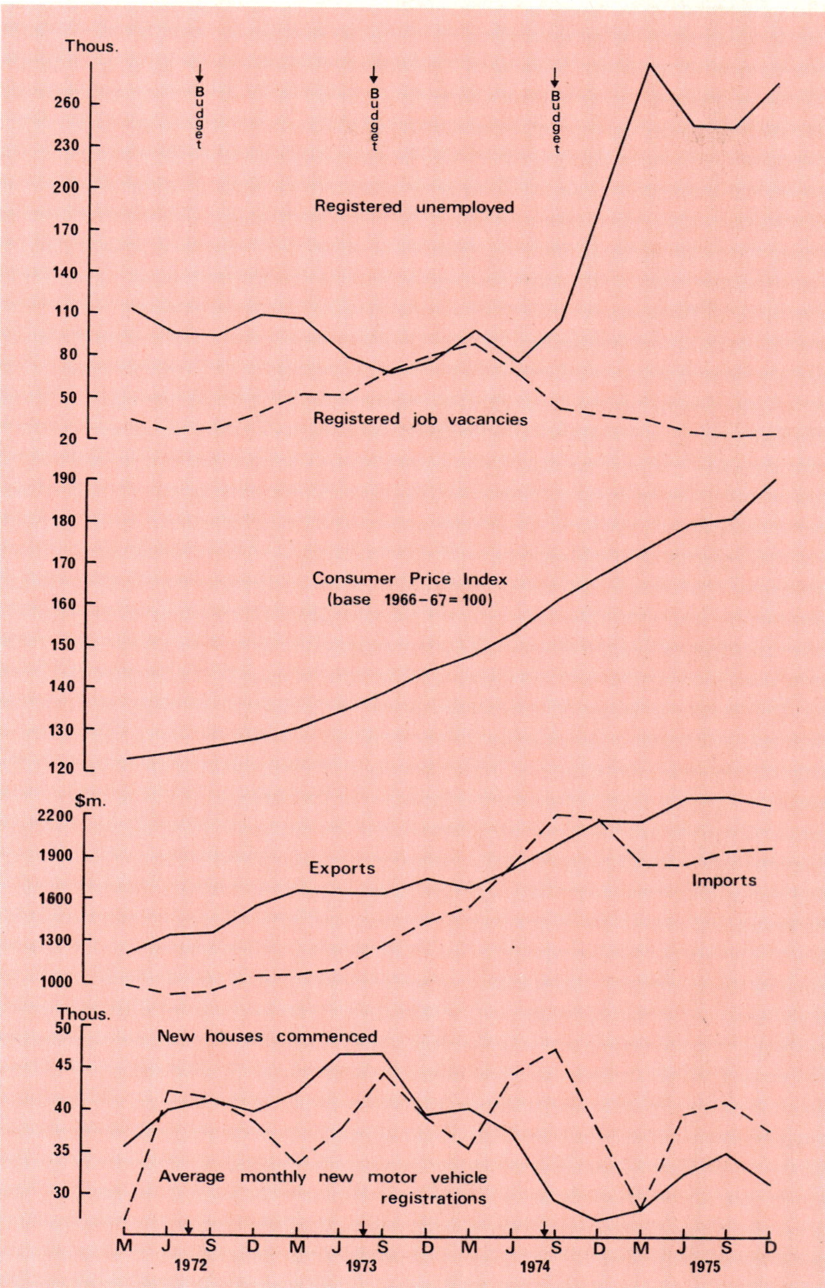

Fig. 27. Economic indicators, 1972-75. (Source: Australian Bureau of Statistics. *Monthly Review of Business Statistics*)

clear. Since the government was swept from office by the Labor Party only four months later, we have no means of knowing how the coalition government would have responded to falling unemployment and growing inflation had it remained in power.

During the second half of 1972, private capital inflow had been growing rapidly, adding to growth in the supply of money and increasing further the surplus in our balance of payments brought about by the high farm export prices. In its first month in office, the new government *revalued* the Australian dollar by almost 5 per cent. This was intended to dampen private capital inflow and to reduce the rate of growth in the money supply. It was also a means of making imports cheaper in comparison to Australian-produced goods, and it was hoped that this would ease the upward pressure on domestic prices. At the same time, the government introduced a **Variable Deposit Requirement (VDR)** scheme under which, initially, 25 per cent of overseas borrowings was required to be deposited, *interest free*, with the Reserve Bank. One effect of revaluation and the VDR scheme was to reverse the former capital inflow. In fact, private capital *outflow* in February 1973 exceeded $300 million.

The growth in government sector expenditure, set in motion by the budget of 1972, was adding substantially to aggregate demand. Monetary conditions were easier during the first half of 1973, and both the LGS assets and advances of the trading banks were growing rapidly. During the financial year 1972/73, real consumption expenditure, stimulated by rising money incomes and lower tax rates, increased by about 5 per cent. There was a sharp increase in new houses commenced, as well as in commercial and industrial building. Investment in machinery and equipment was also growing, particularly in the mining industry.

By the end of the financial year in June 1973, real GDP had grown by 4 per cent over the previous year. This was due in part to an increase of 135,000 in the numbers employed. There were also increases in overtime worked and in the productivity of labour. The gap between registered unemployment and registered vacancies was rapidly closing. Meanwhile, despite revaluation and introduction of the VDR scheme, foreign reserves had grown from $3,737 million to $4,248 million. The volume of imports was growing, in part as a result of the lower cost of imports and in part in response to growing aggregate demand in Australia. However, the high level of foreign reserves suggested that this was not a matter for immediate concern.

Only one problem remained: namely, the rising rate of inflation. During 1972 the productivity of labour had increased by 2.8 per cent. However, money wage rates increased more rapidly, and the real labour cost per unit of output increased by 6.7 per cent. These rising labour costs were feeding into prices, showing up in the CPI and providing the trade unions with a basis for claims for further increases in money wage rates.

The government, having unsuccessfully sought an extension of its constitutional powers to allow for direct control over prices and incomes, introduced two measures in an attempt to reduce the rate of growth in prices. In July 1973 *the government reduced all tariffs by 25 per cent.* In the face of cheaper imports, it was expected that Australian manufacturers would be forced to hold down their prices. Secondly, the government established the **Prices Justification Tribunal** (PJT), which came into effect on 1 August 1973.

The legislation under which the PJT was established required all companies or affiliated groups of companies with total annual sales of $20 million or more to notify the tribunal of their intention to raise prices. The tribunal could either approve the proposed increases or hold public inquiries to determine the extent to which increases in prices were justified. The companies concerned were forbidden to raise their prices before the PJT had reached its decisions. To the extent that time was required both to prepare their cases and for the PJT to make decisions, there developed lags between the intention to raise prices and the implementation of price increases. Furthermore, in an attempt to gain relatively quick approval, rather than risk drawn-out inquiries, many companies appeared to seek smaller increases in prices than they believed to be justified — simply in order to recover part of their rising costs as quickly as possible.

In his first annual report, the chairman of the PJT drew attention to "a tendency for companies to negotiate [with unions] substantial wage increases". He made it clear that, in the event of industrial disputes involving excessive wage demands, *management must bear the blame if industrial peace was bought at too high a price.* In other words, increases in labour costs were not automatically accepted as a basis for raising prices. Meanwhile, the share of gross profits in total value added was falling, and it was not at all clear how far profits could be squeezed without threatening the longer-run survival of individual firms and industries. To the extent that the PJT was successful in holding down prices and gross profits, it also contributed to the liquidity problems experienced by some firms and industries in the years that followed.

The new government, before its election, had promised major reforms in social welfare, education, and the quality of urban life. Naturally, the government was anxious to make a start on these reforms as soon as possible, and it saw *the budget of August 1973* as a means to that end.

By that time the economy was very close to full employment and many industries were operating at their designed capacity. The treasurer admitted that inflation was the major economic problem facing the government. However, he suggested that an increase in imports following the 25 per cent tariff cut would "help to ease inflationary strains".

Although some expenditures were cut back sharply — particularly assistance to farm industries — the government planned to increase expenditure in money terms by 18.9 per cent over expenditure realized in 1972/73. Spending on social security was planned to rise by 16 per cent, health by 25 per cent, education by 92 per cent, and housing and community amenities by 324 per cent.

The rate structure of tax on personal income was more continuously progressive at that time than it is now. Since the money incomes of wage and salary earners were rising fairly rapidly, these people were losing an increasing proportion of their incomes to direct taxation. Even so, total expenditure was planned to rise more rapidly than estimated receipts. In order to implement its promised reforms, the government therefore sought to increase its revenue. Numerous tax concessions formerly available to primary producers and some concessions to other firms were abolished. Payroll tax was increased in the Commonwealth territories. Excise duties were raised on petroleum products, spirits, and tobacco. However, there was no change in the rates of tax on personal income. Despite these increases in revenue, the government planned for a deficit of $687 million.

The new government could not be blamed for seeking to put into effect its pre-election promises. However, at the time of its first budget, the economy was again operating close to its capacity. So perhaps the government should have accepted a need to "hasten slowly" with its reforms. Admittedly, it had reason to expect that market supplies would be increased by a growing volume of imports. Nevertheless, the planned increase in government expenditure could only add further to aggregate demand — unless, of course, the government was prepared to increase taxes to a greater extent in order to transfer a greater proportion of available resources from the private to the public sector.

An inflationary gap existed in Australia in 1973. Total planned expenditure increased because of—
1. **a rapid growth in the money supply due to the government budget deficit and balance of payments surpluses;**
2. **expansionary budgets of August 1972 and August 1973.**

After the budget, the government increased the VDR on overseas borrowings to 33 per cent in an attempt to reduce private capital inflow still further. In September 1973 the Australian dollar was *revalued* by a further 5 per cent, making imported goods even cheaper compared with Australian-produced goods.

By the end of 1973 the demand for labour was slightly in excess of the available supply. During that year average weekly earnings per employed male unit had increased by 15.3 per cent, while labour productivity had increased only slightly. Despite the effects of revaluations of the

Australian dollar and tariff cuts in reducing import prices, the CPI rose by 13.2 per cent. Rising wage rates were finding their way into prices, and rising prices were providing the foundation for further claims for increases in money wage rates.

In the second half of 1973 the Reserve Bank increased SRDs and asked the bank to restrict new lending. More importantly, in an attempt to ease demand pressures, the government requested that the savings banks restrict their lending for housing. In the December quarter, new housing commencements dropped sharply.

The government responses to the inflationary gap were:
1. **Fiscal policy — no restraint, owing to election promises**
2. **Monetary policy — increases in SRDs**
3. **External policy — revaluations, 25 per cent tariff cut, VDR**
4. **Incomes policy — referendum for control over prices and wages (lost), the PJT, and support for wage indexation.**

Late in 1973 and early in 1974 the effects of successive revaluations of the Australian dollar and the 25 per cent across-the-board tariff cuts also began to have their effects. The volume of imports of textiles, clothing, footwear, motor vehicles, and a wide range of consumer durables was growing rapidly and had reached almost double the level of a year earlier. Foreign reserves were falling rapidly, in part because of the growing volume of imports but also because the peak in farm export prices had passed. From the second quarter of 1974 there was a sharp increase in world crude oil prices, followed by increases in the prices of other imported goods. As our foreign reserves fell further, the government reduced VDRs in an attempt to encourage private capital inflow.

Meanwhile, consumption expenditure was rising much less rapidly than the growth in money incomes. This was due, in part, to an increasing proportion of household income being lost by way of direct taxation. But there was also evidence, as indicated in figure 4, that households were consuming less and saving more of their disposable incomes. At the same time, an increasing part of consumer demand was being met by imported goods.

When sales of Australian-produced motor vehicles slumped in the last quarter of 1973 and continued to fall early in 1974, the government introduced a *temporary* reduction in sales tax on vehicles to 15 per cent. At the same time, the government made it clear that this tax would be raised again, by 2½ per cent per month, starting from May, until restored to the former level of 27½ per cent. Many people brought forward their spending plans, and buyers were quick to take advantage of the temporarily lower prices. The motor vehicle industry geared up for higher sales and production. It was not surprising that sales fell back sharply once the former level of sales tax had been restored.

During the first half of 1974, monetary conditions were very tight and interest rates were rising. New lending slowed down, and some of the trading banks found it necessary to borrow from the Reserve Bank in order to meet the LGS convention.

By the middle of 1974, activity in the building industry had slowed considerably. The motor vehicle industry was recovering, but only because of the temporary reduction in sales tax. Some industries, particularly textiles, clothing, footwear, and electrical goods, were struggling against the growing tide of low-priced imports while themselves facing sharply rising labour costs per unit of output. Inventories were growing rapidly, and some of the firms most directly in competition with imported goods were already dismissing workers. At the same time, there were already signs of declining business confidence in the building industry.

Meanwhile, the government and its advisers continued to be preoccupied with the belief that the principal source of our problems lay in excess aggregate demand. Early in June 1974 the government announced that it intended to reduce its own spending in an attempt to ease demand pressures. It was noted that unemployment was higher than expected in these circumstances. The Reserve Bank suggested that this might have been due to the higher level of unemployment benefit being paid and an increased preference for leisure among younger people.

After winning another general election, the Labor government introduced its second *budget in September 1974.* In introducing that budget, the treasurer referred to the government's "firm action . . . to moderate excessive demand and, through exchange rate adjustments and tariff reductions, to increase supplies". He admitted that inflation was a major problem, but was quick to make clear the government's attitude: "*The conventional response to inflation has relied almost entirely on the creation of mass unemployment. Those who advocate such a course in present conditions are unable to say what level of unemployment would markedly reduce inflation. The government is not prepared deliberately to create a level of 4 or 5 per cent or perhaps even higher unemployment.*"

The treasurer stated that the government had no intention of again contributing to excess demand pressures. Yet, having said this, he annouced that the government planned to increase its expenditure by 32.4 per cent over its actual expenditure in 1973/74. Most of this increase in expenditure was again directed towards education, health, social security and welfare, and urban-regional development. In addition, the government introduced a *Structural Adjustment Assistance* scheme, under which the government planned to assist people thrown out of work as a direct result of the government's policies — for example, the reduction in tariff protection. At the same time, the government gave increasing emphasis to the **Rural Reconstruction Scheme** and retraining for all people structurally unemployed.

The government planned to increase revenue by raising excise duties, increasing payroll tax, further withdrawal of tax concessions to firms, and a 10 per cent tax surcharge on income derived from property. On the other hand, the budget provided assistance to people in the lower to middle income groups in two ways — firstly, by making interest on housing loans tax deductible, and secondly, by restructuring rates of tax on personal income to provide relief for people with less than average incomes. Allowing for these changes in taxation, receipts were expected to rise by 30.8 per cent. Overall, the government budgeted for a deficit of $571 million.

Contrary to the expectations of the government, the stage was already set for a sharp decline in production and employment. The building industry was continuing to slow down, and new motor vehicle sales dropped sharply after the former level of sales tax had been restored. The successive revaluations of the Australian dollar, combined with tariff cuts, had reduced the cost of imported goods, while Australian producers faced rising labour costs per unit of output. The share of gross profits in total value added continued to fall. As people began to lose their jobs, others saved more and consumed less in attempts to provide financial reserves against possible loss of their own jobs. Inventories accumulated rapidly, and as firms cut back production more people lost their jobs. With a tight rein held on the ability of the banks to lend, many firms were unable to finance their growing inventories and faced a liquidity crisis; in fact, some were unable to meet their unavoidable commitments, and the numbers of company failures started to grow.

From the time of the budget in September 1974, the fiscal, monetary, and external restraints on economic activity were progressively reversed. In September the government *devalued* the Australian dollar by 12 per cent. This had the immediate effect of making imports less competitive, but it *also* had the effect of adding to the upward pressures on prices in Australia. In an attempt to ease the liquidity problems of firms, the Reserve Bank reduced SRDs from about 9 per cent in the middle of 1974 to 3 per cent in October. The trading banks were asked to increase their lending, and the savings banks were urged to lend more for home purchases. In November, direct tax on wage and salary earnings was cut by 7 per cent and the rate of company taxation was reduced by 2½ per cent. Meanwhile, the government sharply increased its own spending.

Despite these measures, there was no halting the consequences of the collapse in business confidence. In May 1974 the numbers registered for employment with the CES represented 1.3 per cent of the workforce. By February 1975 registered unemployment represented 4.9 per cent of the workforce. Over the same period the ABS estimate of unemployment rose from 2.1 to 5.4 per cent. Meanwhile, there was a sharp fall in the numbers of registered job vacancies.

From the second half of 1974, production and employment fell sharply. Some contributing factors were:
1. The effect of earlier revaluations and tariff cuts
2. The restoration of the motor vehicle sales tax
3. The 1974 wage explosion, which caused profits to fall
4. An increase in savings
5. Tight bank liquidity caused by monetary policy

Meanwhle, in marked contrast to previous experience, the strong inflationary trend continued. During the year ended December 1974, average adult male earnings increased by 28.2 per cent, labour productivity increased only very slightly, and the CPI increased by a further 16.3 per cent.

Late in 1974 the government accepted the need to restrain the growth in money wage rates. In December the Conciliation and Arbitration Commission announced that it would adopt a system of "**wage indexation**" in 1975. Wages and salaries were to be raised in step with the percentage increase recorded in the CPI in each quarter, provided that other increases were restricted to demonstrated increases in labour productivity and "flow-on" adjustments based on past wage decisions.

The purpose underlying the decision to adopt wage indexation was to break the link between wage claims and expected *future* increases in prices. Workers could rest assured that they would be fully compensated for future increases in prices. Provided the unions accepted the Arbitration Commission's guidelines, excessive wage claims would be eliminated. Furthermore, if other elements in the prices of goods, such as imports and indirect taxes, increased less rapidly than money wage rates, the rate of growth in prices could be expected to decline. On the basis of an increase of 3.6 per cent in the CPI during the March quarter of 1975, the commission granted an increase of 3.6 per cent on all wages and salaries from the middle of May.

However, by the end of the financial year 1974/75 it was clear that the road to recovery would be long and costly. Despite unusually high bank liquidity and a sharp increase in government spending that left it with an actual deficit of $2,561 million, there was no sign of response. In fact, industrial production had dropped by about 12 per cent compared with the previous year. The devaluation in September, coupled with a reduction in the volume of imports, had served to lessen the deficit in our balance of payments. However, our foreign reserves continued to fall. Worse still, and in contrast with any previous experience, we faced the highest level of unemployment since the Great Depression *and* an unacceptably high rate of inflation.

As in 1950-51 and 1959-61, it can be argued that in 1972-75 government was a destabilizing element in the economy. It added to excess demand and later imposed a contractionary policy on a contracting economy. Again, time lags caused the policy weapons to be largely counter-productive.

Question

1. Describe the Australian economy in the period 1970 to 1975 under the following headings:
   a. Inflation
   b. Money supply — monetary policy
   c. Fiscal policy
   d. Employment
   e. External balance

13 Inflation and Unemployment

For a period of about twenty years, until late in the 1960s, it was generally accepted that an increase in the general level of prices was caused by excess aggregate demand. In these circumstances, it seemed appropriate that governments should take steps to cut back demand — for example, by increasing taxation, reducing government sector expenditure, or by means of credit restrictions.

In the early fifties and again in the early sixties there was evidence in Australia of an *inflationary gap* of the kind described in chapter 11. The demand for labour exceeded the available supply, and both money wage rates and prices were rising. In each period, the government adopted measures designed to reduce aggregate demand. Price stability was restored, but at the cost of rising unemployment.

We are now less certain about the causes of and cures for inflation. One thing is now clear. The general level of prices *can* rise even when we have a high level of unemployment. In other words, as we have seen in Australia in the 1970s, it is possible to have a high rate of inflation even when we also have what would otherwise be described as a *deflationary gap*. This has led some economists to question the relevance of existing theory.

PROBLEMS CREATED BY INFLATION

The models of the economy developed in chapter 11 suggest that living standards depend upon *real* production and *real* income. This appears to suggest that, so long as we have full employment and the level of production is close to our maximum attainable with currently known technology, the general level of prices is of no great consequence. So why should we be concerned about inflation?

Inflation, particularly at the rates indicated by the CPI in figure 27, **creates a number of problems**:

1. *Individual prices and incomes do not adjust equally and in step with the overall rate of increase in the general level of prices.* For example, some **trade unions** are strong and, by direct negotiations with employers, sometimes backed by threats to withdraw their labour services or other forms of industrial action, periodically win increases in their money wage rates. In many cases, particularly in the mid 1970s, these increases in wage rates were more than sufficient to meet increases in the CPI. Other labour unions are lower in numbers, less well organized, and in a weaker position to bargain for higher wage rates by threatening to withdraw their labour. These groups have little alternative but to make occasional submissions to the *Conciliation and Arbitration Commission* and to rely on quarterly or six-monthly national wage case hearings that determine increases in the incomes of *all* wage and salary earners.

Many people who have retired from the workforce and are living on age or invalid pensions are in a position similar to workers in the weaker unions. Their pensions are reviewed at infrequent intervals. These periodic revisions may or may not allow pensions to catch up with rising prices. Between these revisions, their incomes are fixed in money terms and the real value of these pensions lags further and further behind the

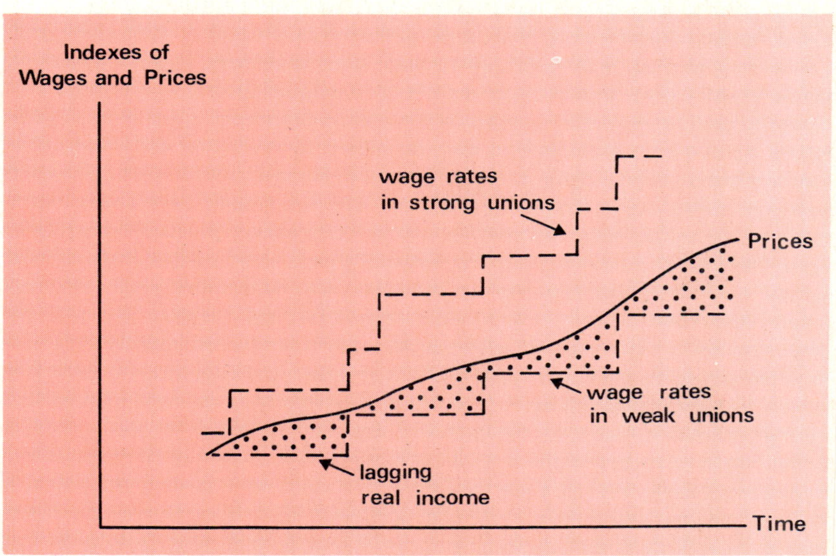

Fig. 28.   Increases in wage rates and prices

general level of prices. So they must either draw on savings or reduce their real consumption expenditures. Those who retire with annuities, lump-sum superannuation benefits, or interest receipts fixed in money terms face similar problems but without the benefit of periodic adjustments.

Nor do all prices increase at the same rates. For example, farm product prices in some periods have fallen, even though other prices have continued to rise. The prices of some manufactured goods tend to be "sticky" — that is, relatively slow to change — owing to agreements between producers to consult with one another before changing their prices. Increases in the prices of some goods have been subject to approval by the PJT or by state price control authorities.

2. *Inflation also has effects on the distribution of wealth. Since debts are recorded in money terms, borrowers tend to gain and lenders to lose if the rate of interest charged is less than the rate of inflation.* For example, a loan of $100 for one year at 10 per cent interest means that the lender exchanges $100 now for $110 one year later. Put another way, the lender exchanges command over $100 worth of goods and services at current prices for what $110 will buy after one year. If, however, the general level of prices rises by 15 per cent over that period, the $110 received by the lender, after twelve months, will buy less than $100 would have bought at the beginning of the period. In a case such as this, where the rate of inflation is greater than the rate of interest paid, **the real rate of interest is negative**.

Over the period 1973 to 1978, the real rate of interest on ten-year Australian government bonds was negative. For part of that period, many people paid negative rates of interest on their housing loans. Since amounts owing on home mortgages are fixed in money terms, rising money incomes meant that the *relative* burden of mortgage indebtedness was decreasing year after year. Meanwhile, the money values of house properties were rising and the real value of mortgages held by the lenders was falling.

Borrowing and lending resulted in a redistribution of wealth. We cannot be sure to what extent the gains went to the more wealthy or the less wealthy. Many of the lenders who suffered losses as a result of inflation were people with small savings accounts trying to save enough to make deposits on their own homes. Many people on quite moderate incomes found the real burden of house repayments reduced by inflation. On the other hand, some people with high incomes and substantial assets were able to borrow more readily because they appeared to be more "creditworthy". Some of these people bought land, paintings, antiques, and precious metals and, because of sharp increases in the prices of such assets, were able to maintain or increase their real wealth. In fact, this urge to buy and hold real assets, rather than financial assets, helped to push up prices. One conspicuous example was speculation in building allotments.

3. *Inflation, particularly at rates that vary from year to year, makes the results of business investment decisions much less certain.* At high and variable rates of inflation, it is much more difficult to predict production costs and market prices years in advance. This serves to add greatly to the usual uncertainties associated with attempts to predict future market demand and likely changes in government policies.

In these circumstances, the more distant future is even less certain than usual. Consequently, many businessmen tend to restrict investment to inventory accumulation and purchases of capital equipment that seem likely to cover the costs involved in the space of only three of four years.

4. *If prices in Australia (and therefore the costs of exporters) are rising more rapidly than world prices, the real incomes of exporters will fall in relation to those of other Australians.* Some trading enterprises — for example, farmers and miners — sell a large proportion of their output overseas. In the absence of an offsetting increase in productivity, exporters' incomes will continue to fall unless the government pays increasing subsidies to these producers or devalues the Australian dollar. However, as suggested in chapter 9, the benefits of devaluation are by no means certain.

A more rapid rate of inflation in Australia than overseas can also be expected to have an impact on imports. In the absence of external measures by the government, Australians will switch from home-produced to imported goods. Unless we are in an inflationary gap situation, this will result in a decline in the level of economic activity in Australia.

Inflation also creates numerous other problems. For example, resources are used up in the frequent recalculation of prices, the issue of revised price lists and the recording of changes in money wage rates. At the same time, trade unions tend to adopt more militant attitudes in their attempts to ensure that they suffer no reduction in their real wages and no reduction relative to other wage and salary earners in the community.

High rates of inflation also have widespread social implications. In these circumstances, most people feel threatened and insecure, particularly with regard to the future. For example, what can people do if they have been saving, for many years, to provide for retirement? At the rates of inflation during the 1970s, the real value of such savings has fallen very rapidly. In these circumstances, people tend to look for "natural" enemies or scapegoats, lashing out at the managers of large firms, trade union leaders, the Canberra bureaucrats, and politicians.

Some of the major problems created by inflation are:
1. Prices and incomes do not all change at the same rates.
2. The distribution of wealth is altered.
3. Increased uncertainty surrounds investment decisions.
4. Exporters are disadvantaged.
5. Import prices become more attractive.

Questions

1. What is meant by the term *inflation*?
2. How is inflation measured in Australia?
3. Why is inflation regarded as a problem?

WHY DO PRICES RISE?

From time to time, it has been suggested that the causes of inflation can be readily identified. These alleged causes usually reflect the self-interests of the people concerned. For this reason, we would not expect the views of spokesmen for employers to coincide with those of union representatives.

Some of the oversimplified explanations that have been offered are as follows:

1. Wage rates have increased either as a result of direct negotiations between unions and employers or as a consequence of decisions by the Arbitration Commission. As a result, production costs rise. So businessmen then have no alternative but to raise their prices.
2. Reflecting the opposite view of cause and effect, businessmen have been raising their prices. The subsequent claims for higher money wages represent the wage-earners' only defence against erosion of their real incomes.
3. There is excess demand for goods and services. This results in higher prices for goods in short supply, increases the bargaining power of the unions, and leads employers to offer higher wage rates in attempts to attract labour away from other firms. (This was certainly true in 1973 and the first half of 1974).
4. Prices have been rising because of excessive growth in the supply of money compared with the growth in real output. If the money supply grows in step with growth in production, inflationary pressures will be removed.
5. World prices have increased, particularly since the first sharp increase in crude oil prices back in the early seventies. Since it is necessary for us to import crude oil and other raw materials and components, these rising import prices add to our production costs. This in turn results in an increase in prices in Australia.

The truth is that it would be extremely difficult to isolate the contribution to inflation made by each of these and other individual factors over any particular period. All of these factors can contribute to inflation and all are interrelated.

An increase in the price of any individual commodity may reflect an increase in the demand for output, an increase in production costs, or some combination of both. **The prices of goods are also affected by independent cost forces — that is, costs that are independent of the level of demand in Australia.** For example, although changes in tariffs and exchange rates introduced by our government have effects on the prices of imports for *Australians*, the prices of crude oil and other imported raw materials and components are determined by forces that are independent of Australian demand. Likewise, the prices of some Australian exports, such as wool, are determined by market forces overseas. Yet an increase in wool prices means that Australian manufacturers using wool as a raw material must also pay a higher price for this input. When world prices for raw materials rise, so too does the cost of production in Australia.

Other examples of cost forces independent of the demand for the output of an individual industry are interest rates, local government rates, payroll taxes, and other charges levied by governments. All of these costs increased during the 1970s, and all contributed to rising prices.

More importantly, wage rates paid in individual industries have become increasingly independent of the demand for the output of those industries. Minimum wage rates, award rates for workers in particular industries, and adjustments based on changes in the CPI are determined from time to time by the Arbitration Commission. Increases in award payments to workers in particular industries tend to flow on automatically to workers with similar skills in other industries. These automatic increases in wage rates must be paid by all firms in all industries concerned, regardless of current demand for their products. So, in contrast to the period up to the time when Keynes wrote his *General Theory*, *money* wage rates no longer change either upwards or downwards in response to changes in the demand for output and labour in a particular industry. Changes in money wage rates are now largely determined by factors beyond the control of an individual firm or industry and are now never in a downwards direction, regardless of the circumstances faced by individual industries.

Some costs, such as imported materials and government charges, are independent of local demand. The Australian system of relative wage justice serves to weaken the link between wage rates and the demand for labour in particular industries.

If an increase in demand was confined to *one* industry and resulted in an increase in the price of that product, this would serve to reduce the quantity of that product demanded in subsequent periods. Assuming the prices of all other goods remained unchanged, some people would switch to the products of other Australian industries or to imported goods.

However, if *all* industries in the economy were operating close to their capacity and *all* faced growing demand for their products, the demand for labour would be strong and possibly in excess of the available supply. In those circumstances, the bargaining power of the unions would be growing and many individual employers would be offering higher wage rates in an attempt to attract scarce labour skills away from other firms. This, in turn, would serve to drive up money wage rates. However, the extent to which higher money wage rates contribute to rising costs per unit of output and higher prices for finished goods depends also on labour productivity. If, for example, labour productivity and money wage rates were both rising by 3 per cent annually, there would be no change in labour costs per unit of output. On the other hand, if money wage rates were rising more rapidly than productivity, this *would* result in higher labour costs per unit and *would* contribute to higher prices.

Labour costs per unit of output rise when money wage rates grow more rapidly than productivity.

Once aggregate demand exceeds the capacity of the economy, we have what Keynes described as an *inflationary gap*. While excess demand remains, prices and incomes tend to rise, period after period. In fact, if all prices and all incomes were rising at the same annual rate — ignoring, for the moment, the possibility that prices overseas may be rising either more or less rapidly — this increase in the general level of prices would *not* serve to dampen aggregate demand in the way that an increase in the price of one commodity alone results in a reduction in the quantity demanded. All that happens in the short run is that prices and incomes continue to rise, while the real level of production remains unchanged.

During the 1950s, the effects of excess demand on the general level of prices was a matter of interest to many economists. A.W. Phillips, for example, studied the relationship between annual changes in money wage rates and changes in the level of unemployment recorded in Britain over many decades. He assumed, as others have done, that there is a close relationship between changes in average money wage rates and changes in the general level of prices. As a result of this and other studies, Phillips claimed that there was a strong inverse relationship between changes in prices and the proportion of the workforce remaining unemployed; further, that this relationship had remained quite stable for many years. A curve fitted to his data indicated generally high rates of inflation at low levels of unemployment. Also, prices were relatively stable at high levels of unemployment. This led Phillips to suggest that governments in economies like Australia face a trade-off between high rates of inflation with low rates of unemployment on the one hand, and low rates of inflation but higher levels of unemployment on the other. Put another way, this suggested that any government aiming to avoid a high rate of

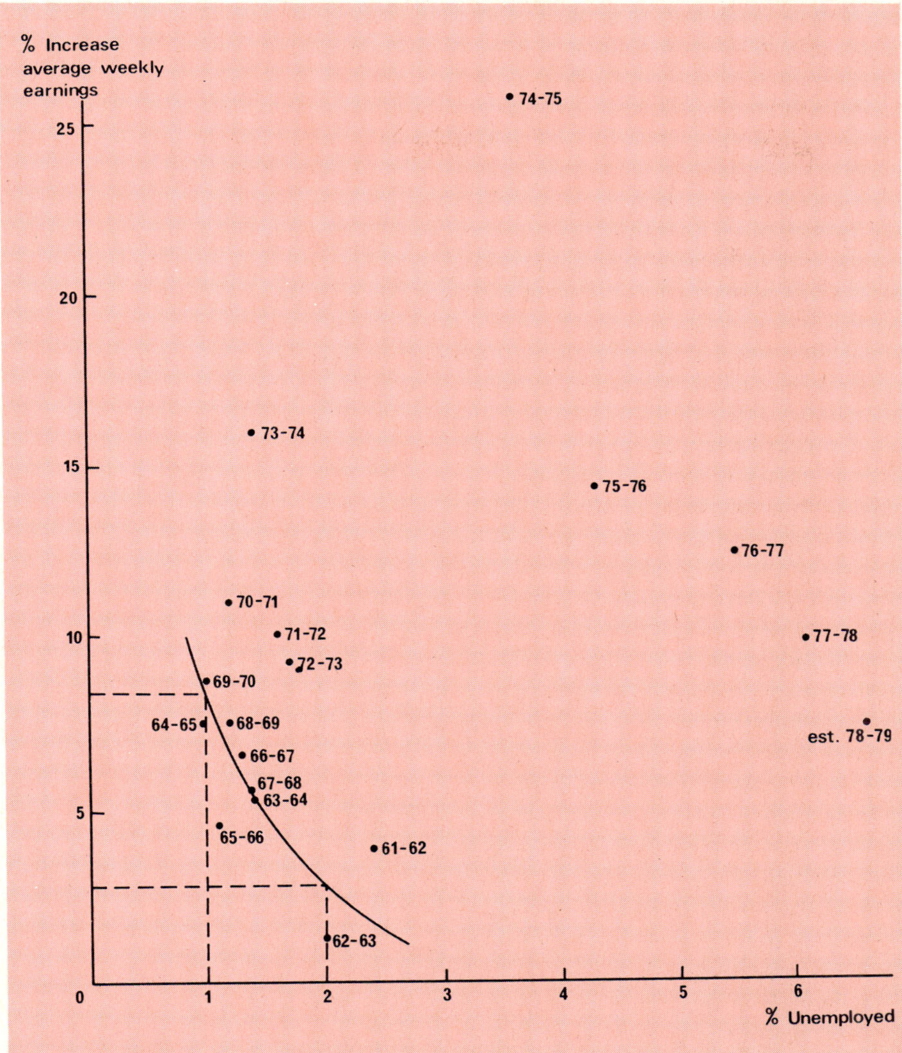

Fig. 29. Percentage increase in average weekly earnings and percentage unemployed in Australia, 1961-79. (Source: Australian Bureau of Statistics, *Monthly Review of Business Statistics*)

inflation would need to take steps to dampen aggregate demand as the economy approaches low levels of unemployment.

The experience of Australia during the 1950s and 1960s also suggested that the nearer we moved towards full employment, the greater was the upward pressure on prices. A "**Phillips Curve**" fitted to Australian data for the 1960s lends further support to that notion. In that period, a reduction in unemployment to 1 per cent of the workforce seemed likely to be associated with an increase in average weekly earnings of slightly more than 8 per cent. If, on the other hand, unemployment rose to 2 per cent of the workforce, this appeared likely to result in an annual increase in money wage rates of less than 3 per cent. If the productivity of labour had been rising at an annual average rate of 2 or 3 per cent, and money wages were the only source of pressure on prices, unemployment at a rate of about 2 per cent would have seemed sufficient to keep prices stable in that period.

However, as figure 29 clearly shows, there has been a dramatic change in the relationship between changes in money wage rates and the level of unemployment in the Australian economy since the 1960s. At each level of unemployment, the rate of increase in average weekly earnings has been much higher than it was formerly. Looked at in another way, the reasoning underlying a Phillips Curve of the 1970s would suggest that we will now have to endure unemployment at a much higher rate if price stability is to be restored.

Why this has happened is not yet clear. Some economists have argued that experience of immediate past increases in prices has a strong influence upon *expectations about the future*. For example, if people have grown accustomed to prices rising at an annual rate of, say, 10 per cent, they expect prices to rise at a similar rate in the next year. Workers seeking an increase in money wage rates on account of an increase of 4 per cent in productivity are then likely to seek an increase of 14 per cent — simply because they expect prices to continue to rise at an annual rate of 10 per cent. Past experience would suggest that an increase of only 4 per cent would be quickly eroded by inflation. If employers have the same expectations regarding future prices, they are likely to agree to such an increase in wage rates — among other reasons, because they expect to be able to raise their own prices by 10 per cent. In that event, they will avoid an increase in the real labour cost per cent of output. **In other words, past increases in the general level of prices have a bearing on present wage demands and future prices through expectations.**

In addition, as pointed out earlier, there are some costs that are independent of the demand for output. Even when aggregate demand is far less than the level necessary to generate full employment, increases in these costs continue to contribute to rising prices. During the 1970s, increases in the prices of imported raw materials, higher interest rates, rising local government rates, and other government charges have all served to raise costs and prices. At the same time there has been an increasing tendency for money wage rates to be determined independently of the demand for labour in individual industries. Put another way, market forces now exercise less influence on money wage rates than they did formerly. Money wage rates continue to rise at regular intervals. Some firms have responded to these rising wage rates by engaging in capital deeping investment, substituting machines for labour.

So, in contrast to the situations faced in Australia in the fifties and sixties, we now have a great deal of excess capacity, together with a high rate of inflation — a situation sometimes referred to as "**Stagflation**".

In the second half of the 1970s high rates of inflation persisted, despite low levels of total planned expenditure. Possible causes of this situation include:

1. Inflationary expectations.

2. Increases in interest rates, government charges, and the costs of imported material.

3. An increased tendency for wage rates to be determined independently of the demand for labour in individual industries.

Questions

1. Explain why businessmen and employees would disagree about the cause of the wage-price spiral.

2. What are "independent cost forces", and why do they present difficulties when attempting to reduce inflation?

3. What was shown by the Phillips Curve? How relevant is the Phillips Curve to recent experience?

POLICIES AIMED AT CONTROLLING INFLATION

Since late in the 1960s, other countries have also faced rising unemployment and high rates of inflation. In some cases, the sources of pressures on prices have been much the same as in Australia. So it is useful to consider briefly measures used in the United States and Britain in attempts to reduce their rates of inflation before looking in more detail at what has happened in Australia.

Prices and Incomes Policy in the United Kingdom

In the United Kingdom, a formal **prices and incomes policy** was introduced in 1965. It was believed that measures aimed directly at controlling prices and incomes would serve to avoid the inflationary consequences of near full employment that had been suggested by Phillips.

Over the period 1965 to 1976, there were frequent changes in the government's policy guidelines. In some periods, the government simply called for voluntary restraint or asked the unions to restrict their wage claims to gains in productivity. For the greater part of that period, the government specified maximum percentage increases in money wage rates that it considered to be in the national interest. In some periods such "ceilings" operated on a voluntary basis. At other times the government attempted to back its guidelines with legislation. In 1966, and again in 1972-73, the government introduced legislation to impose a total freeze of all prices and incomes — on each occasion for only a few months.

As the severity of the government's policy guidelines swung back and forth between total freeze and voluntary restraints, so too did the rate of increase in prices and incomes. Over the financial year 1966/67, the general level of prices increased by only 2.5 per cent — certainly less than could have been expected in the absence of the government's freeze. However, that freeze was accepted only because it was known to be *temporary*. It was quickly followed by a flood of price increases and wage claims, and prices then rose more rapidly than would have been expected had the freeze not been imposed initially.

Between the periods of total freeze or legislation giving force to the government's will, it is not surprising that attempts to encourage voluntary restraint were unsuccessful. Some firms were more dependent than others on imported raw materials and components, or in other ways had been absorbing increases in costs. Furthermore, prices of individual commodities tend to change with changes in demand, costs, and technology. In fact, if all prices are frozen or all prices move upwards in step, how are *differences* in prices to act as a device for allocating scarce resources?

From the viewpoint of wage and salary earners, there are always some who are placed at a particular disadvantage by such policies. Some will have received increases in wage rates immediately before new limits are introduced: others will have been expecting increases in incomes based on claims already lodged. On the other hand, there are ways and means of avoiding an incomes policy if employers and workers are prepared to engage in so-called *sweetheart agreements*. For example, in return for union assurances that no strike or other disruptive action will be taken over some future period, employers may agree to the reclassification of workers to higher grades and the provision of various fringe benefits.

The benefits of the British policies are not at all clear. Except for the brief periods of total freeze, available evidence does not suggest that these policies led to a slower rate of increase in prices than could otherwise have been expected. Over the six-year period 1970-76, when the Australian CPI increased by 79.8 per cent, the British Retail Prices Index (base 1970 = 100) rose by 111.4 per cent. Nor is there any evidence to suggest that policies in the United Kingdom have dampened expectations about future prices.

Incomes policies in the United Kingdom were not particularly successful.

Prices and Incomes Policy in the United States

In contrast to the United Kingdom, the economy of the United States is less closely regulated. In the early 1970s the United States government imposed a total freeze on all prices and incomes for a period of three months. Over that brief period, the freeze was widely accepted and there was almost zero growth in the general level of prices. However, as soon as the government's ban was lifted, the former rate of inflation was quickly restored.

During 1977 and early in 1978, some prominent American economists were forecasting an increase in the rate of inflation in the United States. They made it clear that the upward pressures on prices were due to independent cost forces and urged the government to restrain interest rates and avoid further increases in the various charges over which it had direct control. Others suggested that the government should specify some upper limit on the annual rate of increase in money wage rates. Further, they recommended that the government should impose penalty taxes on workers and firms involved in negotiating increases in excess of this ceiling, while offering tax rebates where increases were less than the upper limit.

As predicted, the annual rate of inflation increased slightly to about 8 per cent. In October 1978 the American President announced "voluntary" arrangements aimed at reducing inflation. Workers were asked to limit the annual rate of increase in their money wage rates to 7 per cent and firms to restrict increases in their prices to an annual rate of 5.75 per cent. Assuming some increase in labour productivity, this would not result in an increase in real labour cost per unit of output. Those who agreed to accept increases in wage rates of less than 7 per cent were guaranteed tax rebates sufficient to compensate them if the rate of inflation exceeded 7 per cent. Firms that raised their prices more rapidly than the rate suggested were warned that they would not be awarded government contracts and would be the target for other punitive measures.

It was hoped that these measures would reduce the annual rate of inflation to 6 per cent by the end of 1979. Many large firms and some unions were quick to indicate a willingness to co-operate, but at the time of writing it was too early to assess the success or failure of these arrangements. Meanwhile, however, it is interesting to note that many economists in the United States now appear to accept that the fullest possible level of employment in that country will have at least 6½ per cent of the workforce unemployed.

The notion that incomes policies are the answer to stagflation received little support from the United States experience.

Australian Attempts at a Prices and Incomes Policy

In 1973 the Labor government in Australia had hoped to introduce direct controls over prices and incomes. The Constitution did not allow for this, and Australian voters rejected a government referendum seeking an extension of its powers for that purpose. So the government used its powers to regulate company activities by establishing **the Prices Justification Tribunal (PJT)** in 1973 and persuaded the Arbitration Commission to adopt a system of wage indexation from early in 1975. Although firms were required to notify the PJT of their intention to raise prices and to wait for the tribunal's decisions before doing so, the legislation did not prevent them from raising their prices above the levels approved. Nor did either the government or the PJT have the power to impose fines on firms that ignored these price recommendations. This led some Australian economists to suggest that the PJT had no effective "teeth" and could therefore have little or no effect on prices.

However, the processes involved and the possibility of drawn-out public inquiries did have the effect of delaying price rises and, in some cases, reducing the size of price increases sought by individual firms. Furthermore, the PJT had the power to report *publicly* on its recommendations. If any firm chose to increase its prices above the levels approved, this was likely to be made known to the Australian people. That is the kind of publicity that large firms would prefer to avoid. In addition, the government has at its disposal other weapons by which it can force firms to co-operate. For example, during the first year of operation of the PJT the world price for copper rose rapidly to about $1,700 a ton. The government threatened to impose export restrictions on Australian copper producers if the domestic price rose above $1,400 a ton. The government's threat was sufficient and the Australian price was held at the required level. So, as suggested by the United States president in 1978, there are ways and means of forcing co-operation if the government has the will to use the weapons available.

The first **wage indexation** decision was based on the increase in the

CPI during the first quarter of 1975. The CPI increased by 3.6 per cent and the Arbitration Commission awarded an increase of 3.6 per cent to all wage and salary earners. That is, the percentage increase in wages and salaries was precisely the same as the percentage increase in the CPI. Since that time, we have referred to such decisions as "**full indexation**".

The reasoning behind wage indexation was as follows. Provided that increases in money wage rates were restricted to full indexation and actual productivity gains, it seemed likely that wage rates would rise less rapidly than under the previous system of collective bargaining and the annual rate of increase might be stabilized.

For example, if money wage rates were rising at, say, 12 per cent annually, while other elements in the prices of goods — such as imported raw materials, indirect taxes, and other government charges — were rising at 8 per cent annually, then *the rate of increase* in prices would begin to fall. If the unions were also willing to set aside claims for rising productivity, rising money wage rates would be partly offset by rising output per worker. Prices would then rise even less rapidly. This would result in progressively smaller percentage increases in the CPI and smaller percentage increases awarded under wage indexation. In this way, it was hoped that the rate of inflation would be dampened.

The coalition government was returned to office at the end of 1975. It faced a high level of unemployment and a rapid rate of inflation which it had inherited from the former government. It was clear that the road to recovery would be long and difficult.

A referendum in 1973 to give the Australian government the power for wage and price control was lost. Following this, income policy consisted of the establishment of the Prices Justification Tribunal and of persuading the Arbitration Commission to adopt wage indexation.

Recent Attempts of Control Inflation

From the time of its return to power, the new government made it clear that a sharp reduction in the rate of inflation was its principal macroeconomic policy objective. Further, that the rate of inflation must be reduced if there was to be any reduction in unemployment.

Early in 1976 the government stated that the declining share of value added that was going to profits and the rising share to wages and salaries was serving to depress the level of activity. It claimed that an increase in profits would serve to restore business confidence and stimulate investment. As a stimulus to fixed capital expenditures, the government introduced an *investment allowance* that permitted firms to claim a larger proportion of the cost of new capital equipment as as tax-deductable expense than was formerly the case. The government predicted that this would contribute to an investment-led recovery. In other words, an increase in investment expenditure was expected to result in a higher equilibrium level of production.

At that time, and throughout the remainder of the seventies, Australian firms had a great deal of excess capacity. So why would they be interested in duplicating their existing plant? Many firms took advantage of the investment allowance to buy new plant and equipment. **Much of that investment was of a capital deepening kind, the effect of which was the substitution of machines for labour. This resulted in the loss of many jobs.**

From 1976 onwards, the government reminded us that real wage rates had increased more rapidly than labour productivity during the first half of the seventies. Since firms showed no interest in hiring additional labour at the current wage rates, the government suggested that it would be necessary to put the earlier process into reverse, reducing the rate of increase in money wage rates in relation to prices if unemployment was to be reduced.

Repeatedly, the government argued that the Arbitration Commission should award less than full wage indexation. This would cause real wages to fall. From time to time the commission appeared to be influenced by those arguments. At times it awarded to all wage and salary earners percentage increases that were less than the recorded increases in the CPI — that is, less than full indexation. At other times, the commission handed down "**plateau**" decisions, under which workers receiving less than average wage rates were awarded full indexation, while all other wage and salary earners received precisely the same increases, in dollar terms, as were awarded to the people with average incomes. These decisions resulted in lower incomes rising most rapidly and a reduction in the relative rewards for skills.

Predictably, the unions have threatened increasingly to turn to direct negotiations with employers in an attempt to maintain the purchasing power of their incomes and to restore wage relativities disrupted by plateau indexation decisions. The government in turn cut personal income tax and indicated its intention to index the new rates of tax — this was in the hope that the unions would then moderate their wage claims. However, it was clear that wage and salary earners could no longer expect full wage indexation. The government called a halt to full tax indexation. The Arbitration Commission abandoned quarterly wage indexation in favour of six-monthly hearings.

Given the coalition government's concern with the declining share of GDP going to profits, it was to be expected that the PJT would be required to play a lesser part in attempting to reduce the rate of growth in prices. In

1976 the government raised to a minimum of $30 million the annual value of sales at which companies were required to notify intended increases in prices. This meant that increases in prices by some firms were no longer subject to approval. Finally, early in 1979 new legislation was introduced and companies were no longer required to notify the tribunal of their intention to raise prices. That is, firms were again free to set their own prices. The PJT was left to act the part of a "watchdog", investigating and reporting on price rises in the least competitive industries and those whose prices have a strong influence on the CPI.

At the time the PJT was established in 1973, there was excess aggregate demand in the Australian economy. In those circumstances it was tempting for firms to raise their prices and increase their profits because they could readily sell their entire output at higher prices. By 1979 the economy was suffering a deep recession and market conditions were much more competitive. Any individual firm that chose to raise its prices would do so at considerable risk to its sales. This change in circumstances suggests that there was no longer the same need for control over prices. On the other hand, the government could not expect the unions to be impressed by arguments suggesting a need to restrain increases in money wage rates but no need to restrain prices.

Meanwhile, the government also contributed to further increases in prices. For example, it introduced a levy on personal income tax to meet the cost of Medibank, the national health insurance scheme, and offered, as an alternative, contributions to private health insurance at sharply rising costs. The government also increased excise duties on beverages, tobacco, and petroleum products. When accused of contributing to higher prices, the government claimed that indirect taxes were an essential part of its fiscal armoury. They suggested that all items subject to taxes should be treated separately when estimating changes in the cost of living.

The government has also increased prices in other ways. For example, by increasing air navigation charges, it added to the cost of air services. Its decision to progressively raise the price of Australian-produced crude oil to parity with import prices served to further increase the cost of transport services. Admittedly, the government's oil price policy has much to commend it, since this should help to conserve our known reserves. Nevertheless, it cannot be denied that these independent cost forces served to raise the CPI still further.

Apart from the downward revision in rates of income tax and a short period of full tax indexation, the government's fiscal policies have been rather cautious. The government has been worried by the large and growing budget deficit. In money terms, government expenditure has continued to grow; but in *real* terms, there has been little change from year to year. While the government waits for signs of recovery in the

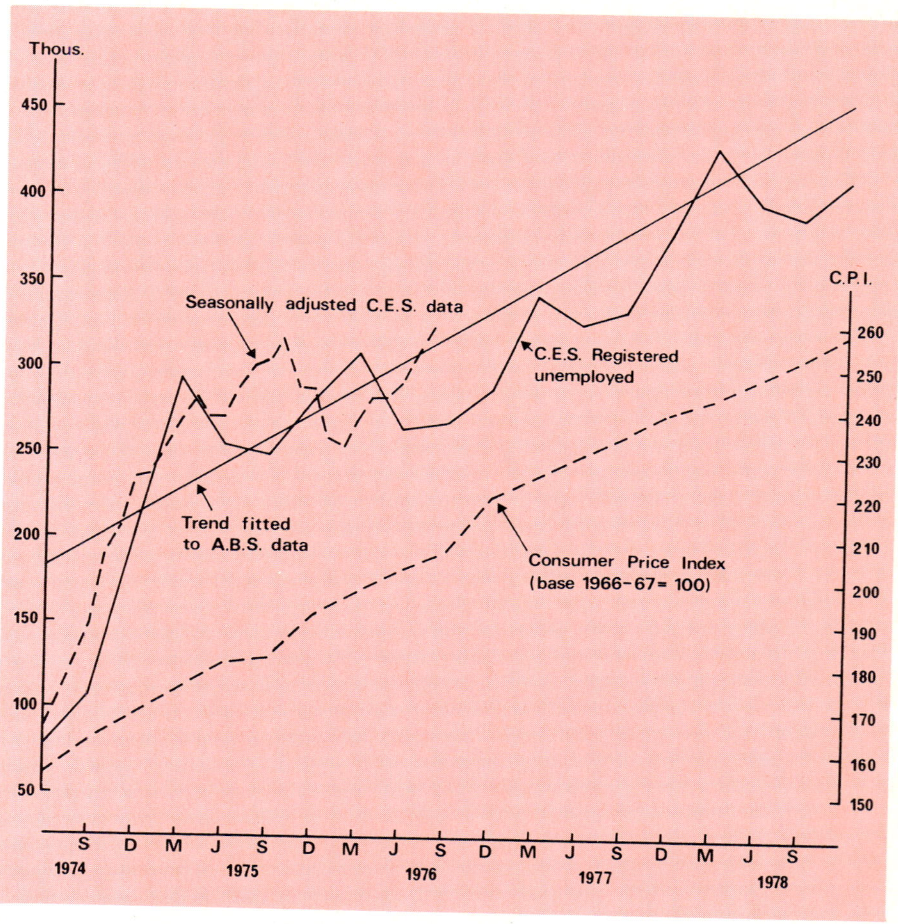

Fig. 30.   Inflation and unemployment, 1974-78. (Source: Department of Employment and Youth Affairs, *Monthly Review of Employment Situation.* Australian Bureau of Statistics, *The Labour Force: Australia* and *Consumer Price Index*)

private sector of the economy, the private sector waits for the government to stimulate economic activity.

The consequences of the sharp decline in economic activity in 1974, the collapse of business confidence, and various policies of the governments since that time can be seen in figure 30.

The rate of inflation during the last two calendar years of the Labor government, 1974 and 1975, was 16.3 per cent and 14.0 per cent respectively. Although prices continued to rise, as shown by the CPI, the *rate* of inflation declined from 14.4 per cent in 1976 to 7.7 per cent in 1978. This fall in the rate of inflation was due in part to a lower rate of growth in import prices and increases in productivity for which no claims have been made by the unions. However, the cost in terms of unemployment has been very high. Whether we use the Commonwealth Employment Service (CES) or the Australian Bureau of Statistics (ABS) figures or various independent estimates, it is clear that unemployment has continued to grow since the middle of 1974.

Meanwhile, the relationship between the rate of increase in money wage rates (or the rate of increase in prices) on the one hand and the level of unemployment on the other, as indicated in figures 29 and 30, suggests that the Phillips Curve trade-off is still relevant. If this is so, the cost of a lower rate of inflation is now much too high. There is no future in a return to a higher rate of inflation, so we must seek ways and means of holding down the rate of inflation while reducing unemployment. This will no doubt require a greater measure of understanding and co-operation than has been evident between all sectors in the 1970s. It may also require governments to adopt tougher measures — for example, tax and other measures that strike at "the hip-pocket nerves" of all who contribute to inflationary pressures without just cause — even if such measures are politically unpalatable.

The coalition government, returned in 1975, pursued price stability as the primary objective. By 1979 the inflation rate had fallen at the cost of increased unemployment.

Questions

1. In a formal prices and incomes policy, voluntary wage restraint is often an important element. What is meant by voluntary wage restraint, and why is it often unsuccessful?

2. One policy to control inflation is a total price freeze. Give reasons why such a freeze may be unsuccessful in controlling inflation.

3. It has been suggested that a system of tax penalties and rebates should be used to hold down the rate of growth of prices and money wage rates in Australia. Describe how such a system could hold down price and money wage increases.

4. What is wage indexation? Why was wage indexation introduced?

5. The Prices Justification Tribunal has been said to be "toothless". Why do businesses generally abide by PJT decisions?

HOW MANY PEOPLE ARE UNEMPLOYED?

Our principal sources of information concerning the numbers unemployed in Australia are the data published by the CES and the ABS. As indicated in chapter 12, these two sets of estimates have different origins and are subject to different sources of error. Even so, these data provide a useful guide to changes in employment in the short run.

Over a longer period, such as that represented in figure 30, there are additional problems that arise from changes in the definition of "the employed" and "the unemployed". For example, trainee teachers were excluded from estimates of the labour force after August 1971. Before July 1973 it was possible for people still at school to register for employment with the CES, provided they intended to leave school before the end of the year. From that time onward it was necessary to have left school before registering. In February 1975 the ABS definition of the labour force was changed to include all people who, during the week of its survey, "worked for one hour or more for pay, profit, commission or payment in kind . . . or worked for 15 hours or more in a family business". More recently, it has been required that those who qualify for unemployment benefits must be "actively seeking employment". Such changes in definition affect the comparability of data over long periods. In addition, periodic revisions in the estimated size of the workforce, based on censuses of population and other sources, have the effect of changing past estimates of unemployment as a proportion of the workforce.

As in chapter 12, we have used quarterly averages of the numbers registered for employment with the CES in figure 30. These quarterly averages to some extent dampen the seasonal peaks and troughs that are evident each year, peaking with school leavers seeking to join the workforce between December and February and falling during the June and September quarters. These seasonal tendencies can be taken into account by using *seasonally adjusted data* — that is, data adjusted in such a way as to remove the underlying seasonal pattern, so that any rise or fall in a time series indicates the true upward or downward tendencies.

Seasonally adjusted data have been a source of embarrassment to past governments. All political parties play the same games, using whatever statistical "evidence" best suits their immediate purposes. In 1976 the government called a halt to the issue of official seasonally adjusted data after August of that year. This is reflected in figure 30.

Since the seasonal pattern of unemployment is widely known, the CES estimates continue to be seasonally adjusted by independent research workers. For example, the *Flinders University National Institute of Labour Studies* has published seasonal adjustment factors for use with numbers registered for employment with the CES during 1979. For January, the institute's adjustment factor was 1.169, suggesting that the numbers actually registered would be 1.169 times the seasonally adjusted figure. In that month there were 493,500 people registered with the CES. So the seasonally adjusted figure would have been 422,100. The institute's adjustment factor for October 1979 was 0.906, suggesting that the actual numbers registered for employment in October would need to be raised by about 10 per cent to allow for the usual seasonal trough in unemployment in that month.

An alternative approach is to fit a straight line trend to a moving average of monthly or quarterly estimates. This serves to avoid the need to interpret increases or decreases in estimated unemployment from month to month. Figure 30 shows a trend that was fitted to ABS quarterly estimates of unemployment over that period.

These are some of the alternative ways of representing changes in the level of unemployment. Unfortunately, all tell the same story, namely, that unemployment continued to grow steadily after the initial sharp increase at the end of 1974.

Although the upward trend in these official data is disturbing, there are reasons to believe that these estimates understate the true level of unemployment. The tightening in definition of "the employed" and "the unemployed" are alone sufficient to suggest this. In addition, there is evidence that many housewives and older people who lost their jobs in the latter half of the seventies have given up searching for alternatives. Giving up the search should not be interpreted as an intention never again to seek employment. Given the opportunity, some of these people can be expected to return to the workforce at some time in the future. Interpretation of all available evidence has led some people to suggest that if one included such "discouraged workers", unemployment in Australia at the end of 1978 may have been as high as 600,000.

One particularly disturbing feature has been the very slow growth in non-government employment. Over the period June 1975 to December 1978, the total numbers *employed* in Australia increased by only 2.5 per cent. Despite ceilings imposed by governments on growth in their public services, slightly more than half of the total increase in numbers employed was accounted for by employment in the government sector. What this means is that growth in real output in the private sector has been due to rising labour productivity, in part associated with the substitution of machines for labour rather than increases in the numbers employed.

There are many difficulties involved in gathering and interpreting unemployment statistics. It is clear, however, that unemployment continued to grow steadily after the initial sharp increase at the end of 1974.

WHAT HAVE WE DONE ABOUT UNEMPLOYMENT?

Before the sharp downturn in activity at the end of 1974, Australian governments relied largely on monetary, fiscal, and external policy measures to influence aggregate demand for Australian output. Since 1974 it has become increasingly evident that these measures have not been sufficient to ensure a matching of the supply and demand for labour. This situation has resulted in increased attention to what might be described as **manpower planning policies,** under which attempts have been made by the Commonwealth and state governments to gather more information regarding current and likely future job opportunities and to provide training intended to prepare people for such employment.

Such a programme involves the forecasting of shortages and surpluses of labour with particular skills in individual regions and industries. It also requires the provision of vocational guidance services, financial assistance to people undergoing training or retraining, and assistance with expenses involved in the relocation of workers.

The main aims of training and retraining schemes are:
1. To assist those who have become unemployed as a result of structural changes in the economy and who have difficulty in finding alternative employment.
2. To enable disadvantaged people who have had limited training and occupational opportunities to improve their skills and therefore their employment prospects.
3. To match the unemployed with likely future job opportunities.
4. To allow individuals generally to improve their skills and therefore their future prospects of employment.

In these ways, it is hoped to improve the *mobility of labour*, allowing workers to adapt more quickly to economic circumstances, to minimize periods of structural unemployment, and to eliminate bottlenecks in production resulting from labour shortages.

Manpower policies are intended to decrease structural unemployment.

Although such arrangements have been given greater attention since 1974, *it would be misleading to suggest that training or retraining schemes are of recent origin.* After World War II, for example, there were many thousands of ex-service personnel who were provided with training assistance under what was known as the **Commonwealth Reconstruction Training Scheme (CRTS).** In 1968 the government accepted a recommendation that measures be introduced to encourage reconstruction in the dairy industry — including provisions for the retraining of those who wished to leave their farms. In 1971, when wool and wheat producers' incomes were very low, the Commonwealth government provided the states with **unemployment relief grants** designed to increase employment opportunities in rural areas. Late in the same year, the Commonwealth introduced its **Rural Reconstruction Scheme**, under which provision was made to assist some farmers to buy additional land and retraining assistance was offered to some who decided to give up farming.

By 1973, when the Australian economy was operating at the full employment level of activity, there were more than twenty training schemes in operation. These included retraining for the structurally unemployed and separate training schemes for women seeking to join the workforce and for ex-servicemen, as well as for Aborigines, migrants, the mentally and physically handicapped, and other disadvantaged groups.

At that time, skilled labour was particularly scarce. Since the principal source of skilled tradesmen in Australia has long been the various apprenticeship training arrangements, the Commonwealth introduced the **National Apprenticeship Assistance Scheme (NAAS)**. The purpose of NAAS was to increase the numbers of young people taking up apprenticeships and to improve the standard of training. Subsidies were offered to employers to encourage them to take on more apprentices and to offer more effective on-the-job training. Allowances were offered to young people as an incentive for them to take up apprenticeships and the additional studies required. As a result, the numbers of apprentices in training increased by 21 per cent during 1973/74.

After unemployment started to grow during the third quarter of 1974, some of the former arrangements were modified and other forms of training and assistance were introduced. *The most significant of the new scheme were as follows:*

1. **The Regional Employment Development (RED) Scheme.** This scheme was introduced in September 1974 to provide financial assistance for projects of economic or social benefit which provided employment for people who otherwise seemed likely to remain out of work. In June 1975 there were thirty thousand people employed under this scheme. No new projects were approved after September 1975, and the RED Scheme was finally terminated during 1976/77.

2. **Structural Adjustment Assistance** was introduced in April 1974 and was initially intended to help people who had lost their jobs as a direct result of the 25 per cent tariff cut. Later, the same assistance was given to other people displaced as a direct result of government decisions designed to bring about structural changes considered to be in the national interest. This scheme provided for income maintenance payments for up to six months or until alternative employment was found. The consequences of government decisions on employment after March 1975 were not

regarded as a qualification for such assistance, and this scheme was wound up during 1976/77.

3. **The National Employment and Training Scheme (NEAT)** was introduced in 1974/75. It combined a number of formerly separate training schemes with the object of providing a broader and more flexible training and retraining system to meet both the needs of individuals and conditions in the labour market. This scheme, still operating in 1979, offers assistance in meeting the cost of fees, books, and equipment, in addition to the unemployment benefit, for those who are given approval to continue with further education, or subsidies to employers who are willing to provide on-the-job training and time off for study where that is required. In July 1978 there were 50,477 people being assisted under this scheme. By February 1979 the number had been reduced to 18,337. This reduction in the numbers being assisted under NEAT reflects a tightening up of eligibility conditions and the government's stated intention to expand opportunities for on-the-job training under its Special Youth Employment Training Programme.

4. **The Special Youth Employment Training Programme (SYETP)** is an offshoot of NEAT and was introduced in 1976. It aims to assist young people who are registered with the CES, have been out of employment for at least four of the previous twelve months, and appear to face difficulties in finding permanent employment. The object of this scheme is to provide on-the-job training in industry or commerce. To encourage employers to employ and train people under this programme, the government offers a wage subsidy of $45 a week for a maximum of seventeen weeks. During 1978/79 the government aimed to train eighty thousand people under this scheme.

5. **The Commonwealth Rebate for Apprentice Full-time Training (CRAFT)** replaced NAAS in January 1977. CRAFT provides living-away-from-home and other allowances for apprentices and offers tax-exempt rebates to employers for releasing apprentices for course work and other off-the-job training. For the year 1977/78, the government made financial provision for forty thousand apprentices under this scheme. The actual number was only twenty-seven thousand. For the year 1978/79, the government allowed for sixty-three thousand to be trained under this scheme. The government has claimed that NAAS and CRAFT have served to reduce a major downturn in the annual intake of apprentices. On the other hand, critics of the current training arrangements claim that the long periods of training required, age limits on entry, and the increasing costs associated with the employment and training of apprentices will lead to a shortage of skilled tradesmen in the future.

To be an effective instrument of economic policy, employment training schemes must be undertaken on a scale large enough to have a significant impact on the labour market. Training schemes must be efficient, flexible enough to cope with shortages and surpluses of various labour skills, and supported by all groups that have an influence on the supply and demand for labour.

Although large numbers of people are now being trained under these and other training schemes, it is difficult to assess the effects of these policies in reducing unemployment. Under SYETP, for example, the period of subsidized on-the-job training in 1979 was restricted to four months. We have no means of knowing how many of these trainees were kept on after training or how many found other jobs as a result of that training. To assess the effectiveness of these training schemes, we would need to know the numbers of people who would have been left unemployed or engaged in part-time jobs or in less skilled jobs had they not undertaken such training. On the other hand, if training under these programmes is becoming a necessary precondition for employment, does this suggest a need to expand the existing programmes? Or should we simply revert to the use of conventional policy measures designed to increase aggregate demand and the total demand for labour?

Employment training schemes need to be large scale, flexible, and well supported. Australia has seen a number of new schemes introduced during the 1970s.

Questions

1. Why are "manpower planning policies" seen to be important in reducing unemployment in the future?

2. Governments finance training and retraining schemes. Describe one such scheme and explain how the scheme will help to reduce the unemployment problem.

14 Current Problems and Questions: What Are the Answers?

No introductory textbook can hope to cover all of the macroeconomic problems that we have faced in the past or are likely to encounter in the future. This book is no exception. Our view has been restricted to "the tip of the iceberg". On the other hand, the concepts introduced in this book should make possible an intelligent appraisal of most of the arguments on the Australian economy that are likely to be encountered in the media.

We hope that readers will now be in a position to consider critically and objectively the arguments put forward, from time to time, by members of governments and by representatives of other political parties, employer organizations, the trade unions, and other groups in the community. Arguments put forward in letters to the editors of newspapers, for example, can be very persuasive. However, some of these arguments are clearly wrong "in principle". Others can be refuted by reference to the facts, and it is hoped that readers will refer to various statistical sources and economic indicators before reaching conclusions on current and future issues.

The purpose of this chapter is to mention some of the questions that have been raised recently and which seem likely to be debated long into the 1980s. Many of the questions raised in this chapter have been left unanswered in the hope that this will stimulate further thought and discussion. Also, although we, like most economists, have our own views, we do not pretend to have all the answers. Meanwhile, however, governments will have no alternative but to face up to these issues and make decisions.

WAS "INFLATION FIRST" THE CORRECT APPROACH?

During the latter half of the seventies, the coalition government clung desperately to the belief that a lower rate of inflation was the essential precondition for a reduction in the level of unemployment. However, figures 29 and 30 show that the cost of a lower rate of inflation has been growing unemployment. This is not intended to suggest that the trends evident over the period 1974 to 1978 will continue indefinitely. To the extent that inflation in itself served to dampen the confidence of households and businessmen, a lower if not a zero rate of inflation in recent years may prove to be more widely acceptable. Meanwhile, it is worth recalling from the introduction to this book that the level of unemployment during the *Great Depression* in the early 1930s was much higher. In time, the economy *did* recover and those who had been unemployed, though badly scarred, survived the experience.

In giving first priority to reduction in the rate of inflation, our government has followed very closely the recommendations of a distinguished group of economists who reported to the **Organisation for Economic Co-operation and Development (OECD)** in June 1977. That group suggested that the widespread recession of the mid seventies was the result of "an unusual bunching of unfortunate disturbances unlikely to be repeated on the same scale, the impact of which was compounded by some avoidable errors in economic policy". It stressed the need to dampen expectations concerning future rates of inflation, to keep a tight rein on demand by means of a cautious "touch on the tiller" approach to economic management, and to avoid sharp changes in direction. Slow recovery in aggregate demand was believed to be necessary if a rekindling of inflationary expectations was to be avoided. Australia is a member of the OECD, and it is apparent that the government has accepted these recommendations.

The Australian government decided to fight inflation first in order to reduce inflationary expectations, before allowing total expenditure to grow slowly.

During the first half of 1979 there were numerous suggestions that the recovery had already begun. Members of the government, the government's Economic Consultative Group (consisting of a panel of leading businessmen), bankers, and some newspapers referred to "a sudden upswing in economic activity" and suggested a need to restrain "a coming boom". What was the evidence for claiming, as one newspaper did, that "the recession is now a bad memory"? In other words, what were the facts?

Question

1. Why did the Australian government maintain "a fight inflation first" strategy despite large and growing levels of unemployment?

WHAT ARE THE SIGNS OF RECOVERY?

Much has been said about the reduction in the actual numbers registered for employment with the CES. However, as we have seen in the past, we expect this to happen after the March quarter in every year. The government suggested that there were many jobs available. However, it is a fallacy to suggest that because there are twenty or thirty thousand jobs available, people have no reason to rely on unemployment benefits. One leading bank suggested that we could expect an increase of 1 per cent in the numbers employed by the end of 1979. But how many school leavers and immigrants will be seeking to join the workforce during 1979? How many people who had given up looking for work may return to the labour force? If the numbers employed increase by 1 per cent, will this result in any reduction in the numbers unemployed?

What was the evidence that there had been an upturn in the level of economic activity? It was clear that consumption expenditure had increased slightly in real terms during the second half of 1978. It was also true that the incomes of farmers had increased greatly relative to the years immediately past. However, history tells us that seasonal conditions and farm product prices vary from year to year. So we should not count on higher farm incomes continuing indefinitely.

Some claimed that there had been a marked improvement in the motor vehicle and building industries; in fact that BHP was having difficulty in meeting the Australian demand for steel. Admittedly, sales of new passenger vehicles increased by 10 per cent over the last five months of 1978. On the other hand, there was a reduction in the numbers of commercial vehicles sold. The overall increase in motor vehicle sales relative to 1977/78 was only 5.5 per cent. Given that the increase in sales followed a sharp reduction in sales tax, for how long is the higher level of sales likely to continue?

On the other hand, it was difficult to find any evidence of a recovery in the building industry. In 1977/78, there was a decline in the numbers of new dwellings completed in every state of the Commonwealth. The numbers of new dwellings completed were less than two-thirds of the annual numbers in the early seventies. Admittedly, building approvals by local and other government authorities provide us with a better guide to what might be expected in the near future. In 1977/78, building approvals fell by 12.6 per cent relative to 1976/77. During the first half of 1978/79, dwelling construction approvals were down slightly on the annual rate in 1977/78. Meanwhile, spokesmen for both employers and workers in the building industry denied that there were any signs of recovery.

It is true that there were some encouraging signs early in 1979, including an increase in overtime worked in manufacturing industries. To describe these signs as evidence of an approaching boom was taking the argument too far. What do we mean by "a boom"? This is an expression that has been used in the past to describe excess aggregate demand, reflected in labour shortages, pressure on existing plant capacity, shortages of some goods and services, and upward pressures on prices. Early in 1979 the only sign that was consistent with boom conditions in the past was the threat of a more rapid rate of increase in prices. However, as we pointed out in chapter 13, this can be explained by independent cost forces. Yet it seems that some people have been confusing upward pressures on prices with increasing pressures on our capacity to produce.

Early indications of an upturn in economic activity do not constitute a boom. Such hopeful signs are often not sustained. A great deal of improvement in total expenditure would have been needed to lift the Australian economy from the recession of the last half of the seventies to a situation that could be referred to as a boom.

Questions

1. What indications would you expect to signal the coming of a recovery in the economy?

2. How could the peak of a boom be recognized.

DOES THE AUSTRALIAN ECONOMY NEED A STIMULUS?

On the question of whether the economy needs a stimulus opinion among economists is divided. Some favour a continuation of monetary and fiscal restraint and agree with the reasoning of the OECD group. Others have called on the government to release the brakes and to provide a stimulus in one form or another. In what ways could the government act to stimulate economic activity?

The level of activity in the building industry has widespread effects on employment in Australia. Not only does an increase in building construction provide extra jobs for bricklayers, carpenters, and the other tradesmen directly involved, but it also has effects on the demand for furniture, furnishings, and a wide range of consumer durables. Both monetary and fiscal policies have been used at times in the past to encourage or dampen building activity. Why not use such measures now to stimulate the depressed building industry? If this were done, what types of building activity should be encouraged? What policy measures should be used and what would be the likely effects?

Some people, including members of governments, suggested early in 1979 that the government should stimulate the economy by increasing immigration. Admittedly, the birthrate has fallen and total population has been growing less rapidly than it was before the 1970s. This has happened during past periods of high unemployment and does not necessarily indicate a long-run trend. It has been claimed that more rapid growth in population would make businessmen more optimistic about future markets for their products; further, that an increase in numbers of immigrants would result in an increase in the demand for houses and consumer durables. This in turn would lead firms to take on more labour, making use of their excess capacity and reducing unemployment. What of the migrants themselves? Surely they would also be seeking jobs? Would the multiplier effect of such a stimulus to production be sufficient not only to absorb the immigrants searching for jobs but also to reduce the numbers of people at present unemployed?

Alternatively, it may be possible to stimulate consumption expenditure and production by *redistributing* income. Table 5 suggested that the m.p.c. among people with lower incomes is much higher than for those with higher incomes. This suggests that total consumption expenditure at each level of output could be raised by redistributing income away from those with higher incomes and towards those with lower incomes. In other words, the position and slope of the consumption function of the form used in chapter 11 could be altered. This could be done by taxing more heavily the people with higher incomes, easing the tax burden on those with lower incomes, and increasing social security payments to pensioners and the unemployed. To what extent would such action be likely to increase total consumption expenditure? Would this result in some unwanted effects on incentives and private investment?

Work by Professors Powell and Dixon on the complex computer-operated, input-output **Impact** model of the Australian economy suggests that stimulation of aggregate demand sufficiently to restore the economy to full employment would raise the annual rate of inflation to 20 per cent. As in the past, such a high rate of inflation could be expected to result in a sharp switch to imports and a worsening in the *balance of payments.* On the other hand, that model predicted that restoring full employment by reducing *real* wages would require a fall of 9.7 per cent in real wages — equivalent to a drop of about twenty dollars a week for the average wage-earner. There is little chance that Australian workers would willingly accept such a cut in real wages.

Since return to a high rate of inflation is unacceptable and workers are unwilling to accept such a reduction in real wage rates, it has been suggested that this leaves us no alternative but to redistribute income away from the employed towards the unemployed. This could be done by imposing a 6 per cent levy on taxable income. If the government used these additional tax proceeds to increase unemployment benefits and to finance the creation of additional jobs — for example, on labour-intensive projects such as those undertaken under the RED scheme, then it is claimed that full employment could be restored. Although there would appear to be a measure of social justice in this proposal, what would be the likely consequences of raising unemployment benefits relative to wages net of tax? Would the unions be likely to seek increases in money wage rates to compensate for higher taxation?

However, some alternatives are less radical. For example, the government might deliberately plan a large increase in its *budget deficit*, either by reducing taxation or by increasing government sector expenditure on projects having a large labour component, or both. Such action would result in an increase in employment and presumably some reduction in the numbers unemployed. This, in turn, would result in more people paying tax on income and fewer people receiving unemployment benefits. So the *actual* deficit could prove to be much less than the *planned* deficit. Although the initial increase in employment may not appear to be sufficient to justify a larger increase in the planned deficit, such an increase in employment may serve to boost both household and business *confidence*. On the other hand, would the government be able to restrict such action to one financial year? Or would the economy come to depend upon more government spending, year after year? Surely the government cannot continue to run a large deficit indefinitely?

During the late seventies there were many calls for stimulation of the economy. Some suggested methods were:
1. Stimulus to the building industry
2. Increased immigration
3. Redistribution of income
4. Job creation schemes
5. General fiscal stimulus

Questions

1. If the economy was to be stimulated, which of the approaches in the summary statement above would you have recommended? Why?

2. Why was the government reluctant to stimulate the economy in the late 1970s?

IS THERE A NEED FOR TAX REFORMS?

From time to time the structure and rates of personal income tax have been changed. Some of these revisions have favoured people with lower incomes more than those with higher incomes. At other times, changes have had the opposite effect. Whatever the rates of tax applied in any period, questions are frequently raised concerning the fairness of current rates of tax relative to the capacity to pay. For example, should the government raise the minimum level of taxable income at which tax is levied? Should rates of tax be more progressive, so that people with higher incomes are taxed more heavily? Would such a change serve to damage incentives to work overtime or in other ways to earn more income? When a married man earns a taxable income of, say, $20,000 and his wife earns no income whatever, he pays much more income tax than the total paid by a husband and wife, each of whom earns a taxable income of $10,000. Does this suggest that the incomes of husbands and wives should be combined for the purpose of assessing tax on income?

Governments have long realized that there is a limit to the amount of tax on income that the Australian people are prepared to endure. If tax on income is raised above that limit, governments are likely to fall. Since voters are likely to react strongly to increases in personal income tax but seem less sensitive to indirect taxes, governments throughout the 1970s indicated a growing interest in raising *indirect taxes.* These taxes are at present confined mainly to excise duties and sales tax on relatively few products. When governments increase these taxes, they discriminate against the individual industries concerned — in contrast to the more general across-the-board effects of an increase in tax on income.

There have been suggestions that it would be "better" if indirect taxes were applied to *all* goods and services in Australia. Some have suggested that we use a value added tax (VAT) such as is widely used in Western Europe or a uniform rate of tax on all retail sales. It would be "better" for governments, because voters appear to be less sensitive to taxation in these forms. If taxes were applied to all products, an increase in VAT or retail turnover tax would not discriminate against individual industries. However, what would be the final effects on prices? What of the principle of capacity to pay? Pensioners, the unemployed, and others with low incomes would then pay as much tax on items of food and clothing as would people with much higher incomes.

Another source of revenue, particularly for state governments, is payroll tax. The higher the level of wages and salaries paid, the greater is the firm's tax liability. Is it logical to tax employers for taking on additional labour, particularly when we face a high level of unemployment?

A possible alternative source of revenue that has been considered in recent years is a tax on wealth — that is, as distinct from and additional to a tax on income. At present, we have no means of knowing the distribution of personal wealth in Australia or the revenue that would be raised by imposing an annual tax of, say, 1 per cent on the wealth of individuals. If such a tax were to be imposed, how would we define wealth? What would be done about indebtedness and what assets would be included or excluded from the tax base? In parts of Western Europe, an annual wealth tax is payable where the wealth of an individual is as little as $2,000. If a wealth tax was imposed at that level in Australia, there would be relatively few people exempted. What of old age pensioners who own their own homes? Would they be required to pay an annual wealth tax, even if they had no other income but their pensions? Would the introduction of such a tax lead some people to spend more now and rely increasingly on the government for support in their retirement?

The question of taxation reform raises many complex economic and political issues. Some of these are:
- **How progressive should the tax system be?**
- **What should be the mix between direct and indirect taxes?**
- **Should Australia adopt a value added tax?**
- **Should Australia adopt a wealth tax?**

Question

1. What are the *attractive* features of (*a*) a value added tax; (*b*) a wealth tax; (*c*) a tax on capital gains?

WHAT SHOULD WE DO ABOUT POVERTY?

First, what is meant by poverty? Most of us have heard or read of the conditions under which many people live in the developing countries. Very few Australians are suffering to that extent. Poverty, in a society like ours, is less absolute and can be best measured in *relative* terms. Some people have insufficient income to meet the cost of *what Australians generally would regard as the basic necessities of life.* **The Australian Government Commission of Inquiry into Poverty**, over the period 1973-75, accepted that a family was living in poverty if its income was less than 60 per cent of the average earnings of Australian workers — with adjustments above or below that figure to take account of size of family and home rental payable.

We know that poverty exists in Australia. How widespread is that poverty? Numerous studies were undertaken by or on behalf of the commission of inquiry. Unfortunately, very few of those studies were based on information concerning the incomes of the families interviewed. The research workers involved in one survey judged people to be living in poverty if they were occupying what the research workers *judged to be* substandard housing. In another study, all people who identified themselves as being of Aboriginal descent were assumed to be living in poverty; yet some of those people had above average incomes. A much more thorough study of farm families in Victoria revealed that many of those families had incomes less than 60 per cent of average earnings at that time. However, the research workers involved in that study realized that some of the families had quite substantial farm *assets.* This led them to suggest that the wealth of individual families should also be taken into account.

If people have low incomes but a great deal of wealth in the form of liquid financial assets, it may be reasonable to suggest that they sell some of those assets in order to raise their levels of consumption. On the other hand, should we suggest that low-income farm families sell part of their land, their livestock, or farm machinery in order to consume more? If so, does it follow that we should be less concerned for the welfare of old age pensioners who own the homes they live in?

The debate concerning the extent of poverty in Australia can only be settled by the gathering of better evidence. Meanwhile, what should be done? Many of the people found to be living in poverty in the mid seventies were receiving social security benefits. Are the present benefits high enough compared with average earnings in Australia? Many young people have been denied employment opportunities because their parents were unable to maintain them while they continued with formal education or trade training. Is there a need for greater attention to living allowances, so that members of low-income families can compete in labour markets on more equal terms? If our primary concern is to improve the opportunities of those in poverty, then this suggests the retention of means-tested grants to help those most in need.

Judgements about the most effective policies to counter poverty in Australia are hindered by the lack of adequate data and by difficulties such as distinguishing between very-low-income earners with wealth and those with no wealth.

Questions

1. Which groups in our community are most likely to be in poverty?

2. Which policies would you suggest to assist in the alleviation of poverty?

DO WE NEED A NEW APPROACH TO FOREIGN TRADE?

When Britain joined the European Common Market, Australian farm industries lost what was formerly their principal overseas market. One reason Britain decided to join the EEC was that many of her manufacturers believed that they would be able to increase their sales and operate more efficiently within a larger "home market".

From time to time it has been suggested that Australia and New Zealand should arrange a similar *customs union*. However, the *comparative advantage* of the two countries, especially in respect to farming, is very similar. We saw in chapter 9 that the best prospects for trade occur where the comparative advantages of two countries differ widely. Australian farmers were worried by the prospect of competing with New Zealand dairy products and lamb with nothing more than natural protection. On the other hand, New Zealand felt that she would have no hope of developing her own manufacturing industries if Australian manufactured goods were allowed to enter duty free.

Why not a *Pacific Basin customs union*? After all, the bulk of our overseas trade is now with countries bordering the Pacific — the United States, Canada, Japan, China, the ASEAN group, and New Zealand. However, some of these countries may not be willing to enter into such an arrangement. Early in the 1970s, Japan made it clear that she was not willing to give preferential treatment to imports from the countries of South-East Asia. The United States would probably prefer to remain clear of any formal arrangements either in the Pacific or in Western Europe. In any event, what would be the likely costs and benefits for Australia? Our miners and farmers would stand to benefit. But how would our motor vehicle and electrical goods manufacturers compete with duty-free Japanese goods?

Australia's participation in a customs union has been well canvassed but does not seem to be acceptable for the present.

Is there any other way that we might increase the volume of our exports? During the years immediately following World War II, Japan sent out trade missions with the object of anticipating the import requirements of other countries. It was noted, for example, that former colonies such as those in southern and south-east Asia were in the process of winning political independence. The obvious lack of transport facilities in such countries led Japan to step up production of rail rolling stock and small ships. Where Japan had previously relied heavily on the export of cotton textiles, she realized that the newly independent countries would be aiming to produce their own textiles — in the process, creating their own job opportunities. So Japan produced cotton textile manufacturing machinery for those markets. Anticipation of the import requirements of other countries, in part, accounted for the rapid growth in Japan's exports during the 1950s. Is it time for Australia to follow Japan's example? If so, where should we be looking for future markets?

In Japan, the government provided assistance to those industries for which future export prospects seemed brightest. Other industries, such as cotton textiles, were "sent to the wall". It seems unlikely that an Australian government would plan for the future as resolutely as did the Japanese. As in the past, we can be certain that structural changes will continue to occur in the Australian economy. Some industries will grow while others decline. Whether or not such changes will be deliberately encouraged by the government remains to be seen.

Question

1. What obstacles exist to the formation of a Pacific Basin customs union?

SHOULD WE ENCOURAGE STRUCTURAL CHANGE?

Structural change is a continuous process. One implication of this kind of change was the structural unemployment discussed in chapter 12. With the passing of time, output and employment grow in some industries but decline in others. These changes involve a reallocation of resources between industries and at least temporary structural unemployment.

Since World War II there have been significant changes in the structure of the Australian economy. In the farm sector, for example, the numbers employed declined steadily after the late 1940s. Output and employment in manufacturing industries grew rapidly until the mid sixties but declined during the seventies. In contrast, there has been strong growth in tourism,

Table 18. Distribution of GDP by Industry, average 1964—69 and 1976/77

	Average 1964—69 %	1976/77 %
Agriculture, forestry, fishing, and hunting	10.4	5.6
Mining	2.2	4.2
Manufacturing	26.4	21.1
Wholesale and retail trade	15.9	15.1
Finance and other business services	8.0	10.7
Entertainment, personal, and community services	10.3	15.2
All other	26.8	28.1
	100.0	100.0

Source: Australian Bureau of Statistics, *Australian National Accounts,* (various issues).

entertainment, and other service industries since the latter half of the sixties. Similar changes have occurred in other industrialized countries.

Table 18 shows some major changes in the distribution of GDP between industries over a period of about ten years. Over that same period there were corresponding changes in the distribution of the workforce. For example, whereas 9.4 per cent of all people employed at the time of the 1966 census were engaged in agriculture, forestry, fishing, or hunting, only 6.6 per cent were employed in those industries at the end of 1977. Over the same period, the numbers engaged in manufacturing dropped from 27.0 to 21.0 per cent of all people employed, while entertainment, personal, and community services accounted for an increase from 17.3 to 21.0 per cent.

What has caused these changes? As real incomes of Australians have grown, people have spent a smaller proportion of their incomes on food and clothing and a growing proportion on services. This helps to explain the decline in the farm sector and the growing importance of service industries. Some farm industries, such as the dairy industry, have found it difficult to establish alternative markets since Britain joined the EEC. As a result of changes in exchange rates, lower tariff protection, and rising labour costs, some manufacturers — for example, in the textile, clothing, and footwear industries — have found it increasingly difficult to compete with imports. In addition, technological changes and investment in labour-saving machinery have resulted in a reduction in numbers employed in some industries.

During the three decades up to 1974, Australia was able to withstand such changes with relatively little cost in terms of employment. Over the greater part of that period, the economy was at or near full employment. The total demand for labour was so strong that relatively few of the people who lost their jobs were unable to find some ready alternative. In fact, technological progress led to rising productivity and higher real incomes.

In contrast, when the level of unemployment is already high, it is much more difficult for workers displaced by structural changes to find alternative employment. It is also difficult for the owners of capital, since many buildings and machines have no alternative uses. In other words, the level of economic activity in any period imposes an important constraint on the capacity of the economy to adjust. So the growing resistance of the trade unions towards computerization and other technological changes during the latter part of the seventies is understandable.

Can we afford to adopt policies designed to slow down structural changes? If some industries are unable to compete with imported goods, what should the government do? In response to the difficulties faced by the textile, clothing, and footwear industries in the mid seventies, the government provided "temporary" increases in protection against imports. Even so, employment continued to fall in those industries. Many of our manufacturing industries are inefficient, aim to sell only on the Australian market, and have come to rely heavily upon protection. If they are offered a temporary increase in protection, will the prospect of a future reduction in protection spur them to greater efficiency? Or will they simply rely on the government to extend protection further and further into the future? Meanwhile, what is the cost of such protection to Australian consumers? Some of the costs and benefits of protection were discussed in chapter 9.

As an alternative, should the government simply accept that structural change is inevitable and take steps to ease the problems faced by the people who lose their jobs? In times of full employment, this would be the logical approach. When we already have a high level of unemployment, such decisions are much more difficult. Many of those who lose their jobs as a result of structural change seem likely to remain unemployed for a long time. In what ways could the government help? Would *Structural Adjustment Assistance* of the kind introduced in 1974 be sufficient? What of training for other occupations and assistance with moving and other expenses to increase the mobility of labour? Would policies such as these reduce the problems faced by the structurally unemployed while there remains a deficiency in aggregate demand?

The **Study Group on Structural Adjustment** in 1979, adopted a tougher stand. One of that group's conclusions was that "if the threat of long-term unemployment at high levels... is to be lessened, manufacturing industry in Australia will need to become more competitive against imports and more export-oriented. There will be a need for new policies to help promote this and to deal with adjustment problems." In contrast to past policies designed to postpone adjustment, this group suggested a need to anticipate and encourage structural change.

Measures recommended by this group included:

1. A gradual lowering of tariffs and other forms of protection against imports.
2. Encouragement to industries processing minerals, foodstuffs, and other raw materials for export.
3. Encouragement to firms introducing new processes and new products.
4. Attempts to develop new export markets, particularly in countries that appear to have good future growth prospects.
5. An increase in the availability of finance to small firms for development and adjustment.
6. Easing or removal of some government controls over foreign investment and the lending policies of financial intermediaries in order to allow more efficient use of the funds available for investment.
7. More emphasis on retraining and relocation schemes to speed up the movement of labour from declining to growing industries. Training

should be available to people while they remain in employment, in order to reduce periods of unemployment between jobs.

However, it was recommended that the introduction of these and other measures be delayed until there was some improvement in the employment situation.

A vital issue for Australia's economic growth and its international competitiveness is the stance the government adopts towards structural change. Will it promote the flow of resources towards efficient industries, or will it protect those industries that find it difficult to meet competition?

The costs of high levels of protection given to our manufacturing industries in the past have been more widely recognized in recent years. The benefits of raising efficiency to the point where we can compete effectively with imports and increase our sales overseas are undeniable. Yet the timing of the recommended policy changes must remain a matter of judgement for future governments. The extent to which unemployment first needs to be reduced will remain a matter for interpretation. For example, what are we likely to regard as full employment in the future? Is this likely to be something like 1 or 2 per cent unemployment, as it was in the 1960s? Or will it come to be accepted that 5 or 6 per cent unemployment is the best that we can hope to achieve? Questions such as these must be left to the economic historians of the future.

Questions

1. What are the major structural changes that have occurred in the Australian economy over the last fifteen years?

2. What attitude should the government adopt towards structural change?

Index